Chicken Tractor

The Permaculture Guide to Happy Hens and Healthy Soil

All New Straw Bale Edition

by

Andy Lee and Patricia Foreman

Tenth Printing — Over 50,000 copies in print!

ISBN 0-9624648-6-4 Straw Bale Edition, 1998
ISBN 0-9624648-2-1 First Edition, 1994

Library of Congress Cataloging-in-Publication Data

Lee, Andrew W., 1948-

    Chicken tractor : the permaculture guide to happy hens

and health soil / by Andy W. Lee. and Patricia Foreman

    p. 320 cm.

    Includes bibliographical references and index.

    Preassigned LCCN: 92-076194

    ISBN 0-9624648-6-4

    1. Chickens. 2. Organic farming. 3. Sustainable Agriculture. 4. Truck farming. 5. Waste products as fertilizer. I. Title

SF487.L44 1994   636.5

QBI93-22295

Published by:

Good Earth Publications
Visit our Book Store at:

www.GoodEarthPublications.com

Here's What Folks are Saying
About Chicken Tractor!

Even if you have never owned a chicken this book teaches you what you need to know to be a successful chicken tractor owner.

Organic Gardening Book Club

Changing climate patterns and chemically contaminated foods are making homegrown food incredibly valuable. The old-fashioned practice of raising a few chickens in the backyard is coming back into vogue. Chicken Tractor shows how easy and profitable it can be to add chickens to your growing season.

Gene Logsdon
Author, *Contrary Farmer*

In a world full of theory and unapplied academics, Chicken Tractor shines as a sterling example of a practical prototype developed by a dirt-under-the-fingernails, creative thinker. Andy Lee's simple elegance in design and description challenge me afresh to smack my forehead and exclaim "now why didn't I think of that"! In our efforts to bring new paradigmes to poultry production, Andy and I share a common vision, a brand-new ethics of excellence for proper models, delicious food and size-neutral, profit potentials.

Joel Salatin
Author, *Pasture Poultry Profit$*

The information in Chicken Tractor *is clearly based on a life full of practical farming experience and experimentation. Andy Lee generously shares with you his hard-earned knowledge. You can't get enough of this kind of information. This down-to-earth, unpretentious style helps make the* Chicken Tractor *a readable and often humorous book.*

Karen Di Franza
The Natural Farmer

Chicken Tractor *is one of our best selling "how-to" books for rare breeds conservation. It gives you the information you need to provide the perfect habitat for endangered breeds of poultry.*

Don Bixby, DVM, Executive Director
American Livestock Breeds Conservancy

This is really something to crow about!

Howard W. "Bud" Kerr, Jr.
USDA Office of Small Farms

Chicken Tractor *inspired me to take action!*

Bruce Johnson
Spencer, Oklahoma

I've always wanted to build a straw bale house. I followed Andy's instructions and now my hens are happily housed in hay!

David Stickney
Hendersonville, North Carolina

Ode to a Chicken Tractor

"Chicken Tractors, Chicken Tractors! I want them Everywhere!"
says Andy Lee, "I want them spreading coast to coast—LA. to Delaware.
What this country really needs — a chicken in every pot;
and with this handy method, well, gosh, that's just what you've got!"

Stick all your chickens in a pen that you can move around;
Take them out into your fields and let them peck the ground.
It may seem silly, but it's not; the benefits abound.

They fertilize, they spread manure, they dig up all the weeds,
and they won't need as much to eat to satisfy their needs.
They're open range, but in a pen so they can't eat your seeds.

You'll make a profit, simple too, it's elegant and neat;
A positive and easy way to help you grow your meat.
As a system, guaranteed, the method can't be beat.

So if you want this great technique, then this is what you do:
Buy the book by Andy Lee; it just came out - it's new.
Chicken Tractor is its name. It's good, and useful too!

by Ron Macher and Paul Berg,
Small Farm Today magazine

Acknowledgments

Howard W. "Bud" Kerr, Jr.—The only person we've ever met who uses a hand-carved rooster head made from a peach branch as his calling card.

Gene Logsdon—Everybody's *Contrary Farmer.*

Phil Laughlin—Cover design, creative advice and computer wizardry.

George DeVault—For inspiration and good-humored support all the way from Moscow.

Patricia Foreman—For research, writing, computer skills, graphics and stupid chicken jokes.

Michael Fox and Melanie Adcock—United States Humane Society, for their contributions to this book and for their dedicated efforts in advocating the humane treatment of poultry and all livestock.

Donald Bixby—American Livestock Breeds Conservancy, for the service he and his organization provide in preserving our heirloom livestock, and for their support of our work.

Ron Macher and Paul Berg—For supporting small-scale farmers through their magazine *Small Farm Today,* and for their wonderfully witty and profoundly clever poem, *Ode To A Chicken Tractor.*

Judy Janes—for so patiently and expertly proofreading, editing and many delicious dinners.

David Stickney—for helping with the processing, and building his urban straw bale hen house.

BackHome Magazine and ***Permaculture Drylands Journal*** for continuing to make available leading edge information about permaculture and self-reliant living .

The Difference Between the books:
Day Range Poultry and *Chicken Tractor*

The major differences in these two books are summarized in the table below. Each tome contains unique material and new information. The entire tables of contents of both books can be seen on the Good Earth Book Store website at:
www.GoodEarthPublications.com

Day Range Poultry	Chicken Tractor
Directed at larger, commercial pasture poultry growers.	Directed at small-scale, homestead poultry.
Farm, pasture, market garden and multi-species grazing.	Kitchen garden and homestead permaculture design.
Commercial processing of hundreds of birds, including USDA facilities.	Table top processing for the home and a few customers.
Details about many kinds of larger shelters (with bottoms) that are moved by motorized vehicles (tractors, ATV, etc).	Smaller, bottomless shelters with pop-holes for good weather use and for building raised garden beds. Movable by hand.
Covers incubation, hatchery management and battery brooding.	Includes straw-bale chicken shelters for winter housing.
Lots of information and lessons-learned about electric poultry fencing.	Information on movable fencing, including bamboo panels.
Lots of detailed information about raising turkeys and poultry breeder flocks.	Main focus on chickens (layers and broilers).
Bulk organic feed ration formulas by the ton for the commercial grower.	Details about feed supplements.
Stresses why a poultry growers cooperative would benefit all growers.	Marketing centers around farmer's markets and direct-sale customers.

About the Authors

Andy Lee is an internationally known speaker, writer, teacher and practitioner. His work encompasses sustainable agriculture, practical permaculture applications, appropriate housing, and cottage-industry strategies. His articles have appeared in dozens of publications including *Organic Gardening, Country Journal, Newsweek, Vegetarian Times, Small Farm Today, Acres USA, BackHome Magazine, Permaculture Drylands Journal* and other sustainable living magazines.

Andy has over 30 years experience as a forester, market gardener, builder and small business owner. He has a Diploma of Permaculture Design from the Permaculture Institute in Australia and has received numerous awards including the Excellence in Agriculture Award from the Renew America Foundation, the US Mayor's award for the Fight against Hunger, the Silver Spade Award from the Janus Institute and the coveted Pullets Surprise for Poultry Pioneers.

Patricia Foreman was born and raised in Indiana. She graduated from Purdue University with degrees in agriculture (genetics and nutrition) and pharmacy. While studying pharmacy and health care she realized that the emphasis for people was on curative and disease management, rather than preventative, nutritional approach that she was taught for farm animals.

Continuing her studies at Indiana University, Pat earned a Master's in Public Administration with majors in Health Systems Administration and International Affairs. While there she was selected for a prestigious Fulbright Fellowship. After graduating in 1976, she went to Washington DC as a Presidential Executive Management Intern, then worked as a Science Officer for the United Nations in Vienna, Austria. Following that Pat joined a nonprofit firm and worked as a consultant on primary health care systems in over 30 developing countries. Her hobbies and interests include writing, meditation, bee keeping, metaphysics, ecology and community service.

Pat and Andy have also written *Day Range Poultry: Every Chicken Owner's Guide to Grazing Gardens and Improving Pastures,* which takes free-range poultry production to a small-farm commercial level. This hands-on book includes hard-to-find information on raising turkeys, incubation, hatchery efficiency, maintaining breeder flocks, building shelters, small-scale processing, and much, much more.

We dedicate this book to

Richard and Marie Foreman

We also dedicate this book to those trillions of
chickens who have served and befriended
mankind for the millennia.
We all owe these feathered fowl great honor for
their products and services.

Thank you, chickens of the world!

Table of Contents

Recipe for a Chicken Tractor

The following "recipe" gives you a jump start for your chicken tractor. The chicken tractor idea and approach can also apply to almost any breed of poultry (turkeys, pheasants, quail) and other small livestock (pigs, goats, rabbits).

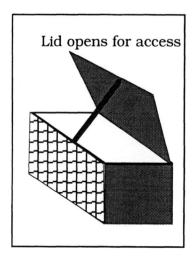

Lid opens for access

Make a bottomless, portable shelter-pen that is sized to fit over your garden bed. Install poultry wire on the top, sides, and ends, and cover the top and one or both ends with a top for protection against the weather. For small flocks, install a door or pop hole to occasionally let the chickens out for more exercise.

Add chickens: One broiler per 2 square feet, or one hen per 4 square feet.

Feed   **Water**

Add fresh water and feed daily. Hang the waterer and feeder high enough to keep dirt and manure from getting into them.

You can also feed kitchen scraps and vegetable wastes from your garden.

RESULT

Chickens clean your garden beds by

Eating grass, weeds and weed seeds, bugs, and plant debris.

By scratching the ground (tilling).

And they add valuable fertilizer

Directly onto your garden

by manuring (pooping).

THEN every day or so move your tractor to fresh graze, or add more bedding. This almost entirely eliminates the flies and smells. After the chickens have matured you can keep them for eggs or process them for a barbecue.

Foreword

The Second Coming of the Backyard Chicken Farmer

by Gene Logsdon

UPPER SANDUSKY, OHIO—
The old-fashioned practice
of raising a few chickens in the
backyard or on the small farm
is coming back into vogue.
Chickens are easy to raise for
eggs and meat, and the quality
and taste of the backyard variety are superb.

The past is in the foreword

Madame Chicken LeClaire´

There are people in our county who make a business of
cleaning and dressing chickens, or you can do it yourself
as we do without much fuss and bother. The fact that
zoning in towns allows residents to raise a barking,
crapping dog the size of a small elephant, but not four
hens for a steady, fresh egg supply, shows just how lacking in common sense we have become as a society. The
indictment against town chickens stemmed originally
from roosters crowing at dawn and waking the neighbors.
The easy solution to that problem is to raise only hens or
butcher the roosters before they mature enough to crow
all the time.

Parker Bosley, a gourmet French master chef and restau-
rateur in Cleveland, has often lamented to me the lack of
tough old hens and roosters available to him for his famous version of coq au vin, which roughly translated
means chicken stewed in wine. I told him he could have
my old hens free if he returned just one as coq au vin, but
I live too far away for it to be convenient for his purposes.

Coq au vin parties are, I hear, becoming popular amongst

16 Chicken Tractor

ports that he has indeed found some small farmers in northeast Ohio who supply him with two- or three-year-old chickens—younger ones just don't have the proper taste qualities for coq au vin. I admire Parker a lot because not only has he familiarized Ohioans with how good local food can be, but because he is not afraid to point out how Ohio State University poultry scientists have ignored small chicken farmers in favor of stinking, polluting commercial chicken factories (as long, of course, as the stinking, polluting chicken factories are not built near OSU professors' homes).

In his efforts to track down or encourage producers of various good foods (he makes a great dish of guinea hen, too) he says that Ohio State "agricultural" experts have not only not been of any help, but have acted as if his requests were outlandish.

Now comes across my desk another example of innovative backyard chicken farming. Andy Lee farms in North Carolina and writes about his outlandish farming ideas, as I do. His book is called *Chicken Tractor.* You'll have to read it to find out what that means, but it's one heck of a good idea, and it has the potential to quadruple your garden yields in no time flat.

The agriculture economists laugh at me but I'm telling you, the dynamic future lies in the hands of backyard chicken farmers like Andy Lee and food crafts people like Parker Bosley.

Gene Logsdon

The Contrary Farmer

Go ahead and laugh, you agro-economist! This isn't just another chicken joke!

Introduction

This whole thing with chicken tractors started back in 1990 when we were starting up the Intervale Community (CSA) Farm in Burlington, Vermont. We wanted to raise chickens in portable pens so we could spread the fertility around the gardens. The pen also needed to be completely enclosed to protect the birds from the numerous predators such as foxes and racoons who shared the farm. Our first generation pen was 4' x 12' and 3' high, made from plywood and chicken wire, with a plywood-covered-with-tarpaper lid. It was far too heavy to be easily portable, but we did manage to grow 30 broilers and spread manure on several of our garden beds during that first summer.

We learned enough from that experience that we enthusiastically went ahead to explore different designs and different materials. We were looking all the time for a pen that would be sturdy, attractive, portable, pestproof, and comfortable for the intended occupants. We even funded research at the University of Vermont to see if portable chicken tractors were economically viable on a farm scale.

After five generations of pen designs—and nearly 3,000 successful chickens later—we decided the whole idea was indeed practical, economical, farm certifiable, and a really fun way to raise food and fertilize the gardens all at the same time. That's when we sat down and wrote the first edition of *Chicken Tractor, the Gardener's Guide to Happy Hens and Healthy Soil.*

The book was published in 1994 and the first second, and third printings very quickly sold out. It was selected as the Book of the Month for December, 1994, by Organic Gardening Book Club. We get letters from readers all over the country and abroad who have had excellent results using the system to raise their food and fertilize their gardens. What is really delightful about all these letters are the numerous ideas for new ways of working the system. That's why we decided to rewrite the book.

In this *All New Straw Bale Edition of the Chicken Tractor* book we are adding nearly 100 pages and 20 photos of new information about what is in essence a very simple subject. One major change to the focus of the book has to do with the subtitle, where we have replaced *Gardener* with *Permaculture*. As we learn more about the benefits of chicken tractoring we realize that this model for soil fertility has ramifications for all sorts of land reclamation, not only in gardens but on farms and ranches as well.

In one of its many manifestations, permaculture is about taking back the responsibility for feeding and sheltering ourselves, and for our own individual welfare and physical and mental well-being. We can only be of service to others if we first learn how to care for ourselves. If we can use the precepts of permaculture to help us learn to feed, house, and employ ourselves, then we can provide for our families with far less strain on the community and our environment. Then we can begin providing a service to others in our community by growing food for them or by showing them how to grow their own. We can also teach them how to build their own shelter and even how to create their own at-home cottage industry or microenterprise employment.

For permaculture to be most successful we need to bring it to mainstream readers so they can act on the information. Bringing permaculture to a wider audience is primarily a one-at-a-time endeavor through workshops, field days and articles in friendly journals. We can expedite information though by offering personal examples as stories for other media. If local newspapers, radio, television, and non-permaculture publications are attracted to our efforts, then we can reach a far larger audience in a much shorter time.

Opening permaculture to a wider audience often requires a hook—an attention grabber—that will nab their imagination and reel them in for a closer look. I was talking to Australian permaculture teacher Lea Harrison one day about how lots of people get hooked on permaculture because of some small permaculture trick or technique. For Lea it was fish traps that caught and held her attention long enough to let the bigger picture develop and seep into her awareness. Other folks I've talked to gravitate towards swales, water harvesting, gabions, herb spirals, and so forth. All of these things hold a fascination for me, too, but the one that stands out clearly in my mind as the outstanding example of a successful tool for developing permaculture systems is the chicken tractor.

A chicken tractor is some form of portable pen to keep chickens in or near your garden where they are most beneficial. The portable pen serves to protect them from weather and predators, while containing them in the area you want to improve. In exchange for your care and feeding they are more than happy to provide weed and pest control and fertility for your lawn, garden, or orchard. Even without the final product of meat or eggs the chickens have paid for their keep.

I first heard the term in 1991 from Jerome Osentowski who reported that he was using a "chicken tractor" to control weeds around his greenhouse in the central Rocky Mountains in Colorado. It is, of course, a term used frequently by Australian author Bill Mollison in his writings and teachings about permaculture (see bibliograpy). Right away I began to imagine all the possibilities inherent in the very idea of tractoring land with chickens.

The chicken tractoring concept has little to do with tractors, but more to do with being "in traction" or being pulled in the direction of soil health and food self-sufficiency. Chicken tractor is a multiuse, multibenefit project that is do-able at almost any level of skill and knowledge. You can build a simple pen today and start using it tomorrow. Perhaps you have just one or two hens to provide a limited supply of eggs for your table. Or, on a larger scale, you might be raising poultry for sale to earn part of your living. Either way, and at many levels in between, you can utilize chicken tractors. Even if you don't eat eggs or poultry you can still enjoy the benefits of the system by growing pullets (young egg layers) for sale to your friends who do eat eggs and poultry.

All across the continent chicken tractors are being amazingly useful in helping to create soil. Poultry digestive systems serve as translators, turning grains, weeds and insects into manure that can be used to fertilize soil for growing crops for people and for livestock.

It is possible to grow poultry simply by letting them free range on your property, living off what they can scrounge from the land. However, to maintain a healthy, well cared for flock—and to achieve optimal yields—you will want to supplement their forage with grains or mixed poultry rations.

Chickens are amazing feed converters. During good weather they are able to change two pounds of feed into one pound of live weight. Even during cold winters they will require less than four pounds of feed to grow one pound live weight or to produce a dozen eggs. What chickens are not good at, however, is extracting the available nutrients from their feed. They excrete about 75% of the nitrogen, 80% of the phosphorus and 85% of the potassium along with about 40% of the organic matter that is in their feed.

In conventional systems, of course, this nutrient-rich by-product becomes a waste—often toxic—and difficult and expensive to dispose of. But in permaculture the excrement is highly valued, so much so that we build appropriately scaled catchment facilities to preserve it. In a sense you are importing fertility into your farm or garden in the form of chicken feed, which unfortunately is usually grown somewhere else. However, as your land becomes more fertile and your own food needs are being met from your gardens, you can then turn your attention to growing chicken feed in the soil that is enriched with chicken manure. Sort of a perpetual motion scheme if you will. Unlike when using chemical forms of fertility you are achieving broader yields via eggs and meat as well as manure for your soil.

While free ranging your chickens might appear to be the ultimate in "natural" food production, you will encounter problems that make portable-pen chicken tractors seem more attractive. For one thing, predators such as foxes, coyotes, possums, raccoons, and dogs are all "free-rangers" too. It's hard to protect a loose flock from depredations. Additionally, it is difficult to keep a loose flock from devastating your garden, and it's all but impossible to train them to drop their manure right where you need it.

It is understandable why a portable pen can be so important to the heath and welfare of your flock and to optimizing yields from your permaculture system. The chicken tractor serves first of all to house and shelter your chickens. The covered lid and sides protect them from rain and snowfall and from intense sunlight. They also shield them from attack by aerial predators such as eagles, hawks, and owls. The screened in sides of the pen allow ample sunshine to warm them, and ventilation to carry off heat and moisture. The screened sides also protect the poultry from earth bound predators such as dogs, foxes, and possums. The chicken tractor does not have a bottom, so the poultry can walk on soil and forage grass, weeds and bugs that come in their path.

As manager of this system, your task is to provide your flock with fresh water and supplemental grain on a daily or twice daily schedule. You also provide the motive power to move the pen and accomplish your land development goals, be they grass and weed and pest control, soil fertility, or enhanced graze for the poultry. In exchange for your kindness, the birds are only too happy to graze the grass, manure the garden, and give you plenty of rich, flavorful eggs or meat to eat.

My favorite use for the chicken tractor is to build raised garden beds. In my hilly, upper Piedmont region the soil is quite thin, often gravelly with very little grass for the birds to eat. I must rely—at least in the beginning—on imported feed and waste hay or straw to build soil above the gravel. I simply move the chicken tractor where I want to create a garden bed and leave it there for whatever length of time it takes to lay down enough manure to fertilize the spot for garden crops.

As you know, putting down too much chicken manure can be devastating to the soil. In some cases leaving them there too long will create a hardpan on the surface and overload the soil with nitrogen and other nutrients to a point of toxicity. This is the kind of mess you will find in the typical fenced-in henhouse yard. We overcome the nutrient overload challenge by adding straw or hay bedding on a daily basis. As soon as the chickens have laid down a good dose of manure we add a thin layer of carbonaceous bedding, just enough to cover the manure. Doing this daily creates a perfectly layered, shallow compost pile.

The hay we use for bedding is usually free. It is either too old for livestock feed, or has gotten wet in the field, making it unsuitable for feed. It has a carbon-to-nitrogen ratio of about 50 to 1, compared to the chicken manure that has a carbon to nitrogen ratio of less than 10 to 1. When we mix the two components together we achieve a nearly perfect carbon-to-nitrogen ratio of 30 to 1, ideal for creating compost. Additionally, the hay or straw acts as a sponge, literally, to soak up and hold rainfall or surface runoff.

This "sponge factor" makes the raised bed method especially rewarding on slopes that are susceptible to erosion, and in drylands areas with low precipitation. It holds the surface water on the site long enough for it to percolate downwards to replenish the groundwater. An added benefit on slopes is that the chickens will automatically scratch and shuffle through the bedding inside their pen, leveling and moving it against the downhill wall. When we remove the pen we have a raised bed miniterrace. As these

raised beds mature and decompose we are left with minidams that control our runoff. These new miniterraces are places in which we can grow abundant crops, all without laborious digging or turning of the soil or earthworks building up of lower terrace edges.

Earthworms find it a delightful place to hang out beneath the raised beds at the interface between the soil and the organic matter. As they consume bits of hay and manure they carry it with them into their burrows for digestion. This opens air pockets in the soil that also serve as water reservoirs during rains. The earthworms leave their castings at the surface where they quickly become new nourishment for plants. In this system then the earthworms and the chickens and the humans are working cooperatively to build soil fertility and a water reservoir.

The accepted, "conventional" way to build new soil today is to rotary-till or plow the topsoil and subsoil and mix it all together to create a deeper topsoil. That doesn't work. What happens instead is that your plowing and tilling create an inferior soil lacking organic matter and tilth. It tends to blow away and wash away. You cannot "deepen" soil with mechanical manipulation. All you can accomplish in that pursuit is to destroy soil tilth and structure. You also kill off the soil life that has—up until now—turned organic matter into humus for the enrichment of the soil and to feed the crops that grow there.

Instead, use a chicken tractor to help you "uppen" your soil. A cranky old fence post in a Montana wheat field first told me about "uppening" many years ago. At the field edge I had to step *up* to reach the fence line. Seeking to understand this phenomenon I sat down over there and asked the fence post why that was. "Why is the field lower than the fence row?" I asked. "Well," grouched the old fence post, "you folks plow this soil so much that it gets real fine and blows away. And the rains wash the rest of it away. After 50 years of that kind of treatment all the fine topsoil is gone, the field surface is several inches below the fence row, and what you see mostly in the field is gravelly and sandy subsoil. And I don't mind telling you I'm sick of the whole damn mess!"

"And that's only half the story," the old fence post went on to say. "At the same time you humans are so busy lowering the field, other natural forces are at work raising the fence row. What you ought to do is look here in my fence row and see a better way. Don't plow the ground. Instead, let the birds and animals and insects feast on the plants. They will thank you by leaving their manure as payment in kind. When the plants die back for the winter the ground-dwelling insects and worms eat the organic matter and convert it to humus. That humus in turn provides nutrition for next year's plants and builds up the organic matter in the soil, thereby further developing your soil moisture reservoir. In this way soil uppens."

So, here's how you can use chicken tractors to help uppen soil. Just move the portable pens in a rotational pattern that will give your chickens fresh graze each day. If you don't have anything for them to graze, just use the system as a sheet mulcher. Either way they leave behind their manure and bedding that will in turn feed the soil organisms that can convert the roughage to humus.

That, really, is the major precept of successful chicken tractoring. All that remains is to explore the many different ways to make it work.

We've always referred to these pens as chicken tractors, but with proper design modifications you can make tractors for turkeys, pheasants, sheep, pigs, goats, and even dairy or beef cattle. With some restrictions a chicken tractor could even be useful for corralling recalcitrant children. The guiding design precepts are that you want to end up with a pen that:

1. Is large enough for the livestock.

2. Is small enough to move easily.

3. Fits the landscape conditions at your site.

This is high density, short duration rotational grazing somewhat akin to Allan Savory's "Holistic Resource Management" and Andre´ Voisin's "Intensive Rotational Grazing". You can make it as simple or as complex as you need to attain your goals, from a very small pen that you move daily, up to miles of portable electric fencing enclosing vast paddocks for seasonal rotational grazing.

The size of a henhouse is dictated by the size of the farmer who has to get inside to tend the chickens and gather eggs. Hens don't need an eight-foot ceiling. It's much less expensive to build a chicken-size house than a people-size house. With the chicken tractor just lift the lid and reach in. Design your pen size based on the physical strength and production interests of the operator, and the hoped-for outcome of the chicken tractor project.

For someone who is relatively small, a chicken tractor that is two feet high, eight feet long and four feet wide is a good choice. This small pen is easy to slide on the ground using ski tips or scoots, or make it even more portable with a set of wheels from a junked lawn mower. If you have a helper and a furniture dolly it's no problem to move pens as large as ten by twelve by feet high. That is the largest I've ever built that is suitably portable. The smaller pens are ideal for six or eight layers or up to 20 broilers for a short time. We use the larger pens for growing turkeys.

Pen design relies on using the fewest possible materials, lightweight yet strong, and able to withstand weather and varmints. Generally we wrap our pen walls with one-inch galvanized poultry netting. For longevity you can use the more expensive poultry netting that has a plastic coating to resist weathering. We hinge our pen tops for access to the birds and their furniture. When we first started out we used a blue polyethylene tarp installed over chicken wire for the lid of the pen, but the tarp fades, rips and leaks after the first year. Now we use plastic roofing panels that cost a little more but last indefinitely. They are also easier to install since we don't have to put chicken wire on the roof.

In rougher weather we attach plastic roofing panels to the ends and sides of the pen to shield the birds from wind and rain. In colder climates you'll want to insulate the pens for winter use. One time we tried putting styrofoam panels for insulation but the chickens pecked it to pieces. Another time we used the radiant barrier material that builders use for reflecting sun heat in attics and it worked just fine. Another thing that works well for insulation and weather protection is to simply stack old hay bales around the windward side of the pen. Then in the spring just use the hay bales for garden mulch.

We presently have five chicken tractors measuring six feet by twelve feet and three feet high. This past year we raised 50 turkeys for sale to our friends, 25 pheasants to release on our farm, and 30 broilers for our freezer. As well as the aforementioned Tur-Gu-Chi gang. We didn't lose any poultry from the chicken tractors. From the hay bale henhouse, though, we lost three pullets to a possum, one pullet to a Dalmation dog, and one pullet to a hawk. To prevent more losses we installed an electric poultry net fence around the structure and charged it with a solar charger.

We didn't keep really close figures on our labor, materials and feed costs for the year. All told we managed to make a small profit and pay off all the equipment. Next year we'll increase our production to 450 broilers and 75 turkeys. We plan to make a enough profit, hopefully to pay off the chicken plucker we just bought.

Meanwhile, there's a whole lot of new techniques and methods emerging in chicken tractor parlance. If you have an experience or anecdote you'd like to share please send it along, we'll be delighted to hear from you. We're all tinkerers and the ultimate "chicken tractor" has yet to be designed, so feel free to share your ideas and questions. Until then, Happy Hen Tracks!

Typical Chicken House That Stays in the Same Place Year After Dreary Year

Chapter 1: What is a Chicken Tractor Anyway?

Since we started working with chicken tractors six years ago, the question almost everyone asks is, "What is a chicken tractor, anyway?" Sometimes I ask the questioner to give me his or her definition of the term, then chuckle at the sometimes silly answers I get.

I first heard the expression "chicken tractor" back in 1991. In that moment I instantly conjured up an image of a whacked-out, hormone-crazed rooster in a duckbill cap racing a low-rider John Deere across the landscape, banging into the barn and careering down the fencerows. Sort of a silly idea, isn't it? Heck, chickens can't drive tractors. Can they?

I've never seen a chicken drive a tractor, or a bus for that matter, and I bet you never have either. What is true is that chickens in the right location can do more good for your garden soil—and do it better and cheaper—than any tractor.

Chickens eat bugs, weeds, and grasses, spread manure wherever they walk, give meat or eggs day after day and almost never talk back or need new tires. They can be far more beneficial to humans when combined with the portable shelter-pen that we refer to as the "tractor" part of the chicken tractor system.

The term "chicken tractor" is just a tongue-in-cheek expression coined by Bill Mollison, the irascible founder of the permaculture movement that started in Australia back in the 70s. It simply means the *whole* idea of putting the chickens where they do the most good and where they are easiest to take care of in the garden.

For most Americans, buying eggs or poultry at the super-market has become a joyless, almost suspicious act. Suspicion, that is, of the potentially carcinogenic chemicals used to raise commercial chickens. We've learned through countless newspaper articles not to trust the producers of our food. They use growth hormones and inhumane feeding and housing regimens. Filth and disease permeate the processing plants.

The alternative to mass-produced food is to grow your own. Until now, growing your own chickens for meat and eggs has been mostly a chicken house affair. Chicken houses themselves can be a joyless scenario, too, although not always as bothersome or frightening as buying poultry from the supermarkets when we don't know where it's been.

Where is the joy when you have to carry the feed in and the manure out of that dreary little building out back called the henhouse? What a waste of energy that building is. It's expensive to build, you can't move it and the ubiquitous attached run gets smelly, muddy and unsightly. Yuck, who wants to raise chickens that way? Especially when there's a simple, inexpensive portable coop that does the work for you.

If you want to fertilize a field or pasture, weed and feed a garden bed, or build a raised-bed garden on poor soil or clay, the chickens will do it for you. All you have to understand is how the system works, then you can engineer changes to fit your site and needs.

There is nothing fancy, newfangled, hard-to-understand or expensive about this method. You just need plain old common sense, a keen eye and an open mind. This is a system that is so simple you can build it on a Saturday and put it to good use on Sunday. With proper care it will last you for years to come.

Sound too good to be true? Well, read on, and find out how others have cashed in on the method. No, it's not a "get-rich-quick" scheme, but it can be a "quick fix" to get good food and healthy soil. It will save you money, either by considerably decreasing your food bill, or giving you extra produce to sell. This is definitely a food production system for people on a low budget with limited space.

Should You Have Roosters in Suburbia?

What to do about restrictive zoning laws if they exist in your town? Try some community activism to get the law changed. Get a grant to show people in your community how they can use chickens in the chicken tractor system without the odor and flies traditionally associated with raising livestock in suburbia. I'd rather listen to my neighbor's chickens cluck than his overpowered, undermuffled riding lawnmower every Saturday morning for the whole summer.

Zoning officials are likely to leave you alone unless they get a complaint. I once knew a fellow who kept a sow with a litter of pigs in his garden shed. None of the neighbors complained and he raised two litters of pigs every year.

One time, for lack of a better place, I started 300 chicks in my garage and kept them there for three weeks until the field pens were ready. Word got out and we had many folks stop by with their kids to see the baby chickens—including our landlords. They were fascinated! They brought their grandson over regularly to see the chicks grow. No one complained. Here's the moral of this story:

Go recruit your neighbors. Enlist them into the idea. Promise them a few free eggs or invite them to a community chicken barbecue.

It is not a good idea to try keeping a rooster in suburbia. Your neighbors aren't <u>that</u> fond of you. I love chickens but I once had a neighbor who inherited a rooster named Paul. I'm not even sure now what breed Paul was, sort of a calico thing, a bit shy and underweight and his left eye looked mostly to the right, but could he crow! Loud, at all hours of the day!

Do you have a crowing problem with your chickens? That's easy enough to fix. Just order all females. They don't crow. Yes, the hens dress out smaller than the cockerels, but hens are good for frying or grilling and you can keep a few of them to become egg layers.

Ten Good Reasons to Go Mobile

What <u>drives</u> our enthusiasm for the chicken tractor idea?

1. It's a system that provides a solution to several problems in the conventional raising of poultry. The system has <u>many</u> beneficial components. In permaculture we call this "stacking". It is a shining example of reciprocal benefits, where the chicken and the grower and garden all benefit.

2. It's appropriately scaled and practical. It can be used for just one chicken, or as many as the grower has time and land to handle.

3. It's a way to get *good* nutritious food (vegetables, chickens and eggs) inexpensively.

4. It prepares the soil for optimum—versus maximum—yields of vegetables and small fruits.

5. It fulfills the part of me that wants to be self-reliant and semiself-sufficient.

6. It enables market gardeners and small-scale family farms to expand their items-for-sale menu and enhance profitability.

7. It is a humane way to raise poultry.

8. It will stimulate interest in the heritage poultry breeds that are good foragers.

9. Potentially, chicken tractors can have a positive global impact on how people reclaim land and produce their food, and can encourage local self-sufficiency.

10. It encourages the policy of local community self-sufficiency by growing local, buying local, and supporting local folks.

The following summarizes the real advantages of chicken tractors compared to raising poultry the conventional way.

Advantages of Chicken Tractors

1. Low-cost, part-time business with good return.

2. Low-cost way to grow your own food that is healthy, nutritious and tasty.

3. A chicken tractor is smaller than a henhouse or barn with its associated mud run and less conspicuous. Less costly and easier to construct.

4. Has other uses in off-season as storage or cold frame.

5. Can be brought directly to the garden, and fits into small sections where you need weed control and fertility.

6. Potentially pest-proof.

7. Kids love to see the chickens in the chicken tractor and can safely help take care of the flock.

8. Chickens themselves are beneficial as:

    a. Manure machines for soil fertilization.

    b. Grass and weed grazers.

    c. Limited tillagers.

    d. Food producers: eggs and meat.

We've tried to contain in this little book all the philosophical, environmental, and humane why-to's, combined with practical how-to's of everything you need to know to get started with a chicken tractor in your garden this year. The result is to give you a step toward self-reliance and semiself-sufficiency, so that you can feel better about yourself, your environment, and the food you eat. All this contributes toward an enhanced quality of life.

Chapter 2: Why Chicken Tractors Belong in Your Garden

Animal Tractors in Permaculture Design

In Bill Mollison's *Introduction to Permaculture,* he uses the chicken to explain his Theory of Relative Location. Relative location means *place every element in relationship to others so that they assist and support each other.* Famous inventor and infamous curmudgeon R. Buckminster Fuller called this *synergy.* Each component supports the entire system so the value of the whole is greatly enhanced. Bill Mollison says it very well:

"The core of permaculture is design. Design is a connection between things. It's not the human, or the chicken, or the garden. It is how the human, the chicken, and the garden are <u>connected</u>."

This is a very thought-provoking idea. It gets even more exciting when added to other permaculture concepts, such as the ones described below.

Some Permaculture Concepts*

- Each element (plant, animal, thing) has many purposes (functions) in a system.
- Each important purpose is supported by many elements.
- Emphasis is on the use of biological resources over fossil fuel resources.
- Using and accelerating natural plant succession to establish favorable sites and soils.
- Using polyculture and diversity of beneficial species for a productive, interactive system.
- Using edge and natural patterns for best effect.

* Adapted from *Introduction to Permaculture,* page 5.

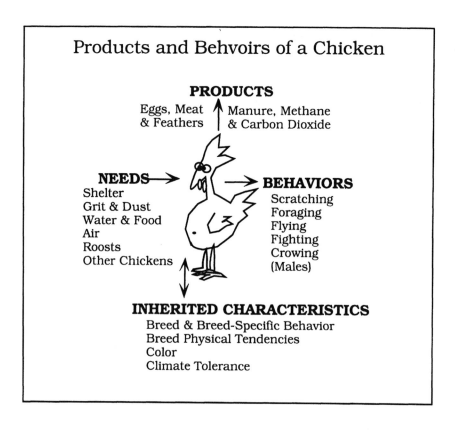

Products and Behvoirs of a Chicken

PRODUCTS

Eggs, Meat & Feathers | Manure, Methane & Carbon Dioxide

NEEDS→
Shelter
Grit & Dust
Water & Food
Air
Roosts
Other Chickens

BEHAVIORS
Scratching
Foraging
Flying
Fighting
Crowing
(Males)

INHERITED CHARACTERISTICS
Breed & Breed-Specific Behavior
Breed Physical Tendencies
Color
Climate Tolerance

In other words it is the location of the chicken that is either very valuable <u>or</u> very much a problem. With chicken tractors, you feed the chicken from and in the garden, and the chicken tends the garden and feeds the human. Another term for this synergy is "stacking".

That's just what the chicken tractor does. It puts the chicken *in the right place*, in the garden. In terms of relative location this is where its food is abundantly available and where the chicken can perform its primary functions as a meat and egg producer, biomass converter, and portable manure spreader.

By having the chicken in the right location you can feed, water, and care for it easily as a minor part of the daily chores of the garden. The chicken provides a handy tillage tool with its continual scratching and pecking. It

Functional Analysis of the Chicken

Chicken Characteristics

Color, size, height & weight
Heat tolerance & cold tolerance
Flying ability, raised for eggs or meat
Single or dual-purpose breed
Mothering ability
Personality, roosting ability
Scratching & foraging, pecking

Inputs (Needs)

Shelter, air, food & water
Dust bath, grit
Roost & nest area for layers
Mineral supplements
Companions - other chickens
Predator protection

Outputs (values)

Meat & eggs, manure (fertilizer)
Feathers & feather meal
heat generation (in greenhouses)
Undigested nutrients, insect, weed & grass control
Carbon dioxide & methane, potential pollution
Companionship, pecking & sound
Biomass converter
Scratching & tillage
Carcass/viscera (for compost)

Relationships

Food for humans, fertilizer for the garden
Organic matter for the garden
Carbon dioxide for plants
Companionship for the gardener
Waste recycling
Soil scratching, compost materials
Weed-disease-pest control
Meat and eggs income, compost income
Increased garden yields
Improved plant health
Improved nutrition for the consumer

becomes a biomass recycler, consuming spent garden plants, weeds, grasses, insects, and excess vegetables. The manure returns to the earth as fertility for the crop. The eggs and meat nourish the gardener, while the viscera, feathers, and carcass add tremendous value to the compost heaps.

The traditional way of raising chickens in henhouses does not view the products and behaviors of a chicken as part of a larger ecosystem. Chicken tractors bring into play the harmonious relationships with you—the gardener—with the chickens and the garden.

Certainly this expands our thinking to include all inputs and outputs with an eye to creating beneficial relationships and improving our garden environment. In the next section we will examine two more permaculture concepts: visible and invisible structures. These structures can either enhance or limit your ability to produce chickens in your own backyard.

Visible Structures

When you start planning your chicken tractor garden there will be visible and invisible structures that can affect your site and plan. The following section gives examples of visible structures.

• **Fences**. Especially permanent fences which may be hard to move if you ever need to. These may have brushy hedgerows growing up in them that can provide food or bedding for the chickens. Maybe the hedgerow will cast a shadow, block the harsh winds or cooling summer breezes. Sometimes fencerows shelter wildlife that will stalk your chickens.

• **Roads**. Especially heavily traveled ones, where the noise might bother your chickens, or the dust and fumes may cause health problems. Proximity to out-of-sight-from-your-house roadways might also invite theft or pilferage. Roads can also be our friends. Roads make it easy to get feed and water to chickens, and helpful when hauling the chickens to the processing house or to market.

• **Driveways, for Access to the Chicken Tractors**. Place these in such a way as not to interfere with your chicken tractor rotation, yet close enough to deliver feed and water without undue labor. Design and build driveways for all-weather use.

• **Terrain and Slopes**. Something we see every day but often fail to recognize as being important to our garden and chicken tractor layout. If the terrain is rocky or hilly it will interfere with our rotation schedule. If the land is flat, such as in a floodplain, we need to think about whether water runoff is going to present a problem for our gardens or poultry.

• **Trees**. Either in hedgerows or freestanding are useful in several ways. They give us shade in the hot summer, windbreaks, lumber and posts to build our chicken tractors and, in some cases, food for the chickens. Leaves from trees are especially useful for bedding and for compost materials. Trees are not welcome in conventional gardens. However, as we study the natural diversity of the landscape, we discover that trees play an incredibly valuable role in weather attenuation, landscape design and wildlife habitat for nesting and for food.

• **Houses and Other Buildings**. These can be our most important visible structures. If they are already existing it may be impossible to move them to make our rotational gardening scheme work out better. They also cast shadows, block or funnel wind, and act as heat reflectors of the rays of the sun. They offer opportunities to harvest rain water for irrigating the garden or for drinking water for ourselves and livestock. We also need to consider the relative location of the chickens to other households. Nearby neighbors may not like any unsightliness or odor from your chicken pens. Always consider your neighbor's property in relation to your own when you lay out your garden plan.

• **The portable pens** themselves become visible structures especially if they are in your neighbor's line of sight. You want to make sure they look neat and well cared for. Think about how the pen location will affect the natural drainage of the site, and if the runoff from the pens will cause any problems in the downhill areas of your site.

Invisible Structures

It's easy to see a "visible" structure and plan how you will compensate for the influence—positive or negative—that it might have on your garden. Sometimes, however, it's not so easy to see the *invisible* structures and what you can do about them if they need correction. Invisible structures include:

• **Attitude, yours and your neighbor's.** Attitudes can have an immediate impact on your choice of a garden spot. If the neighbors don't like the idea of raising livestock for food then you have a budding quarrel on your hands if you consciously or otherwise put your chickens in their line of sight.

• **Social and cultural customs** surrounding the raising of poultry for eggs and meat in your area are certainly an invisible structure. If people in your area are receptive to a local agricultural industry you will have an easier time communicating with your neighbors about the advantages of raising poultry in this manner.

• **Zoning and Board of Health regulations** in your community can be bothersome. Many areas in this country have zoning restrictions against raising livestock. Some communities ban chickens, especially roosters. These old zoning laws are in response to odor and fly complaints and the noise pollution of roosters. If you are raising roosters for meat birds you can harvest them before they begin to crow strongly. Egg layers are much quieter, of course, but you won't get fertilized eggs for hatching unless you keep one or two roosters around. To my knowledge there isn't any humane way to keep a rooster from crowing.

• **Subsurface obstacles** such as hardpan or high water table, that might cause the chickens to create boggy conditions. In this situation you can wind up with a heck of a mess if you place your chicken pens in an area that doesn't drain well. You'll get all kinds of odors and fly problems, soon followed by even bigger problems with your neighbors and your local Board of Health.

• **Prevailing winds, storms and rain**. In the Upper Piedmont of North Carolina where I live, the prevailing summer storms come out of the south. Knowing this, I always enclose the south end or side of the tractor to keep the rain off the birds. Likewise, I know that the chickens are most apt to overheat during the later part of the day when the fierce westerly sun makes its way into the pens. I can add shading to the west end of the pens to keep them cooler.

• **Climate, heat and cold**, clouds or sun, rain or dry, length of season. These all influence how successful your poultry project will be. These are things you need to know in order to plan your annual rotation of chickens. For example, you don't want to put your chickens outside until they are old enough to withstand the weather. Knowing these weather patterns will enable you to determine just how many batches of birds you can grow in any given season.

• **Disease vectors**, such as pigeons and sparrows that might come to your chicken feeders for a free meal. You want to check around your area to see if any particular poultry diseases prevail in your region.

• **Electromagnetic fields**, referred to as EMFs have a potentially detrimental effect on poultry. Presently there are conflicting reports as to whether or not EMFs cause cancer in livestock. Over the years I've heard enough anecdotal evidence to give me concern when working in areas where EMFs might exist. Personally I just don't want my birds subjected to something that is as concentrated as EMFs under a high-tension power line, or near a transformer box.

• **Natural light** is a big factor in optimal egg production, and has some influence on how well meat chickens will gain weight. Putting them in a continually dark area is detrimental. Putting them in bold sunshine without some form of shade will be devastating, especially once the ambient temperature climbs over 90 degrees Fahrenheit.

• **Location of feed and water supplies** are both visible and invisible structures. If you have to truck your water from off-site you will spend much more time caring for your chickens than if your water is available from a nearby garden hose. The same thing applies to feed. If you have to truck feed from far away it can add an enormous cost to your chicken production operation. When Patricia and I lived in Vermont we belonged to a feed co op that brings organic chicken feed all the way from midstate New

York at an added cost of eight cents per pound. The co-op can only buy it in ten ton lots, so they have to have a large storage facility nearby.

• **Relative location of your overall garden plan** and your soil fertility management are important invisible structures. You need room to move the chicken tractors without encroaching on the land you need for your annual garden. Also, you don't want to apply more manure in a small space than the soil can reasonably handle.

Competing uses for the site usually come about through lack of master planning in the beginning. My first market garden in Pembroke, Massachusetts, experienced this problem when my two sons decided they wanted a baseball field where my garden expansion area was. The compromise was to move my chickens farther back on the land, adding about 200 extra feet to my daily chore of caring for the chickens. Fortunately I was shrewd enough to bargain into the deal that the boys had to take over the chicken chore.

• **Nearby processing facilities**. Being close to the slaughterhouse—either your own or a nearby commercial facility—will help a great deal when you start harvesting your chickens. Presently I butcher my own broilers, turkeys and pheasants, but I have friends who must drive over an hour to get to a processing plant. Knowing the time and distance to the slaughterhouse is critical to your planning. Transportation is a cost you need to add to your overhead, and there's always a chance not all the birds will survive a long, hot journey to the processor.

• **Supply houses for equipment, supplies, and feed**. Buying supplies and equipment has become easier with the passing years as more mail-order catalogs carry them. Feed is a different story. Long-distance trucking of livestock feed is costly and it's bad for the environment, even if it does employ a lot of people. If your feed transportation costs get too far out of hand you may want to start growing your own feed. This then becomes another invisible structure. Maybe it's a visible structure too, if you don't have the land to do it on.

• **Local experienced people** will often be able to help you with advice on how to get started. Many of us grew up in families where raising chickens was part of everyday life. If that was true for you then you probably know all you need to get started. Others, however, have a desire to grow chickens, but absolutely no idea how to begin. That's when friendly experienced neighbors can be invaluable. Look around your area and see who's doing it, and become friends with them. They'll probably gladly share their knowledge with you in exchange for your occasional help moving chickens or building more pens. You may be able to help start a cooperative with other small-scale growers in your area. Together you can buy bulk feed at less cost and group orders of chicks for a better price. Your group might even consider jointly buying processing or freezer storage equipment that you can share.

• **Neighborhood dogs**, even friendly, gentle ones. I learned this lesson very quickly from a six-month-old Lhasa apso puppy named ZaZa. She was a former neighbor's pet and a very playful little mop, cute as animal house slippers. Her only problem was she wanted to play with the chickens. She runs along the pen yapping her fool hear off and scaring the dickens out of the chickens. Luckily she is a smart pup and we got her trained out of this annoyance.

When you look back at the list showing the functional analysis of the chicken tractor, you can easily understand why chickens belong in the garden. Understanding why we move the chicken tractors so frequently is a different notion. We need to rotate them daily so we can take advantage of <u>all the benefits</u> they offer in the garden.

Weed control, manuring, pest control, recycling waste vegetation from the garden, and tilling the soil are all good reasons why we use chicken tractors. To understand this better, we need to look at three problems associated with stationary pens:

1. Chicken manure is potentially a hazardous waste. When you keep chickens in just one fenced-in run, they will quickly turn it into a foul-smelling, fecal-laden spot that contains toxic levels of macro- and micro-nutrients, especially nitrogen. So much nitrogen will accumulate that it will turn into ammo-

Yuck! Too much poop is disgusting! And unhealthy!

nia, killing soil life and smelling up your garden. It's difficult to collect the manure for your compost pile before most of the vital nutrients have leached away.

Pesty flies! By moving the tractor daily, or by adding more bedding, most of the flies and odors will be eliminated.

2. The stationary, enclosed run also becomes a site for flies. They are always around, and the chickens eat a lot of them. However, with so much fecal matter lying on the surface the flies will get ahead of the chickens' ability to eat them. Flies will become a major nuisance.

3. In the enclosed run the chickens get dirty and don't thrive. They need fresh pasture and fresh soil to scratch every day. If you leave them too long in the same spot you will be toxifying one garden bed while denying your other garden beds the opportunity to reap the benefits of the chicken tractor rotation.

Get Super-Fertile Soil Fast—Using Animal Manure

Chickens are great biocyclers if you move them to fresh graze each day. They can get as much as 30% of their food from vegetation on the garden beds. They eat spent garden plants, weeds and cover crops, depending on where you are in your garden bed rotation. By eating fresh weeds, grasses and garden plants, your chickens will get a diverse diet, enabling them to acquire many of the nutrients and vitamins they need for vigorous growth and well being.

For as long as anyone can remember, livestock growers have claimed extra yields from their land by applying animal manures; either raw, seasoned or composted. Most people, even many vegetarians, feel that you just can't grow good food crops without access to animal manures for fertility.

However, it's been my experience that land can just as easily be reclaimed with non-manure compost, if you have enough time and follow a good rotation schedule. Back in 1990 we helped start the Intervale Community Farm on 3 acres of worn-out corn field in Burlington, Vermont. The soil, a fine sandy loam, had less than three percent organic matter. We had to irrigate frequently because the soil didn't hold much water, and the fertilizer requirements were almost too high to be affordable. Our yields that first year were fairly low compared to what we thought they could be. For example, tomato plants yielded less than one pound per square foot.

We didn't have access to manure of any kind for making compost, so we used the next best thing, leaves and grass clippings. We worked out a deal with the Chittenden County Solid Waste District to have residents use the edge of our field as a drop-off site for leaves and grass clippings. When we had time away from other farm chores we used the tractor to form the materials into windrows about four feet high, ten feet wide and 300 feet long. Then we hired a friend who owned a Wildcat compost turner to turn the windrows for us.

As the compost became available we spread it on our field from one-inch to two-inches deep and worked it into the soil with a light rotary tilling. This practice has continued for seven years, and the result is that the organic matter in the field is now approaching six percent. The vegetable yields have improved dramatically, with the best tomato plants yielding about three pounds per square foot.

However, it's far more likely that yields in the three-pounds-per-square-foot range will come more quickly with the use of animal manure. A good grade of compost that contains animal manure will usually be superior to a compost made without animal manure. This is especially true if the land you are undertaking to garden or farm is not very fertile to begin with. Almost always, what poor soil needs more of is organic matter.

In the chicken tractor garden—with the portable pens rotating over the beds even for a few days each year—the accumulation of manure can add superb richness to the soil. With super-rich soil you can expect super-high yields. Of course, the other elements in the system are equally important, such as plenty of sunlight and water. The most important ingredient, of course, is plenty of intelligent management by the gardener.

Does animal manure help you reclaim and fertilize land faster? Yes! The Intervale Community Farm yields improved dramatically in five years because we were using compost, even though the compost didn't have animal manure in it. Now, here's an example of how I used compost made <u>with</u> animal manure to develop a super-rich soil in just two years.

When I started my one-acre market garden in Pembroke, Massachusetts, back in 1979, my tomatoes yielded less than one pound per plant. Fortunately I lived near a goat-breeding farm managed by Heifer Project International that had an abundance of well-aged goat manure, free for the hauling. I hauled the manure to my garden in a borrowed dump truck and spread it about four inches thick and then mixed it in the soil with a rented rotary tiller.

About two weeks later I put in my tomato transplants with a side-dressing of organic fertilizer. That year I had an astounding increase in yields of rich, red tomatoes, with some plants producing up to seven pounds each! The average for the harvest was about five pounds per plant. The following year, after a second application of well-aged goat manure, I had some tomato plants that produced 20 pounds each, and the garden average was 14 pounds. Manure made it possible to achieve this increase in yields. My tomato harvest went from two pounds per plant to 14 pounds per plant (700%) in only two years.

Earthworms as Indicators

As a symbol of fertility in the garden, the earthworm is a great barometer. The earthworm count in my garden went from almost zero in 1979 to over ten worms per cubic foot in 1981, and kept climbing each year after that. I'll bet today if you dug up that soil you'd find over 1,000 worms per cubic meter. It's easy for me to see from this experience how very, very important animal manures are when used properly in a soil management program.

Chapter 3: Chicken Tractor Systems

In Chapter One we looked at the characteristics of portable shelter-pens and some of the permaculture philosophy behind them. Now let's look at various ways to design and use the chicken tractor. It is easier to understand how the system functions if we know what we—and the chickens— <u>need</u> from the system. In poultry production we humans need to receive food. The chickens need protection from the heat, cold, rain, sun, and predators, and they need feed and water regularly.

There are seven basic chicken tractor models with variations on a theme with each one. The table below summarizes the systems. We discuss each of these systems in this chapter.

Chicken Tractor Systems

1. Rotational Garden: Uses bottomless shelter-pen that you move daily in the garden. Need room to move pens around garden.

2. Deep Mulch System: Stationary bottomless shelter-pen. Add fresh bedding daily. Creates a raised garden bed.

3. Sheet Mulch System: Bottomless cage that stays on garden beds longer than one day, but shorter than life of chickens. Puts a sheet-mulch on top of beds.

4. Intensive Grazing in Paddocks: Have a fixed or movable henhouse and rotate grazing in paddocks. Eggmobiles are an example. Good for layers.

5. Polyface System: Mixes species, e.g., chickens follow cattle in field. Good application for eggmobiles. Great parasite control.

6. Hens on wheels: The henhouse is mounted on wheels for easy moving around the garden. More costly to build and harder to keep clean and maintained.

7. Greenhouse Systems: Creates ecosystem, balances oxygen from plants and carbon dioxide from chickens. Can protect chickens through winter season.

1. Rotational Garden System

The basic rotational garden system is simply to house the chickens in bottomless, portable shelter-pens that are the same width of your garden beds. You can choose whatever length you want. When the garden bed is not producing crops you put a chicken tractor on top and let the chickens glean, till, and fertilize the bed for the following crop.

My garden is twice as large as it needs to be for food production alone. This enables me to rotate and improve each garden bed every other year as shown by the figure above.

My garden beds are 4 by 80 feet. That is too long for a structurally stable pen so I use a 4 by 10 foot pen and move it from one end of the bed to the other. Once the entire length of the bed has been "treated", I move the pen across the path to the next bed. I repeat this pattern, treating all the beds until the birds are ready to harvest.

In really hot weather, above 90°F., use extra shading material for the chickens. If you see them panting they are too hot, and will sometimes die from suffocation if you can't cool them quickly. One way to cool the chickens is to place wet burlap bags over the pen. Any slight breeze moving through the wet burlap will move the moisture and drop the air temperature by as much as 10°F. Another way to cool them is to add a small door in the trac-

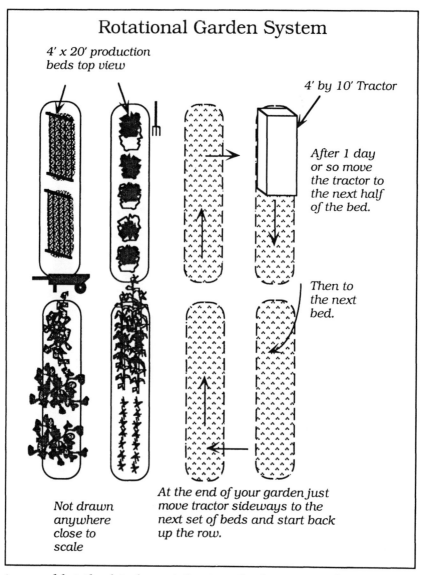

Rotational Garden System

4' x 20' production beds top view

4' by 10' Tractor

After 1 day or so move the tractor to the next half of the bed.

Then to the next bed.

At the end of your garden just move tractor sideways to the next set of beds and start back up the row.

Not drawn anywhere close to scale

tor and let the birds out during the hot part of the day so they can find shade under nearby trees or buildings. Of course, if dogs or predators are nearby this isn't such a good option.

2. Deep Mulch System

In some gardens there simply isn't enough room to move the chicken tractor to a new piece of ground each day.

Other places—such as our hilltop homesite in North Carolina—the soil is so infertile, rocky, or filled with clay that nothing will grow in it and there isn't anything for them to graze to begin with. In these instances you can use the deep mulch system to create rich garden beds above the surface. With this method you never need to rotary till or dig up the soil.

In the deep mulch method, place the pen over the area where you want to build a garden bed. Just mow the vegetation and leave the clippings in place as a source of nitrogen. The herbaceous layer will decompose rapidly under the mulch with the aid of the bacteria and earthworms that will begin feeding there. This system will build individual raised garden beds wherever you want them.

Several years ago when Pat and I were building a new house in Charlotte, Vermont, we wanted to start right away to prepare the soil for a salad garden about ten feet from the back door. We built the house in a meadow containing milkweed, several types of grasses, common vetch and small poplar and green ash saplings. Rather than rent or borrow a rotary tiller to prepare the salad garden spot, we used a chicken tractor.

On the spot where we wanted the salad garden to be, we installed the 40-square-foot portable pen and added the waterer and feeder and 20 broilers. The broilers were three weeks old when we started the site, and we kept them there for five weeks, adding about an inch of loose, dry hay each day for bedding.

We also wanted our birds to have access to grass and weed seeds. We believe chickens need chlorophyll and other trace minerals that grass contains. We used our lawn mower with a grass catcher on the back, every other day or so we would mow enough to gather a bag or two full

and dump it in the chicken tractor. The chickens loved it and
busily picked through and
gobbled down lots of the green
stuff. Our idea of heavy farm iron
is a lawn mower — another version of a small-scale tractor.

If the chickens can't get to the lawn I'll take the lawn to the chickens.

We harvested the chickens on
September 1, and moved the
pen. The once fluffy mulch
looked like a straw mattress,

Grass catcher bags grass for your chickens.

neatly pressed into shape and about ten inches deep.
When I rolled back the mulch to see underneath, the
earthworms, bacteria and fungi had already begun to decompose the mulch. It looked like the inside of a perfectly
working compost pile. Next spring this site was a wonderfully fertile raised bed; ready for growing really great salad
greens.

The top layers of the "mattress" of hay bedding did not
decompose into humus by spring. So we layerd on about
one inch of compost and good topsoil and planted our
salad crops. Within days the seeds sprouted and sent
their roots deep into the mulch layer beneath and began
extracting nutrients and moisture.

I've seen this garden method work with hay bales, too.
Just set the bales where you want a garden, layer soil on
top, add fertilizer and plant your crops. The seeds will
germinate in the soil layer, then send roots throughout
the hay bale in search of nutrients and moisture. Another
tip is to use the hay or straw bale as a urinal for a few
weeks before planting crops in it. This adds a significant
amount of nitrogen that helps break down the carbonaceous straw or hay.

Some folks may have a certain queasiness about using human waste for fertilizer. I think urine from a healthy human is a darn sight better garden fertilizer than some of the chemical stuff you can buy, and it's a lot cheaper. Some of my garden students use urine—diluted with ten parts water—to give their vegetable plots extra nutrients. They just sprinkle the diluted urine on the ground around the plants. In some cases, too, they claim a reduction in pest problems since the human urine odor is a deterrent.

Predators and the Deep Mulch System.

In the deep mulch method, the chickens stay in one spot for several days or even weeks. This invites predators to try to dig under the pen to attack the chickens. You can stop burrowing animals by laying chicken wire around the four sides of the pen and anchoring it with clothespins made from old coat hangers. Tuck the wire under the edge of the pen a few inches. Any animal that tries to burrow under the pen will get frustrated by the wire and give up. For more information on predators see Chapter 9.

In extreme cases, particularly with neighborhood dogs, it may be necessary to install a wire or electric fence around the garden perimeter to keep them away from the pen.

The surface of the bedding will remain relatively dry throughout the cycle as long as you keep the lid closed. The cover on the windward side and on the roof lid will keep most of the rain out. If the bedding does get wet simply add a fresh layer of hay mulch to give the chickens dry footing. Some moisture will wick up from the ground underneath the mat of bedding. It will not make its way into the top mulch layer, however, because the bedding is not packed tightly enough for capillary action to occur.

Flies and odors can become a problem in the deep mulch system. There are always plenty of flies in the area and the chicken pen attracts them. I do think the birds catch all the flies that hatch in the mulch but newcomers can increase too quickly for the chickens to catch them all. Adding extra bedding—sometimes even twice a day—will keep the flies from becoming a huge problem. The same thing applies to odors. Just keep adding a little more bedding until you get the right formula. Add extra bedding as the birds get older, especially if the weather is hot. The older chickens excrete more manure, and the bedding can get uncomfortably warm as it begins composting and decomposing. Just be liberal with the bedding and add it more frequently if you have to.

For a five week period with 20 broilers in a 4 by 10 foot chicken tractor we use about a bale of mulch hay that we get from a local farmer for one dollar per bale, or for free if the hay is moldy or dusty. We pull off chunks of hay from the bales and shake them out on the mulch, in a loose layer about one-inch deep. It works best if you shake bedding on half the pen at a time so the chickens can retreat to the other end of the pen. Once you've placed bedding on the first half of the pen, go to the other end and start shaking bedding there.

An interesting side note is that after a few days the chickens will get very complacent about the new bedding. Oftentimes you'll have to push them out of the way so you can shake the hay or straw over the entire floor. However, if you unexpectedly add something new to the pen it will frighten them and they'll try to run or fly away from it.

I observed this for the first time when Patricia put a stick of firewood in one end of the pen to see if the chickens would roost on it. You would have thought she'd thrown a stick of dynamite in there! The chickens were terrified and tried to fly out of the pen. As soon as we took the stick of firewood out they calmed right down and went back to feeding and grazing.

If the hay or straw bedding has any seeds in it the chickens will pick them out. If you throw scratch feed or cracked corn on the surface they like to scratch for it. They also like to scratch and fluff the bedding so they can lie down in it. Unfortunately, there usually aren't enough weed or grain seeds in the hay bedding to add significant feed value.

I think there are lots of opportunities on most small-scale farms to provide supplemental feed for the chickens. It would be an interesting experiment, for example, to grow grain, such as millet, as a "snack" for the chickens. Let the grain mature on the stalk and use it as bedding to see if the chickens will get any feed value from it. Chances are they will peck and scratch through the straw searching out the seeds. This will supplement their diet, and give them some exercise and something to do with their time. The scratching will also help mix the bedding with the manure for better composting.

In his book *The Contrary Farmer*, author and farmer Gene Logsdon talks about doing this with wheat. His method is to simply cut and bale the wheat—grain and all. Then he feeds it to his hens through the winter. I have fed my hens millet grain mixed in with their feed and notice that they will always peck out the millet seeds first before eating their regular feed.

We always add a smidgen of grit to the feeder lip each day when we add more feed. This is necessary to keep the chickens' digestive systems in good working order. In the deep mulch system they don't have much access to dirt or sand to put in their digestive craw. They need this grit to grind their food for digestion. Grit is ground oyster shells and only costs pennies for the amount we give them. It prevents the birds getting impacted craws from too much commercial feed and hay. In larger production facilities, growers offer grit in separate feed trays giving the chickens free access to it.

One way to increase the feed conversion capability of chickens is to harvest green grasses and weeds and put them on top of the fresh bedding. It's a little extra work to do this but the chickens seem to really enjoy pecking at the fresh green grasses. The chlorophyll contained in the green plant matter is a detoxicant. It helps the chickens' digestive systems expel toxins they might pick up from the feed, from the bedding or from the ground.

Deep Mulch Tractor Size

We put 20 broilers in a 4 by 10 foot pen. This gives them each two square feet of space. We've also tried putting 30 broilers in a 6 by 12 foot pen. This works if we harvest them at intervals as they increase in size. At the eigth week we take out ten, then ten more at the tenth week and the final ten at the twelfth week. This gives us a combination of fryers from the smaller birds, broilers from the medium sized birds, and up to seven pound roasters from the 12-week-old birds. During their final week of growth the birds may appear a bit crowded, but we've never had any incidents of pecking or fighting. Other pastured poultry growers have been able to reduce pen space to just one and one quarter square feet per bird without seeing symptoms of over-crowding.

Another way to get fryers and roasters from the same batch of chickens is to buy "straight run" chicks. Straight run means male and female chicks together. About half of them will be male, the other half female. The females grow more slowly and mature at lower weights than the cockerels. Usually the weight difference is from one to two pounds.

During the eighth week to tenth week the cockerels will start learning to crow, so make sure the pens aren't too close to neighbors who complain about the noise. By this time, too, the cockerels are trying to mate the hens. So either harvest the roosters or move the hens to a different pen.

The reason I grow some smaller chickens is that I like fried chicken, and I really like to cook chicken on the grill. But

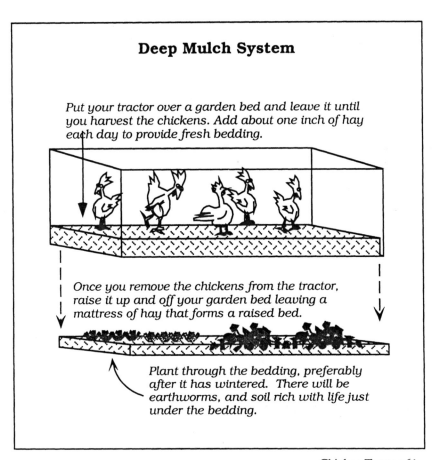

Deep Mulch System

Put your tractor over a garden bed and leave it until you harvest the chickens. Add about one inch of hay each day to provide fresh bedding.

Once you remove the chickens from the tractor, raise it up and off your garden bed leaving a mattress of hay that forms a raised bed.

Plant through the bedding, preferably after it has wintered. There will be earthworms, and soil rich with life just under the bedding.

the larger pieces from the roaster-sized chickens get over-done on the outside and under done on the inside when cooked in a frying pan or on the grill. The smaller size pieces are easier to fry and barbeque.

Deep Mulch System and Your Garden Soil

In this deep mulch method nitrogen will build up in the mulch. At first you might think the extra concentration of nitrogen is a great deal higher than your vegetables will need. For example, people have warned me that tomatoes planted in this nitrogen-rich bedding will produce all foliage and no fruits.

In my experience this just isn't the case. The high carbon content of the dry hay acts as a neutral buffer against a nitrogen overload. As the material breaks down into humus it effectively traps the excess nitrogen and holds it for future crops. The overall effect is that plants extract the nutrients they need without producing excessive foliage. Leftover nutrients are held in reserve in the organic matter.

This is not too much nitrogen for crops, according to tests at the University of Connecticut. After 12 years of annual compost applications, researchers found as much as 2,000 pounds of nitrogen per acre locked in the organic matter in the soil. The bulk of this nitrogen goes to microbes that are busy breaking down the carbon material and releasing the nutrients for crops. A typical garden crop will need less than 100 pounds nitrogen per acre to yield well. In repeated tests, university researchers did not find any instance of excess nitrogen leaching into the groundwater when soil organic matter was at an adequate level. However, their check plots that were low in organic matter did show leaching activity.

To get quick decomposition of the deep mulch it's best to remove the chicken tractor immediately after harvesting the chickens. Water the bed thoroughly. As with a compost pile, the mulch material needs to be moist to start the composting process. A shallow pile will not heat up to the degree a full-sized compost pile will. However it will get warm enough to provide a comfortable environment for the bacteria to do their work of slowly decomposing the material.

Move the chicken tractor off the deep mulch bed as soon as you harvest the chickens. This is to eliminate bacterial attack on frame lumber. This also allows ultraviolet rays and natural rainfall and earth elements to aid in the decomposing process. Also, you might need the chicken tractor for starting the next batch of chickens. Or you might want to use the structure for other purposes such as storage or cold frame.

A way to enhance the structure and fertility of your new garden bed is to layer in some garden soil along with the fresh bedding each day. This garden soil is rich with bacteria and will "seed" the deep mulch. Adding water helps the bacteria come to life so they can reduce the pile to finished humus in no time. We also add grass cuttings from our lawn mower by using our grass-catcher bag when we mow the lawn.

Earthworms play a very important role in this decomposition as well. Within only two or three weeks, even before you remove the chickens, the earthworms will come up in the soil beneath the pen and begin consuming the mulch, turning it into wonderfully rich castings. They will be most active where the deep mulch rests on the soil.

It's best if you can build these deep mulch beds the year before you plant vegetables in them so that the mulch can

Deep Mulch System - notice the futon mattress like raised bed when we lift the chicken tractor up.

decay and become nutrient-rich humus. However, you can plant in one of these beds before it decomposes if you want. Just shovel in a layer of garden soil or potting mix and set your transplants directly into the new soil.

The layer of grass and weeds that is under the bedding provides the first nitrogen boost to begin sheet composting the bedding. The root systems of the native plants will decompose in the soil. This decomposition provides food for the soil dwellers. Channels form as the microbes and earthworms eat the roots. The soil dwellers use these channels for access to the raw materials at the surface. These channels also allow moisture to go up and down, serving as a reservoir to hold water from heavy rainfall.

Putting in layers of bedding each day to balance the nitrogen in the manure will give the optimal carbon to nitrogen ratio of 30:1, for great compost. At this rate you are adding the equivalent of 40 cubic yards of compost per acre, enough to assure you of optimal yields from your vegetable garden.

Deep Mulch System Daily Care

Daily care for the chickens in the deep mulch pen requires nothing more than visiting them once each day and adding more feed in the feeder, giving them fresh water, and putting down fresh bedding. It takes only a minute to wash and fill the waterer if you have a garden hose close by. Keeping the feed in a sealed container next to the chicken tractor makes refilling the chicken feeder quick and simple. Store the hay or straw on a pallet nearby so you can replenish the chicken bedding quickly. You can do all these daily chores in less than five minutes. If you also throw in some harvested greens it might add another minute to your schedule. These are ideal tasks for youngsters to help you with.

We store our mulch hay bales on a wooden pallet next to the chicken tractor. This way it is easy and convenient to add bedding to the pen as needed. We cover the stored bales with a small tarp and tie the corners to the underlying pallet so the tarp doesn't blow off in a strong wind.

We keep our feed in a galvanized trash can next to the deep mulch pen. We keep the lid on with a strong bungee cord to keep raccoons out. It's a simple matter to scoop out fresh feed each day.

We also keep a small bag of crushed clamshells or gravel in the feed barrel and mix it in with the feed so the chickens will have access to grit. This helps their digestive systems since they don't have access to natural grit.

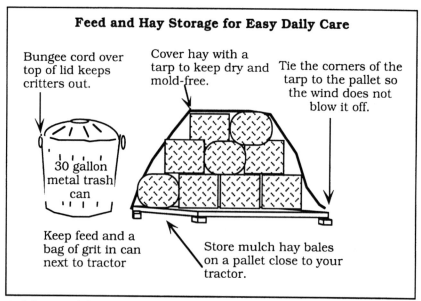

Feed and Hay Storage for Easy Daily Care

Bungee cord over top of lid keeps critters out.

Cover hay with a tarp to keep dry and mold-free.

Tie the corners of the tarp to the pallet so the wind does not blow it off.

30 gallon metal trash can

Keep feed and a bag of grit in can next to tractor

Store mulch hay bales on a pallet close to your tractor.

Add a Cold Frame to Create a Portable Bioshelter.

One way to get maximum usage of your chicken tractor is to reverse its orientation during the spring and fall. By putting the enclosed side on the north you will protect the chickens from cold northerly breezes.

With the open side on the south they will get warm sunlight throughout most of the day. When the sun gets too hot for them in midsummer, just rotate the pen and put the enclosed side to the south so they are in the shade.

In the spring and fall you can also put a solar cold frame on the south side of the chicken tractor. The tractor box will serve as a reflector and sun trap for the sun's heat, and will protect the cold frame from the north wind. There is a potential here, too, for the birds to help heat the cold frame and provide some carbon dioxide for the growing plants.

Remove the tarp on the south side of the chicken tractor and snuggle the pen against the north side of the cold

Advantages of a Bioshelter

1. Heat and light for the chickens and the plants.

2. Chickens utilize oxygen from the plants and breathe out carbon dioxide that can be used by the plants.

3. Plants and chickens have northerly windbreak.

4. The close proximity of the garden and the chickens provides an activities center for the gardener to do all chores at the same location.

frame. The chicken wire on the side of the pen remains in place to keep the chickens from having access to the plants in the cold frame. The plastic film on the cold frame will protect the chickens from the chilly wind.

You can make the cold frame—and the chickens—warmer by putting a tarp on the north side of the shelter-pen, and at the ends. This will block the cold air from hitting the chickens and the plants. The table below lists the reciprocal benefits and advantages of this low-cost, temporary "bioshelter".

The cold frame can measure 40 square feet, the same size as the chicken tractor. The cold frame will produce about fifty dollars worth of lettuce during the time the birds are growing to harvestable size. Sell the lettuce to the folks who buy the chickens from you. It is also possible to start seedlings such as broccoli or, better yet, tomatoes in the cold frame part of the portable bioshelter. After harvesting the chickens, remove the cold frame and turn the site into a permanent garden bed with plants already planted and growing.

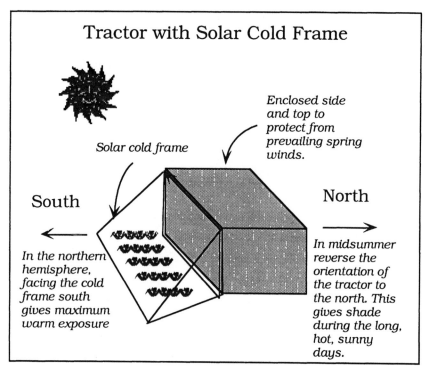

Tractor with Solar Cold Frame

Solar cold frame

Enclosed side and top to protect from prevailing spring winds.

South

North

In the northern hemisphere, facing the cold frame south gives maximum warm exposure

In midsummer reverse the orientation of the tractor to the north. This gives shade during the long, hot, sunny days.

Another example of stacking in time and place is to add a trellis to the south side of the chicken tractor for growing vining crops such as green beans, cucumbers, or indeterminate tomatoes. This will provide shade for the chickens during the hotter days of summer.

Don't attach the vining crop to the chicken tractor frame, though. It will harbor moisture that can lead to decaying wood frame members. Also, some vining crops, particularly peas, are hard to remove from trellis netting when they die. It's easier if you can simply take the trellis down and clean the dead vines into your compost pile.

3. Sheet Mulch System - Halfway Between Grazing and Deep Mulch

In the sheet mulch system we think of using the chicken tractor more than one day but less than a month on each position. The objectives are:

1. Kill the grass and weeds in the garden bed.

2. Fertilize the garden bed.

3. Build up a layer of organic matter (mulch) that will hold the nutrients and protect the soil from erosion and drying out.

4. Add fertility and organic matter to the soil as the mulch decays and turns into humus.

Begin by putting the chickens on the garden bed where they will deposit a layer of manure. Add mulch to the manure each day until the mulch measures about four-inches deep. Then, move the chickens to the next spot and repeat the process.

This sequence adds loads of organic matter and manure to several different beds while the broilers are in the garden. If you are using laying hens in the portable pen you can cover far more ground each year. In most areas of the country you can keep chickens outside from six to nine months.

The chickens drop manure where you need it, and the mulch holds the nitrogen and other nutrients in a stable condition while the mulch slowly decays. This lets gardeners forego planting cover crops altogether, and still gives them the opportunity to move the pens regularly to benefit from the manure applications.

The traditional way of converting a sod lawn area to garden beds is to rotary-till the site repeatedly, killing the grass and mixing it with the soil. Rotary tilling is noisy, time-consuming, energy-intensive and expensive, and destroys the soil structure and tilth. There's a better way to create garden beds, using chicken tractors. Put the chickens on the site for about two to three days. They will eat all the grass right down to bare ground and leave a thick layer of manure. Then move the tractor to the next site, and mulch the one they were just on. When the next batch of chickens arrives 30 days later, just put them on the existing mulch.

This way, a continuous rich mulch is being placed on each garden bed. This mulch kills the sod underneath and allows the soil life to do its job of decomposing the leaves and root mass, turning them into fertile humus.

No tillage at all is required. Just plant the crops through the mulch. Use the chickens this way to rid the beds of weeds and grasses during the first batch. The following batches just add more fertility and mulch to each bed, making them super rich and super productive for the following year's vegetable crop.

In this model the gardener will have to feed more grain since there is less graze for the birds. The saved labor of tilling and planting cover crops after each rotation of birds will offset the extra feed bill. At best we can only hope to save thirty-six cents per bird if they are eating grass and weeds. We can save at least that much if we don't have to rotary till and buy cover-crop seed. In addition, the following year when the garden is ready to plant to vegetables, there will be no need to mow and till under a heavy cover crop. To start seedlings, just pull back the mulch and set the transplants, then push the mulch back around them.

A word here about cover crops. For many years I believed, like most of my peers, that cover crops were an effective way to add organic matter to the soil. Recently, however, I've talked with Dr. Vern Grubinger and other researchers at the University of Vermont who believe that in many cases organic matter in the soil does not increase significantly by tilling under cover crops.

What seems to happen instead is that the act of tilling introduces air to the soil. This then causes an explosion of microbiotic life that quickly consumes the newly introduced organic matter. This is particularly true with succulents such as buckwheat which add very little if any organic matter to the soil since they are mostly water. Additionally, the extra tillage required to kill and cover the green manure crop causes loss of soil structure and tilth. Over the years I've observed that our favorite cover crop, winter rye, is very hard to kill and will sometimes resprout in the vegetable beds. The repeated rotary tilling necessary to kill the rye damages the soil more than the value of the rye as a green manure. This isn't to say, though, that cover crops are useless. Far from it. They just aren't the panacea for poor soil we once thought they were.

One researcher told me that he now favors simply mowing the cover crop and leaving the biomass on the surface where it breaks down slowly. When you study natural systems this is what you see. Annuals die in the fall and form a mulch on the soil, which protects it from the elements. As time goes by the soil microbes and earthworms and other mulch-dwellers slowly turn the mulch into humus. This leads me to believe that topsoil doesn't deepen, it uppens.

Mulch, whether left from dead cover crops such as oats––or straw and leaves spread by the gardener—will keep the ground cooler in the early spring. This can be an advantage in warmer climates in the summertime, but a disadvantage in cooler climates in the spring.

Having mulch on your garden beds may mean you will have to delay planting some of your crops until the soil has warmed. That's not too big a problem, though. My experience has been that the later-planted crops almost invariably mature on or near the same day as crops planted earlier in unmulched soil. I think this may have to do with the mulch preventing the ground from freezing to deeper levels than unmulched soil, and thus thawing earlier in the spring.

Some beds will require a fine seed bed for small seeds such as carrots, beets, scallions, radishes and so forth. Just spread a light layer of compost, about one-half-inch deep, over the sheet mulch. Broadcast the seeds, then cover them with another light layer of compost or soil. Seeds sprout and send out roots that penetrate the sheet mulch to the soil underneath and find a wealth of nutrients there for quick and healthy growth. The result, no tillage at all. Great!

Crops you can transplant through the mulch are potatoes, pumpkins, winter squash, summer squash, tomatoes, eggplants, peppers, cucumbers, lettuce, broccoli, kale, collards and so on.

Leave the paths between the garden beds in grass and white clover. Mow these periodically and leave the clippings on the ground to fertilize the grass. You can also use the grass clippings to spike your compost pile, or feed the clippings to the chickens.

Each sheet-mulch chicken-tractor with 20 broilers in it will need from one to four bales of mulch hay or straw to carry it through the rotation. Mulch hay, costing one dollar per bale, adds three dollars to the cost of the batch. With chickens dressing out at four pounds each, that's 80 pounds of meat, with the mulch hay adding from one to four cents per pound to the overall cost of the dressed weight of the birds.

In a sheet-mulch system, each batch moves five times, so each 40-square-foot pen will cover 200 square feet per batch. With three batches per season you will cover 600 square feet per season. A typical home garden today is less than 600 square feet. The garden can get most of the soil fertility and most of the replacement organic matter from the chickens and bedding in this system.

This method even works on a one-day-only basis. Move the chickens to fresh graze daily and let them reduce the spot to bare ground and cover it with nitrogen-rich manure. Move them to their next position. Instead of spreading cover crop seed and tilling, simply cover the disturbed area with a layer of loose hay mulch about one-inch deep. This will act as a buffer to hold the nutrients in the upper levels of the soil and will provide carbonaceous materials for the soil life to use while reducing the mulch to humus. This can provide a very rich soil in no time at all.

As the second and following batches of chickens arrive at this spot in their rotation you will enhance the fertility of the soil tremendously. If you start a second batch of chickens on the site and the hay mulch remaining from the preceding batch is wet, you may want to put down a light layer of new mulch hay to keep the chickens dry.

This does of course nullify any gain from grazing, but conversely you don't have to buy cover crop seed and spend the time needed to spread it and till it under. The mulch will cost some money but chances are the saved labor is worth more to you than the cost of the mulch. Think about the graze the same way. You'll have more feed to buy, but will spend less time tilling under the plots. This can work, too, if you are converting pasture or lawn to garden. The overwintering mulch will kill the grass underneath, making it much easier for you to prepare a seed bed in the spring.

Shelter-Pens larger Than four-feet wide

Several of my friends are using larger pens, measuring 10' x 10' or 10' by 12'. These larger pens have either a flat roof or a hooped roof. The advantage, of course, of the larger pens is that they are relatively inexpensive to build compared to the larger number of chickens they will hold. They can cover more ground quickly if you are raising your chickens in a pasture situation.

However, there are some disadvantages to the larger pens, particularly the hoop-style portable pens. First, of course, is that they don't fit over your garden beds when you want to preserve permanent pathways between beds. There's also the difficulty of moving them, since they can be quite heavy and bulky, making them awkward to handle.

I've found that the hoop-style pens are more expensive and much harder to build than the flat-roofed pens. Possibly the only advantage I can think of for the hoop-style pens is that you can also use them as portable greenhouses and field tunnels by removing the tarpaulin and replacing it with plastic greenhouse film. You can easily do this with flat-roofed pens, too. They will shed water almost as easily as a hoop-roofed pen, especially if the ground is sloped even a little bit.

Another style of pen, one my folks used to use, is the A-frame on skids. This style is easy to build, but hard to manage. I don't use it because the steep roof eliminates a lot of headroom inside, and it's very difficult to get at the waterer and feeder, or to catch the chickens at harvest time.

I haven't converted my poultry operation to larger shelter-pens because I use the tractors on four-foot-wide beds. It isn't any great bother to move the chicken tractor across

the pathway to begin the next pass on the adjacent garden bed. The goal in using the tractors on the garden beds is to get the paths and beds into a permanent state so that the soil does not have to be rotary tilled. The soil just gets healthier and healthier each year.

This makes for a much more attractive and abundant garden. The mulched permanent garden beds look very nice next to the grassy permanent paths. The grassy paths also give us an excellent avenue to walk to our birds and garden beds without getting muddy feet or encouraging erosion from either water or wind.

4. Intensive Grazing in Paddocks

The English pop-hole method is worth discussing here simply because it is the forerunner of the chicken tractor. The pop-hole method relies on short duration intensive grazing in rotated paddocks. English poultry growers use this method to raise thousands of birds per year with good results. By law English growers can carry only 400 hens per acre in this method, or double that for broilers. The obvious reason for the limit on birds has to do with the toxicity of the soil after growing so many birds on such a small piece of land.

The way this system works is to place the portable shelter in the center of the area for grazing, then erect portable electric fencing in a square area around the shelter. There are four pop holes, one at each corner of the shelter. Close all but one door, thereby directing the birds to graze in the specified area. Depending on your creativity, this scheme can be more elaborate, with as many individual paddocks and doors as you can fit into your site.

Once the chickens finish grazing the first group of paddocks, move the whole shelter and pen system to the next location and repeat the process, on and on across the field. At some point, after the grass has recovered from grazing, you will be able to return your flock to the beginning point and start the rotation all over.

Another design option for the pop-hole method is to have a long, enclosed wire tunnel running out from the hen house and perpendicular to the garden beds. At each garden bed there is a pop hole in the tunnel. A second tunnel rests perpendicular to the main tunnel. It moves from bed to bed as needed. The chickens enter the garden bed tunnel through the pop hole. Some folks call this the permaculture method. Its only difference from the English pop-hole method is the addition of the long service tunnel at the head of the garden beds.

If you are raising hybrid breeds that have had their natural foraging characteristics bred out of them, this system will not work as well. I've seen many times, and had other

Fixed Henhouse with Rotational Paddocks

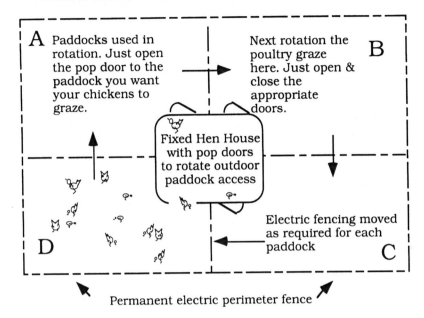

A Paddocks used in rotation. Just open the pop door to the paddock you want your chickens to graze.

Next rotation the poultry graze here. Just open & close the appropriate doors. B

Fixed Hen House with pop doors to rotate outdoor paddock access

Electric fencing moved as required for each paddock

D

C

Permanent electric perimeter fence

growers tell me, that some of the hybrids will refuse to graze altogether, unless you force them to graze by withholding feed temporarily and setting the birds directly on the grass you want them to eat. I have raised hybrid Cornish Cross broilers that were so lethargic they refused to eat potato beetles or earthworms that I collected and placed in their pen.

A second disadvantage is the open pens used in the English pop-hole system don't protect the chickens from flying predators such as hawks and owls, or from wild birds that might be diseased.

Another concern is that the birds will graze their favorite plants exclusively, allowing the undesired plants to overtake and crowd out the desired plants over one or two grazing seasons. It is necessary to keep the paddock size small and the number of birds high to force them to graze all the plants in the paddock. By doing this you will certainly encourage diversity in the grasses and herbaceous forbs, and year after year the graze will get better.

Finally, the sheer cost of building the henhouse and associated chicken runs can be prohibitive. I talked with one grower who has spent over $800 and a week of labor to build an 8' x 12' henhouse and 25' x 50' run. This setup will only house 50 laying hens. For that amount of money I think he could have built a half-dozen chicken tractors that would hold twice as many chickens and be far more portable and useful in the garden.

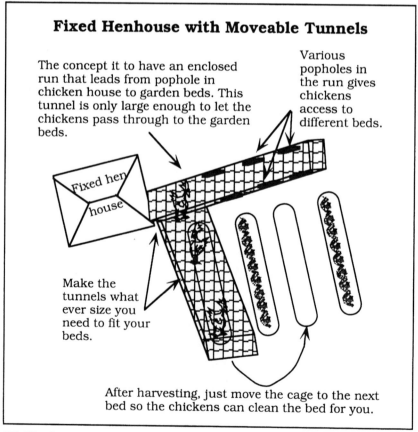

Fixed Henhouse with Moveable Tunnels

The concept it to have an enclosed run that leads from pophole in chicken house to garden beds. This tunnel is only large enough to let the chickens pass through to the garden beds.

Various popholes in the run gives chickens access to different beds.

Fixed hen house

Make the tunnels what ever size you need to fit your beds.

After harvesting, just move the cage to the next bed so the chickens can clean the bed for you.

Sundown At the Chicken Corral —and It's OK!

Vicki Dunaway in Willis, Virginia, was faced with the problem of her hens not adapting to the chicken tractor model. Her solution was to build a movable corral connected to her tractor. She describes it best in her letter to us below.

"We had 36 adolescent chicks ready to go out and only one new chicken tractor. They were okay in the one tractor for a little while if I moved it twice a day, but they were going to need more space.

We already had another chicken tractor containing seven old hens someone had given us. I don't know if it was because they were not raised in a chicken tractor, but they just didn't seem happy in that small space, even if I moved it twice a day. They picked on each other, whined a lot, and ate eggs. All the signs of boredom, in my opinion.

I asked my 'natural engineer' husband, Charley, if he could design a corral that could be moved with the tractor. My idea was for panels that could be easily disconnected. What he came up with was five 4 x 10 panels made of 2x2s and chicken wire. One panel has a hinged door that we can go in and out easily. We tied the panels together with one half inch nylon rope pieces (bright yellow is easy to find in grass). We put a pop hole in the chicken tractor so the hens could go in and out.

This worked very well except the corral was not tall enough. Even after clipping wings I spent a fair amount of time chasing chickens that flew over the top. We lost one hen to a neighbor's dog who harassed them until one flew out. We solved this problem by stapling flexible plastic fencing to the top. Our next corral will have taller sides. We want to try bamboo and have planted some for use in the garden and with chicken tractors.

I move the corral about every three days and it takes me about 20 minutes to complete the entire process. I would leave it longer in one place but I couldn't stand the chickens fussing at me because they didn't have any more green stuff.

After we put the roosters in the freezer (I'm a light sleeper) we made enough roost space for 28 remaining hens. Now the chicken tractor is adequate for sleeping, eating, drinking and laying with enough protection against bad weather. For our next tractor/corral we might put a corral on each side and add wheels to the tractor.

For our severe winters the chicken tractors are not adequate. We keep our hens in the greenhouse for the winter and they look great! I just keep spreading wood shavings from a local cabinetmaking shop and some cracked corn scratch. The chickens fluff up the wood shaving looking for the corn and it stays quite clean and nice."

Vicki and Charley Dunaway's Chicken Corral

Susanna Kay Lein's Bamboo Chicken Bungalow

Another chicken tractor corral was developed by Susana Kay Lein, an American working in Guatemala. She uses bamboo and hemp for her corrals as paraphrased in a letter to Vicki Dunaway:

"The chicken tractors and corrals we use here in Guatemala 'rotate' with a little more effort than the other tractors and still can use improvement. I prefer to use natural materials I can grow rather than pay for the expense of wire and wood. I use 'caña de carizo' which is hollow like bamboo and grows like sugar cane. For construction it is very similar to bamboo. I cut the carizo about shoulder height (five feet) and about one inch in diameter. I use my machete and put about a 45° angle on the ends so it will stab in the ground easily. I use a long skinny piece of carizo for cross braces and tie them all together with 'pita',

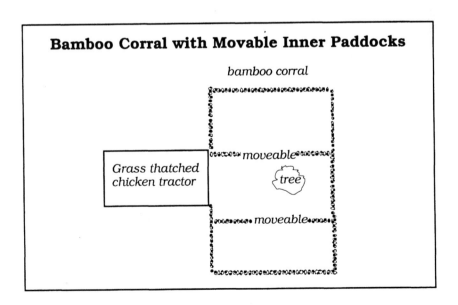

Bamboo Corral with Movable Inner Paddocks

bamboo corral

moveable

tree

moveable

Grass thatched chicken tractor

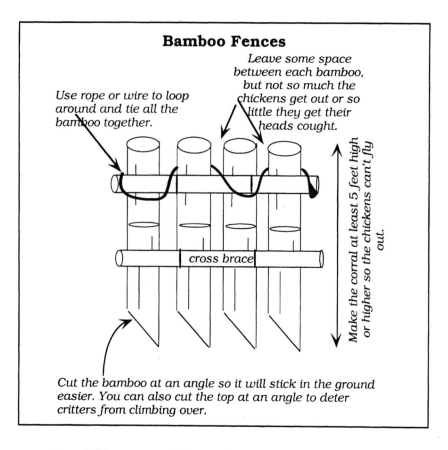

Bamboo Fences

Leave some space between each bamboo, but not so much the chickens get out or so little they get their heads cought.

Use rope or wire to loop around and tie all the bamboo together.

cross brace

Make the corral at least 5 feet high or higher so the chickens can't fly out.

Cut the bamboo at an angle so it will stick in the ground easier. You can also cut the top at an angle to deter critters from climbing over.

a natural fiber rope. I loop the pita around each vertical cane and tie them horizontally to the brace. I tie at least two cross braces on each panel. This helps stabilize the fence.

"Carizo is abundant so I made one big corral and move one or two of the corral walls back and forth allowing us to plant where the chickens have been. Because the birds have fertilized these areas well the soil is rich and softer than before. I use it for quick vegetable crops or beans. I also have sunflowers planted around the edge and peas nearby. My chicken tractor has a reed grass roof and we move it every year to a new spot wherever we want to develop a garden spot."

5. Polyface Model - Poultry with Beef Cattle.

Joel and Teresa Salatin at Polyface Farm in Swoope, Virginia, have developed an entire livelihood on just 20 acres, using a unique combination of rotationally grazing beef cattle and chicken tractors. Polyface Farm (farm of many faces) specializes in raising the "best poultry, rabbits, lamb and beef in the world," according to their recently published book, *Pastured Poultry Profit$*. The subtitle of their book is "*Net $25,000 in 6 months on 20 acres*". Joel also has an excellent book describing his method of raising beef entirely on grass. It's called *Salad Bar Beef* and includes how he uses his chickens and "egg mobile" for parasite control.

They are in the Shenandoah Valley of Virginia at 2,000-feet elevation, and grow as many as 10,000 broilers per year using portable, flat-roofed pens measuring 10 by 12'.

They refer to their method as pastured poultry. The Salatins range their chickens in conjunction with their high density, short duration beef grazing. They prepare the grass by grazing the beef cattle ahead of the chickens. The advantage is that chickens graze best when the grass is fairly short, about up to their bellies.

As the chickens follow behind the beef, they peck and scratch through the cow manure, scattering it over a larger area and digging out any worm or fly larvae in the manure. This breaks the cycle of bovine stomach parasites, eliminating the need for synthetic worm medicines for the cows.

The chickens scatter the manure piles, eliminating the concentration of nitrogen in one spot that will cause heavily nitrogenated grass to regrow. The cows refuse to eat these overly-lush clumps of grass. Joel calls these areas "the repugnance zone".

According to Joel, there is another advantage of chickens grazing after the beef cattle. The enzymes in cow manure are perfectly balanced for the chickens' digestive systems. The enzymes help the chickens digest their food. In nature the birds always follow the ruminants. Wild birds always follow deer and elk, for example. The beautiful Cattle Egret, for example, got its name from its habit of foraging with cattle.

To encourage the chickens to eat more grass, the Salatins withhold grain feed for the first half hour each morning after they move the chicken pens. They also move the older broilers twice daily to spread their manure better and to encourage even more grazing. These frequent moves keep the birds cleaner, especially in rainy weather. Moving the heavy birds more frequently also helps keep

"Egg mobile" used by Jerry Catteral at Webfoot Farm in Dorset, Vermont. The chickens follow his herd of Scot Highland cows.

them from killing the pasture grasses and forbs. Joel feels the primary benefits of this system are that there is no manure to haul out, or flies to control, and all the nutrient laden manure is going directly to growing vegetation.

Using this method, the Salatins work hard for six months during the growing season, then relax during the rest of the year. They still manage to earn more than $25,000 per year from 20 acres at their farm. They process the chickens at the farm, and sell them to a group of loyal clientele who drive to the farm several times each season to pick up their dressed broilers and eggs. They started their whole farm poultry operation for about what it would cost to buy a used, midsize farm tractor.

While Joel relies on Cornish Cross hybrids for fryers and broilers, he turns to the classic American poultry breeds for egg layers. He feels their aggressive foraging characteristics combined with their hardiness and weathering abilities make them far more suitable for free-range egg farming than any of the modern hybrid egg layers. His favorites are Dominique, New Hampshire, and Rhode Island Reds. Joel says these birds will range out 200 yards from their shelter and will consume significant quantities of protein-laden worms, crickets, grasshoppers and larvae, as much as seven pounds per 100 chickens per day.

Joel doesn't use any electric fencing around his laying hens. Instead, he relies on their natural homing instinct to go back to their egg mobile shelter at night, where he closes them in before the night predators come calling. He doesn't worry about hawks and owls because the chickens are large enough and aggressive enough to fend for themselves during the daytime.

6. Hens on Wheels.

Egg producers can use the chicken tractor on wheels to move their hens to any place in the garden or yard that seems appropriate. Ed Robinson, author of the classic homesteader's manual, *The Have More Plan*, has developed plans for an ingenious mobile chicken coop. There is a complete set of plans for Robinson's henhouse on wheels in Will Graves' book, *Raising Poultry Successfully.* (see appendix).

Bruce Johnson in Spencer, Oklahoma, developed his henhouse-on-wheels on a small boat trailer, complete with winch. He can pull or push the trailer wherever he wants it. If the terrain is too difficult for hand power he simply runs out the winch cable, anchors it to a stake in the ground and pulls the trailer by reeling in the winch line. Using all junk materials he estimates the cost of his portable egg factory at about $100.

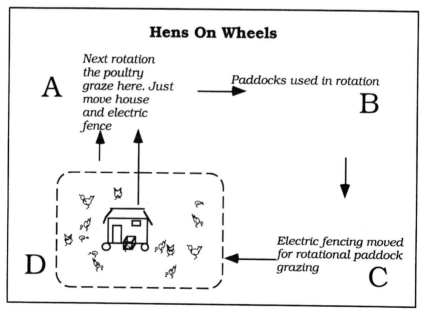

Hens On Wheels

A

Next rotation the poultry graze here. Just move house and electric fence

Paddocks used in rotation

B

Electric fencing moved for rotational paddock grazing

C

D

The Gypsy Model includes a small ramp for the chickens to get into the house part. There are three nest boxes that are accessible from the outside, and windows for ventilation. There also is a separate storage compartment that holds feed and supplies.

Another ingenious low-cost version is Harvey Harman's Poultry Pioneer Covered-Wagon Model. Harvey and his family run a community-supported farm in Bear Creek, North Carolina. Harvey used wheels from a derelict lawn mower on the back of the frame. He then used a variation of the hoop model with chicken wire in front and roofing metal for shelter in the back.

7. The Greenhouse System

Can you raise chickens in your greenhouse? Yes! It's a natural combination. You get oxygen from the plants and carbon dioxide from the chickens. Plants need carbon

Bruce Johnson's Gypsy Model
built on a recycled boat trailer.

Harvey Harman's Poultry Pioneer Covered-Wagon Model

dioxide and chickens need oxygen. The manure adds nitrogen and other valuable nutrients to the greenhouse soil. Use the bedding to biofilter the ammonia and other gasses given off by the manure.

The chickens also give body heat to help keep the greenhouse warm. Using this model you can keep your laying hens out in the garden beds through spring, summer and fall, and in the greenhouse through the winter. This provides an excellent use of fall and early-spring greenhouse space. Then use the greenhouse in the summer for producing field tunnel crops.

My first experience with raising chickens in the greenhouse came about with Tim Laird, one of my university interns and former manager of Intervale Community Farm in Burlington, Vermont. He let seven of his chickens loose in our 12 x 30' greenhouse, thinking they would glean the weeds and grasses during the fall and early winter.

Seven hens were just not enough to get the job done in a 360-square-foot greenhouse. They hung around the water bucket and feed trough, only eating the tender grasses and weeds within easy reach. The weeds at the back of the greenhouse grew large and rank and the chickens simply ignored them.

From this experience we learned that to get clean weed and grass control from chickens it is necessary to confine them for short periods of time on fairly small sections of the greenhouse floor. This forces them to eat all the green vegetation that is there, and causes the manure to be spread more equably throughout the greenhouse.

Now I use the "under-the-bench plan" for raising poultry in a 12 x 12' greenhouse. Starting about mid-March, I start early seedlings in the greenhouse and fence in the space under the benches. It is a great place to grow chicks using the deep mulch system. By the time the seedlings are ready to go to the garden the chickens are old enough to move outside to chicken tractors.

During the summer I remove the benches from the greenhouse and use the deep mulch beds to raise greenhouse tomatoes, cucumbers, or herbs and salad greens. By early winter, when the greenhouse requires heat, I move the chickens back inside and let them stay in there for the winter. Then, the following spring I move the greenhouse to a new location, turn its former site into garden beds, and start the whole rotation all over.

This method will also work very well with hydroponic or soilless mix crops that grow on the benches while the chickens remain beneath the benches. With this type system you can have virtually year-round egg, vegetable, and salad green production.

In some circumstances—for instance if you are using the greenhouse for winter shelter for your hens—you can fasten portable outside runs to the greenhouse to enable chickens to have access to outside graze. These runs will become heavily enriched areas that can become future raised beds, especially if you add bedding to balance the manure. Just don't leave the poultry there so long that the site becomes overloaded with nutrients and turns toxic.

It's important to install motorized vent fans in the greenhouse to keep the chickens from overheating on warm, sunny days. Their own body heat will often be enough to warm the greenhouse during all but the coldest days of winter, particularly if they are one of the old standard breed chickens that are hardy.

According to Anna Eddy, owner of the Solviva Greenhouse on Martha's Vineyard, Massachusetts, heat gain from chickens will amount to eight Btu's per pound of animal per hour. Each chicken provides heat in the equivalent of 2.5 gallons of heating oil per heating season. This enables chickens to survive temperatures down to 0 degrees F without undue stress.

Use electric varmint fencing around the perimiter to stop predators that might claw through the plastic film. Two growers I know, Matt and Scout Proft in Dorset, Vermont, built their greenhouse up on a foundation so the coyotes couldn't dig in to get at the baby turkeys.

The greenhouse is an excellent example of "stacking space" by having chickens on the floor and seedlings on the benches. It's also an example of "time stacking" since we are growing baby chickens while seedlings are growing as the succession crop for the greenhouse. You can even use this greenhouse space to grow the baby chicks you will be moving to your broiler pens later in the season.

Economics of a Market Garden Bioshelter

Let's take a look at what sort of income you can anticipate from a simple hoop-style greenhouse measuring 12 x 12'. This gives you 144 square feet of sheltered space. You'll need about 30 percent of that space for pathways and door access.

This size greenhouse can have four-foot-wide benches running down each side of a four-foot pathway. Under these benches you will have room to grow 48 broilers or 24 laying hens.

For this exercise let's assume you will grow one batch of broilers in the spring while your seedlings are growing on the benches. Once the seedlings go to the garden you can move the broilers to an outside shelter-pen or process them for the freezer. Then move the benches out of the greenhouse. Double dig the area under the benches and shape it into growing beds. These growing beds, enriched by the chicken manure and bedding, make an excellent place to grow tomatoes in the greenhouse. Sometimes there is too much mulch to be turned under for garden beds. You can remove the excess mulch and use it in your garden or put it on the compost pile.

With 96 square feet of bed space you can grow 24 tomato plants that will yield about 20 pounds per plant. This will give you a total harvest of 480 pounds. These tomatoes will sell for $1.50 per pound average, bringing in $720 in tomato sales.

You can sell your 48 broilers for eight dollars each for a total broiler income of $384. Additionally, you have 96 square feet of bench space. In this amount of room you can grow a total of 3'456 seedlings valued at wholesale at fifteen cents each—making them worth $520.

So, your potential gross income from the greenhouse over an eight-month period is:

Seedlings	$520
Broilers	$384
Tomatoes	$720
Total	$1,624

This gives you a total income of $11.28 per square foot. Also, you'll have 96 square feet of incredibly rich garden beds for future garden crops.

You didn't have to spend a great amount of money to make over $1,600 from your greenhouse. You didn't need to buy any heavy equipment, or go to any great trouble to accomplish all of this. The greenhouse itself can cost as little as $200 to $300 if you build it yourself. In some areas of the country you can pay the taxes on your house with the income from just one 12 x 12 greenhouse. At the very least you can enjoy a great little spare-time income for only an hour or so of work each day. You might spend about 100 hours over the course of the season doing all these things and expect to earn better than $10 per hour from your hobby business, after paying all expenses.

Use the chicken tractor greenhouse as the centerpiece of your market garden. Expand your garden each year with chickens preparing land as you need it. Sell some of your produce to make this a business venture that will give you a tax write-off that helps overcome the tax bite on your regular, full-time income from your real job. It's a great way to practice and develop skills for future farming adventures, as well.

For more information on market gardening for income, refer to my book, *Backyard Market Gardening* (see appendix).

Chapter 4: Straw Bale Chicken House

Hay and straw bales have been used to house animals (and people) for centuries. Bale housing has especially evolved since the early 1900s. This is when mechanical hay balers made it possible to compress hay and straw into string or wire-bound blocks called bales.

The first time we used bales to protect livestock was when we stacked a couple of old wet bales on the upwind side of a chicken tractor to keep the wind off a batch of pheasants we were starting. Later on a neighbor gave us about 100 bales of spoiled rained-on hay. We quickly designed a simple hay bale hut to keep our laying hens, guineas and turkeys in during the winter. The beauty of our hay henhouse is that it uses mostly waste materials (rained-

Poultry Group Processing

on hay) which we will compost and use for mulch at the end of the bale house's useful life.

This chapter briefly describes what we and others have learned and done. If you want to learn more, get our comprehensive book on using hay or straw to house animals. The title is: *Straw Bale Chicken House: The Affordable, Sustainable, Compostable Way to House Your Hens and Mulch Your Garden*, by Andy Lee & Patricia Foreman.

Benefits of Bale Construction

Modern building with bales is evolving by leaps and bounds. Think of hay or straw bales as oversized bricks, easily stacked. Building with bales requires much less skill and labor than building with stone, wood or concrete. Bale building is also very forgiving. If you make a mistake you just stuff it.

The energy efficiency of bales is excellent. The R-value of a two-string bale (about 18 inches wide) is about R-42. That is at least twice better than the wall systems of modern, four-star-rated insulated homes.

We noticed in the heat of summer that inside our hay hen house would be about ten degrees cooler than the ambient temperature. In winter our birds are really cozy even against the coldest of northern winds.

Straw vs Hay: What's the Difference?

In our many conversations with folks about using bales for animal housing, we usually need to clarify which we are talking about: straw or hay. There is currently a straw bale construction boom going on for people housing. For long-term people-house construction straw is preferable to hay. Because of this we got in the habit of saying straw bales. But we used hay bales. So what's the difference?

Straw is the stalks from threshed grain. Straw is hollow inside — like a little tube that allows air circulation. Straw also has a shiny waxy coating on the outside that makes it a little more water-resistant and durable for longer-term construction.

Hay is grass or clover that is cut and dried for fodder (feed for livestock). Farmers typically bale hay with blossoms or seed heads intact. After the cut grass dries in the field it is bundled into hay bales. Hay stalks are not hollow nor do they have a coating.

We housed our hens happily in hay because we had hay bales given to us. In our part of the country, western North Carolina, there is a lot of hay made for the horse and cow farms. It also rains a lot here, so a lot of hay gets rained on and "spoiled" before it gets hauled into a barn.

Once hay is rained on it molds and, if fed to animals, can cause serious health problems. However, rained-on hay is fine for mulching our garden, building small animal houses, and lots of other uses around the farm such as for temporary windbreaks and erosion control.

For your critter bale-house project we suggest you use whichever you can find locally and cheaply. Traditionally hay is valuable as an animal feed which sometimes makes it more expensive than straw. However, in our area a lot of the straw bales are imported from the Midwest or Canada and are therefore about a dollar a bale more expensive then hay. For the purposes of this chapter we are going to use "bales" to mean either hay or straw bundles.

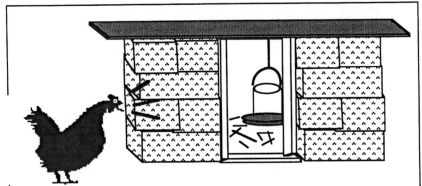

*No matter how hard she tried, **Attila the Hen** could not blow down the straw bale house.*

I'll Blow Your House Down: Common Concerns About Bale Construction.

OK, go ahead and chuckle, but indigenous cultures have used straw, grasses and vines to build with effectively for thousands of years.

One of the most commonly expressed concerns is fire safety. We tried setting a bale on fire and got mostly charred hay and smoke. In every fire test, bale construction for people homes exceeds the building code for fire safety. Luckly none of our poultry smoke. Steen, Steen and Bainbridge discuss fire safety in great detail in their book, *The Straw Bale House,* published by Chelsea Green.

As for bugs and termites, we don't see many in the bale henhouse — such crawlies are a delicacy to the poultry palate.

Rot is a concern on exposed bales and especially on bales that sit on damp ground. Bales stacked on edge will last a little bit longer than blaes laid flat. On our first hay bale henhouse we put the bales directly on the ground. After about eight months we noticed the bottom bales seemed to have melted as the bottom couple of inches decomposed. This caused the walls to lean a bit but we easily pushed them back in place and added a stick prop support. Given the amount of rain we have in western North Carolina—65 inches per year average—we didn't expect those bales to last more than a few months. We are pleasantly surprised that our first bale building is now over a year old and could go longer, although it's leaning and looking rather tired and droopy.

Odors and allergies might be a concern for you. Clean, dry hay and straw has very little mold or dust. Hay or straw bedding is effective in controlling odors because it absorbs them as a primitive biofilter. We haven't noticed any foul smells resulting from the bales.

What Will Your Neighbors Think?

That is a question we can't answer for you. We can tell you that our little hay-bale henhouse has inspired others to build their own. Because of the ease and low cost, this has also made it possible for these folks to have chickens for the first time. Your neighbors will probably be amused by the concept and delighted by the fresh, wholesome eggs you can share with them. Most kids are fascinated and delighted by the whole project. Some dogs get a little too enthusiastic and need some chicken etiquette training. David Stickney, a close friend of ours, built his six-hen hay bale house in the suburban subdivision where he lives and so far reports only positive feedback from the neighbors.

Bale Binding

Bales are bound with either sisal twine, wire, or plastic (polypropylene) string. We found the twine bindings tended to stretch and rot. Sisal, unless it is treated with a preservative, does not hold the bales secure for as long as the plastic or wire. However, the bales we got were free for the fetching, so we weren't picky about binding.

On the downside, plastic string and wire do not decompose. If you plan to recycle your bale building into garden mulch, you will need to gather all the binding and dispose of it when you spread the bales. Otherwise it can get caught in your lawn mower or lie around your yard forever. We let the sisal binding decompose in the garden or under mulch. However, we don't compost the treated twine because of the chemicals.

If you are having someone bind your bales for use in construction then you might want to specify the plastic binding. Plastic is easier to work with in modifying the bales. The wire is harder to cut and retie. You can also request half bales be made. Modern balers can make bales as small as 12 inches. However custom bales will probably cost you as much as a full bale due to the time and extra labor needed to make them.

Wet Hay or Straw Bales

Naturally you want to use the driest bales you can find. However, the bales we usually get for free or a good price are either old or rained upon, sometimes multiple times. Since we are not using the bales for feed this has not been a problem so far.

However be careful that the hay is not too moldy or dusty. Molds are capable of infecting any bird and even people. Mold can produce a form of pneumonia that is acute in

Super Simple Hay Bale Henhouse

baby chicks and chronic in mature birds. Especially common is a fungal disease called *aspergillosis*, also known as "farmer's lung". Symptoms include the bird gasping for air and swollen eyes.

All fungus (*mycotoxicosis*) infections increase a bird's need for vitamins, trace elements (especially selenium), and protein. In addition to old bales, the source of the infection can be feed and bedding. If you notice one or more of your birds wheezing we suggest you put down fresh bedding and make sure your feed is fresh and of a high quality. If your bales puff "dust" when you hit them then it is probably time to rebuild with fresh bales.

Be careful when handling dusty bales since "farmer's lung" is at best uncomfortable and at worst deadly. When handling lots of dusty bales we wear nose masks — the paper, disposable kind used in construction.

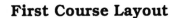

First Course Layout

Lay the first course where you want to build laying the bales length wise.

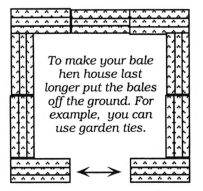

To make your bale hen house last longer put the bales off the ground. For example, you can use garden ties.

Leave an opening one bale length for the door so you can go in and collect eggs.

Here's How to Build a Super-Simple Bale Henhouse

You can use bales to build almost any shape from square to egg-shaped (Get it?—Another chicken joke!). Our hut measures 10 x 10', with a 12 x 12' roof. The whole structure cost us less than $100 and currently houses eight hens, four guineas, and five turkeys. This is crowded living for so many large birds so we let them out during the daytime when we are home, plus they have two attached chicken tractors for extra play room.

Making Half-Bales

For the corners, people door, and chicken door, you will need to make half-bales. You can modify bales to almost any size or shape you need. There are several techniques to resize bales for large-scale construction. For our simple building purposes we found it easiest to cut the binding, size the bale to meet our needs, and retie the binding. There are always spare pieces of binding you can use from bales that have broken apart from loading and unloading.

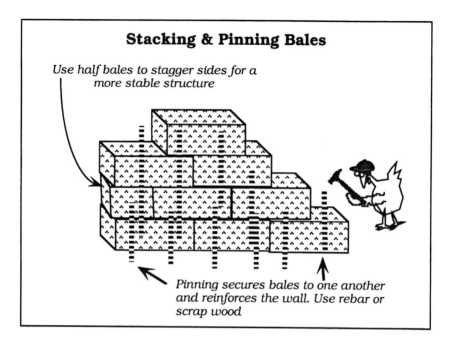

Stacking & Pinning Bales

Use half bales to stagger sides for a more stable structure

Pinning secures bales to one another and reinforces the wall. Use rebar or scrap wood

Building Walls

To start your bale building just lay the first course where you want to build. For our first bale house, we just laid the bales directly on the ground. This worked fine, but after a while the bottom bales seemed to melt as they slowly composted. However, we wanted our second bale house to last longer so we got some used wooden pallets. You can get pallets free from almost any shipping company. Just cut the pallets lengthwise to fit the length of the bales and place the pallets directly on the ground with the first course of bales on top. This will form a foundation that will help keep the bottom bales dry. (It also forms a cavity for rats to nest in, so keep an eye out for these unwelcome guests and dispatch them as needed.)

Leave a bale-wide opening for the doorway. Stake the first course to the ground with wooden scraps or metal rebar. We used leftover pieces from our house construction, about 1 by 36 inches and drove them into the first bale and into the ground.

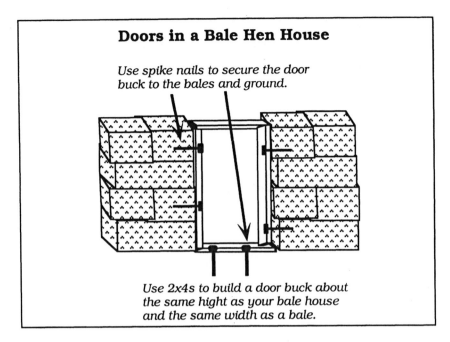

Doors in a Bale Hen House

Use spike nails to secure the door buck to the bales and ground.

Use 2x4s to build a door buck about the same hight as your bale house and the same width as a bale.

On each subsequent course use half bales to offset seams so you have a running bond. To clarify the process, I've drawn a sketch for you. You also will need half bales to fit around every other layer at the door frame.

Then each subsequent layer gets staked (pinned) to the one under it. This stabilizes the walls so they won't fall over before you get the roof on. Staking the bales adds structural integrity in high winds or earthquakes. Materials you can use for pinning includes metal rebar, wood, bamboo, tree branches, or any long, hard object you have easy access to.

Our first hay bale hut is four courses high which is plenty for the birds, but I have to stoop when I go in for eggs and to change water and add feed. My friend David Stickney used three courses for his urban model. Our turkeys and guineas would prefer more headroom because they like to perch as high as possible at night. Just keep in mind that the higher you go, the more stability becomes a problem. Our next bale house will probably be five courses high .

Our door frame is simple. We used 2x4 boards the size of the door opening (about three feet by four feet) to form the buck about as high as the top bale. We anchored the 2x4 door buck to the ground and side bales with long cabin spike nails. Drill holes in the buck first to fit the spikes through. We found that as the bales settled, so did the roof — right onto the door jam. We had to keep adding height to the roof by putting scrap boards between the rafters and where the roof lay on the bales. Otherwise we couldn't open the door easily.

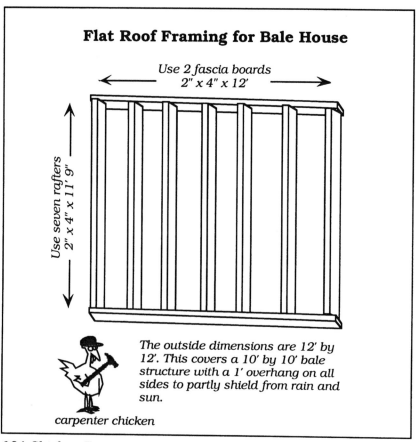

Flat Roof Framing for Bale House

Use 2 fascia boards
2" x 4" x 12'

Use seven rafters
2" x 4" x 11' 9"

The outside dimensions are 12' by 12'. This covers a 10' by 10' bale structure with a 1' overhang on all sides to partly shield from rain and sun.

carpenter chicken

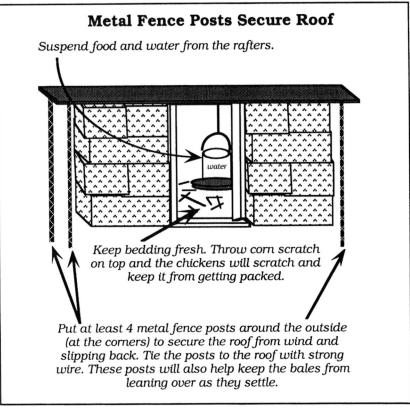

Metal Fence Posts Secure Roof

Suspend food and water from the rafters.

water

Keep bedding fresh. Throw corn scratch on top and the chickens will scratch and keep it from getting packed.

Put at least 4 metal fence posts around the outside (at the corners) to secure the roof from wind and slipping back. Tie the posts to the roof with strong wire. These posts will also help keep the bales from leaning over as they settle.

We used more 2x4s to make a door frame to fit inside the door buck. We put cross supports at the corners to keep it square. Then we hinged the door to the door buck. We covered the door with one inch chicken wire for light and ventilation.

If you put the doorway on the south side the winter sun will help warm the biddies in the winter. Usually it is least desirable to face the door north because of winter winds, or west because of the hot afternoon (dragon) sun. We put the door of our first bale hut facing west and had to lean a piece of plywood in front of the door to shield the interior from the hot, late afternoon summer sun. In really hot weather we even added a fan to keep the ladies cool. Use your common sense for door placement depending upon your (micro) climate and relative location.

For severe winter weather and draft protection we use 12 mil plastic to cover the door. For some parts of the attached chicken tractor we used a combination of plywood and plastic to keep the wind out. It looked a little tacky but our birds were warm, cozy and healthy all winter.

Roof Construction

The roof is simple. Use 2"x4"x12' boards to make a 12'-square platform with rafters 24" apart. Then nail Tuff-Tex roofing panels to the "rafters". Use special galvanized roofing nails that have a neoprene washer under the head. These prevent nail holes from leaking. These Tuff-Tex panels are 2' wide and 12' long. We found for our southern, hot summer climate that a lighter color of roofing was much cooler than a darker color.

There are translucent roofing panels made of Fiberglas and plastic that let in more light. These might be fine for winter use but in the summer they might let in too much heat. We don't recommend using translucent panels for the entire roof. For the small size of the bale house, the door lets in enough light.

Galvanized roofing panels are suitable roof coverings, though they tend to let in more heat than the other panels. Plywood and asphalt roll roofing would also be acceptable except for the expense and weight and extra work to put it all together. Roofing paper (tarpaper) is not suitable, it will blow off fairly quickly.

Our first supersimple and fast model had the roof sitting directly on top of the hay bales. As the bales settled, the roof height dropped a little. We propped the roof back up

Chicken Tractors Combined with Hay Bale house for Winter Housing. Note the long sticks we use for arm extenders to help herding the birds

by putting scrap pieces of wood where the rafters met the bales. We especially had to do this on the door side so we could open the door, and to keep the roof slant to the back for drainage.

We used a 7' steel fence post at each corner of the hut, driven at least 2' deep and then wired the top of the post to the corner of the roof section. This held the roof on in remarkably high wind gusts of up to 70 mph. You could use more steel fence posts for additional support to keep the bales from bulging out, and further strapping for the roof if you have high winds in your area.

Don't worry about building any fancy roof for "pitch". On most farms there will be plenty of ground slope so when you put up the hut there will be enough angle for rain to run off. If your area has heavy snow loads then you will need heavier rafters and more of a pitch to shed the snow.

For our 'next generation' bale henhouse we used a simple post-and-beam construction so that the roof rests on posts instead of directly on the bales. This keeps the roof from settling down as the bales compact a little.

Other materials you can use for building include bamboo trusses, hoop, canvas and just about anything you can scrounge from the dump or recycle center. Just keep in mind that even chickens have aesthetic standards and your neighbors will appreciate cute rather than crappy structures.

Roof Types

There are many variations for roofs ranging from our simple flat roof, to hip roofs and even dormers for the creative enthusiasts. Just as we have heard from our readers about the many models of chicken tractors, we hope to hear from you about how you build your animal bale housing project. Perhaps we can include your project in the next edition!

Interior Finish: Building to Chicken Code

We have two doors in the hay bale henhouse: one for people and a small turkey-size pop hole that leads to an attached chicken tractor. The chicken tractor serves as a sun (play) room. To put a poultry door in the bale house we simply removed about half a bale on the second row and put in a small doorjamb made from scrap wood. This small jamb supports the hay bale above from collapsing down. We also put a short ramp for our small bantams to get up and down easily. The turkeys had no problem stepping through the door into the adjacent chicken tractor.

Roosts and nesting boxes are furniture musts for poultry. Our birds seem to prefer the highest roost available, which has sometimes been on top of our house. See the chapter on chicken tractor construction for roost and nest box construction suggestions. A tree branch about 1.5" to 3" in diameter will also do for roosts.

We put in two roosts, one along the back wall and one along the side. We simply stuck them into a wall to rest on a bale and provided additional support with cinder blocks inside. Hang a feeder and waterer inside the hay house suspended from the roof rafters, or from the supports in the adjacent chicken tractor.

We built in a three-bay nest box that is the same size as a bale. It sits in the second course of bales and has a door flap to open from the outside so we can gather eggs without going inside the bale house. A four-bay nest box sits just under the lid of the attached chicken tractor. To gather eggs we just lift the lid. A roost in front of the nest box enables the hens to hop up first to the roost and then to the next box.

Size Considerations Depends Upon Your Flock Size.

You will need at least two square feet per broiler, four square feet per hen, and eight square feet per turkey. You will also need some space for a chicken yard so they can get fresh air, exercise and sunshine. When we are home we let our birds out almost daily to free-range around the yard, woods, and pasture that are next to our house. The flock always puts themselves to bed at dusk. We just have to close the doors and turn on the electric poultry net that surrounds the entire structure. If we are going to be gone during the day we almost always keep the birds in and the electric netting on. This keeps the local serial chicken killers away.

TurGuChi Co-Housing

Put a chicken door in the side by removing about 1/2 bale and making a doorjam to support the hay above. Have this door next to the door in your chicken tractor.

Add a sunwing to your bale house by putting a door in your chicken tractor on the side or end, and in the side of the bale house. You can attach as many tractors as you have for larger flocks.

Co-Housing: The TurGuChi Condo for Interracial and Intercultural Housing

With winter coming on it seemed natural to combine our chicken tractors with the bale house to form the Tur-Gu-Chi Condo. Some folks crave the Gucci brand for fashion. But we have our farm fashion with our <u>Tur</u>keys, <u>Gu</u>inea and <u>Chi</u>ckens (pronounced turgoochi).

We used two of our larger chicken tractors that had turkey-size doors in the ends and middle. We put these next to the hay-bale house as outdoor runs. We call this extension "sun-wings" thinking that the term is better suited to poultry — it's a bird thing.

Inside the Urban Hobbit Bale Henhouse

This complex now houses eight hens alaying, five sort-of-wild turkeys and four gabby guineas. We let all these birds free roam during the day. The chickens go back to the condo to roost every night. The turkeys and guineas hang around the pen since they are bonded with the chickens and eventually put themselves to bed at dusk. Otherwise we'd lose them to foxes, coyotes, dogs, raccoons, possums, weasels, rats and the boogeyman.

Hay-Bale Suburban Hobbit Model

by David Stickney

I wanted to have fresh eggs and move toward a simpler, more self-sufficient lifestyle. After working with Andy Lee and being inspired by seeing his hay-bale henhouse in action, I set out to design and build one for myself.

Because we live in an urban area and have limited yard space I decided to make my bale henhouse smaller than

Andy's. My house is approximately nine feet square. It has eight bales to a layer and is only three bales tall. As Andy is fond of saying, "Why build a people-size hen house for hundreds of dollars when a $100 hen-sized house makes more sense for my small flock?"

The interior dimensions are 6' x 6' which is enough for eight to twelve birds. I made the door from a 3'x3' sheet of half-inch plywood screwed to a 2x4 frame, hinged and barrel-bolted. The door opens to a 10 x 30' chicken yard that also contains my compost pile.

My roof is supported separately from the bales by 4x4 posts in each corner. When the bales are too old I'll simply use them in my garden and replace them with fresh ones. I left about four inches of space between the top bale and the roof for ventilation. My fencing comes up under the roof to keep various potential diners from wiggling through and snacking on my flock.

Inside the west side of the bale house I built a plywood nesting box along the top bales. I can reach in from the outside to pick up the eggs.

As a newcomer to sustainable living, I appreciate that living on the land is not only about the fertility of the soil and livestock. It is also the fertility of my imagination and creativity. Hay bales have always smelled good to me — now they smell even better. I used salvaged boards and roofing, so the whole kit and kaboodle, including the hardware, cost me only $1.49.

Bale Construction For Livestock — Problems and How to Solve Them

• Varmints: Rats, Opossums and Other Carnivores

A house of bales will not deter a hungry carnivore. We lost three of our young hens to an opossum, and two birds to either rats or weasels. It would not take much for a dog or raccoon to claw its way through the bales.

Our approach to this problem was to put electric poultry netting around the compound. We use a solar charger for the fence that works well in warm weather. But we found the battery didn't recharge fully and function properly in the cold winter months. So we had to run an electric cord out to the bale house for a water warmer and to run the electric fence.

If you use electric tape or netting be sure to get a low-impedance, intermittent charger. The low-impedance will not burn out the fine wires in the tape and netting. The intermittent charger pulses and gives the birds a chance to get away from the shock. A continuous charge has a higher probability of electrocuting a small animal.

We also considered running a non-electric chicken wire fence all around the outside of the hay henhouse, but we already had the electric net and it's much simpler to install.

• Drainage.

Our bale house is on a hillside. To keep water from running onto the bales and in the house we dug a small swale (shallow ditch) along the uphill side. This directs the water around the house. This works very well and only took a few minutes to dig the two- to four-inch-deep trench. We put the extra dirt on the downhill side of the trench to form a mini-dike. We periodically need to redig the trench as it tends to fill in when we walk on it.

Other problems we've encountered so far with our bale chicken hut are:

1. Mistakenly faced door to west. Afternoon "dragon" sun overheats the hut. Have to shield with piece of plywood in really hot weather. Put your door to the east or south. Allow one foot roof overhang so summer sun that is high in sky does not penetrate door opening.

2. Using old wet hay that is moldy may cause *aspergilliosis*, a respiratory infection that requires antibiotics and nursery rest for infected chickens. Use decent hay and put the roof on quickly so hay stays dry. We expect this hay bale hut will last one full year, perhaps two before we tear it down and compost it and build a new one.

3. As hay bales settle from weight of roof, and from age, the roof pins the door and makes it harder to open. Solution is to use 2x4 posts at corners and let roof sit directly on the posts so it is independent of door buck. You still need fence posts for anchors, though, just like wind anchors on mobile homes.

You need very little building experience to build a hay-bale henhouse. There are almost endless design variations you can use in bale building. When a hay-bale henhouse is used in conjunction with portable chicken yards and chicken tractors, almost anyone with even limited outdoor space can keep hens safely, comfortably and humanely.

Future Generation Bale Houses

Pat wants to build a henhouse using those big four foot diameter round bales, and I want to experiment with housing our Tamworth pigs with bales. We plan to experiment with other small farm uses for bale construction including critter housing and some temporary shelters to get our farm equipment, bicycles, lumber, and other weather-sensitive items out of the elements.

Let us know your experiences with bale housing for critters and garden uses. We might be able to include your project as an example in one of our publications and share your experiences with others. We expect a lot of new information and clever ideas to become available as the straw bale movement matures and evolves.

Chapter 5: Soil Building with Chicken Tractors

Today's chemically intensive and tillage-oriented farming practices have resulted in soils deficient in organic matter, trace elements, and macro and micronutrients. These deficiencies become apparent in the nutritional content of the grasses and grain grown on these soils. Consequently, we are seeing deficiencies in the health of the animals maintained on these crops. It goes without saying, then, that we humans who eat the products of these infertile fields are also suffering from dietary deficiencies. These deficiencies are becoming readily apparent in our nation's rising cancer and heart disease statistics.

You can overcome many soil nutrient deficiencies with applications of compost and livestock manure. Throughout our American history we've had plenty of positive experiences using livestock in crop rotations to renew the earth with manure. Thomas Jefferson, in 1793, wrote of:

"A moveable airy cow house, to be set up in the middle of the field which is to be dunged, and soil our cattle in that thro' the summer as well as winter, keeping them constantly up & well littered."

If we knew that much 200 years ago, why did we forget? Somewhere in our nation's history we lost sight of what James Madison, our fourth president, said in 1818:

"Nothing is more certain than that the continual cropping without manure deprives the soil of its fertility. It is equally certain that fertility may be preserved or restored by giving to the earth animal or vegetable manure equivalent to the matter taken from it."

In today's agriculture, we have a situation that is the exact opposite of what Jefferson and Madison both recommended. With monocrop farming in the last four decades, we have seen livestock disappear from thousands and thousands of acres of farmland, to be replaced year after year by cash grain crops. Mono-cropping results in soil erosion from wind and rain. The soil lies bare and unprotected by vegetation for most of the year. Without livestock manure there is not a good way to replenish fertility and organic matter. The structure and tilth of the soil degenerates year by year. Before you know it you are trying to grow your crops in sub-soil instead of topsoil.

Soil loss from these grain fields is enormous. Some reports indicate that growers lose as much as four bushels of topsoil for each bushel of grain produced. Nationally, topsoil losses average four tons per acre per year, which is ten times greater than average natural soil formation. In midwestern grain fields it is common to have topsoil losses of as much as 11 tons per acre per year!

One hundred years ago, topsoil in some areas of the Great Plains measured nearly a dozen _feet_ deep. Today, we measure remaining topsoil in _inches_. In some areas less than four inches remain, and in extreme cases the land has become desert.

I've spent years watching the land after heavy rains. To see the good brown earth continually being washed off the fields into nearby lakes and streams is alarming. This is the condition that writer and farmer Edward Faulkner described as "_watching the farmer's fortune wash downstream_".

I think the first thing we need to do as farmers is to learn how to keep our farms out of the creek. And we need to stop growing cash grains on fields that are subject to erosion or flooding. We should return these marginal fields to pasture, vegetated wetlands, and forest land, then concentrate our crop-producing energies on the remaining good land.

We need to restore our fields to their past levels of high organic matter and fertility. Then we need to use rotational grazing of poultry and other livestock, combined with green manure cover crops and sensible crop rotations, to increase yields. Increased yields from properly enriched fields will more than make up for taking our marginal acres out of production.

I feel there will be many immediate and positive results from this movement away from plowing and planting every last acre of land that is available to us, regardless of its suitability for farming. Our air will be cleaner because there will be less dust in it. The streams, rivers, lakes, and oceans will be cleaner because of reduced erosion and silting.

Our use of fossil fuels for farming will decrease since we will be concentrating our food-growing energies on smaller pieces of real estate. Our ruminant livestock health—and human health—will improve, as food animals return to a grass-based diet that is easier for them to digest. Grass diets also help them produce meat that is lower in fat and cholesterol.

Some farmers are being pushed onto marginal land because much of our good land is being lost to increased residential, commercial, and industrial development. This results directly from our steadily increasing population. In my lifetime our world population has doubled. My remaining life expectancy of 30 years will see another doubling of our population. So, in my lifetime there will have been a quadrupling of the world population.

In the next thirty years the demands for land for housing, institutional, commercial, and industrial development will be enormous. As prices skyrocket for buildable land the areas available for farming will become smaller and smaller. This process is already exceedingly acute where we need farmland most, at the fringes of our towns and cities.

Nearly one-third of our nation's farmland, 320 million acres, lies at the urban edge. On this land, we raise 86% of all fruits and vegetables, 80% of all dairies and 45% of our meat, poultry and fish. This land is under intense pressure from development, pollution, and erosion. Each day we lose nearly 17,000 acres of tillable land, or 60 million acres per decade.

In the past year alone we lost nearly 2.5 million acres to development, and several times that much to erosion, salinization, pollution and loss of soil fertility. It doesn't take a rocket scientist to figure out that if these losses continue unabated we are at risk of creating huge famine within the very near future.

It seems like a farfetched idea, I know, to think we will ever have famine or new deserts forming in America. It wasn't too many years ago, though, that the droughts that caused the dust bowl did just that, giving us a dire warning of even more deserts to come. If you doubt this is true, look across the ocean to countries like Sudan and Ethiopia to see what the final harvest of overpopulation, overfarming and overdevelopment might be.

Both of these countries, as late as 1940, were 40% forested and had more than adequate food supplies for their people. Now they are both nearly 100 percent desert, and the population rests in the grip of a terrible famine that appears to be unsolvable.

Twice As Much Food on Half as Much Land

In the next 30 years it is entirely possible that our farm-land will decrease by half, while our expanding population's food demand will double. Our nation will then have the necessity of growing twice as much food on half the land. Can we do it? I think so.

Allan Savory, developer of Holistic Resource Management, in Albuquerque, New Mexico, says, *"It's becoming increasingly clear that we will all soon be managing land of smaller units of greater complexity."*

John Jeavons at Ecology Action in California has shown beyond any shadow of doubt that we can improve vegetable yields by 4 to 31 times the current national average. Even grain yields will double or triple with intensive growing techniques.

Such increases are possible to all of us, if we take the time to study successful, intensive growing methods and replicate them in our own gardens and fields. The important distinction between John and me is that he is growing a vegetarian diet, while I still, at least for the near future, prefer to eat meat.

It may be a forgone conclusion that at some point in our nation's future we will all become vegetarian. I believe this will happen not from an altruistic, value-based decision, but because the declining land base will make meat so expensive that many of us won't be able to afford it. This is already true in Japan, where steak sells for as much as $24 per pound.

The only apparent long-term answer to an increasing population and declining farmland is for all of us to become vegetarian. However, most of the U.S. population is still eating a meat-based diet, and most of us are unwilling to give it up. Currently here in America, less than two percent of our population is vegetarian. Some 40% of that group eats some meat occasionally, primarily fish and poultry.

It seems unlikely that the remaining 98 percent of our population who are meat-eaters are going to change their diet overnight. So, it's not likely that our national meat-based diet will change significantly soon. Rather it will erode gradually as more and more people find our present diet is too expensive, not only in dollars and cents but in health and environmental costs as well.

How Can Chicken Tractors Help Soil Improve?

The answer, at least for the near future, is to adjust our farming methods to more pasture and less grain. This means more intensive livestock management on the pastures, and less reliance on confinement feeding of livestock such as in feedlots. In the poultry industry today we have only a few major companies, each producing millions of broilers each year through a complex network of contract growers and processors. Let's think instead about having thousands of small-scale growers, each producing only thousands of birds each year, and doing it on pasture with supplemental grain.

Three important benefits—along with many lesser benefits—will result from such a paradigm shift. First, consumers will have access to good tasting, healthy chickens. Second, many new farmers will be able to make all or part of their living on their land. Third, and perhaps most important, there will be a significant reversal of deterioration in our nation's farms, health, and environment.

The chicken tractor system is nothing more than management-intensive, high-density, short-duration rotational grazing. I think it's important to point out here that the chicken tractor method can apply just as well to all manner of livestock. Dairy cows, beef, horses, sheep, pigs, and goats can all be grown successfully using high-density, short-duration rotational grazing.

Time after time it's been proven that rotational grazing can improve the land, produce a superior product, and make more money for the farmer than confinement feeding, regardless of which livestock are in the system. We cannot deny these facts, although our national policy makers can choose to ignore them at least in the short term.

Sensible and humane livestock production has to become part of our nation's cultural ethic. Consider recycling, as an example. Five years ago none of us knew how to recycle. Now we're all doing it as a day-to-day routine, and failure to do so seems somehow morally wrong. If the Congress of the United States will get behind this rotational grazing idea and mandate an end to grain-based confinement feeding, we would see an immediate, incredible national shift to a healthier diet, a healthier environment and a healthier nation.

In the meantime, until that glorious day arrives, we can only continue our experiments and demonstrations. Our efforts will have an effect on our neighbors and friends, and there will be a swelling pool of knowledge. Eventually the nation's population will see the benefits of rotational grazing and will force our government to take it seriously.

So, as poultry growers, either for our own use or for sale, we need to start improving our land and our incomes with chicken tractors. Use the chicken tractors to fertilize your gardens or farm fields, so that you can grow more of your own food, and enough to sell to earn either a full-time or part-time income from your land.

How Does Soil Fertility Happen?

Soil forms by the decomposition of organic matter—materials that were once living—into humus. The decomposition takes place when the decomposer organisms—earthworms, bacteria, fungi, etc.—eat the organic matter.

It's an interesting notion, but soil doesn't deepen, it uppens. As each year's growth dies and falls to the earth, it decays and turns into humus. This humus contains the nutrients, vitamins and minerals that the next year's plant growth requires. It is an ongoing cycle, with the soil dwellers providing the nutrients for the plants, and the plants growing the biomass to feed the soil dwellers. For centuries humans have searched for the perpetual motion machine. All along we've had it, right at our very feet, in the ground we walk on.

Anything that was once living can become soil organic matter and then humus. That's why, when we mulch the soil, it will eventually become richer as the mulch decays and turns into humus—topsoil.

We can destroy this valuable layer of topsoil—humus and organic matter—in one of several ways. We can plow and till the soil until it becomes finely granulated, subject to wind and water erosion. We can plant continuous crops in the soil, remove all the biomass as feed for distant livestock and humans, and not allow any organic materials back to the earth to feed the soil dwellers.

Another way we can destroy soil is to use astringent fertilizers that overstimulate soil dwellers, causing a rapid depletion of the organic matter. We can also use toxic chemicals that kill the soil dwellers, thereby totally disabling the cycle in which plants provide food for the soil life and the soil life provides food for the plants.

The chicken tractor system interrupts all of these methods of soil destruction, replacing them with a system that very closely resembles the natural processes. As the chickens eat the greenery inside their pen they remove the need for herbicides. The manure from the chickens replaces the need for synthetic fertilizers. The organic material in the chicken manure—about 40 percent of the volume—feeds the soil life, which in turn feeds the plant life that feeds the chicken. All of this in nature's symbiotic harmony.

The trick, of course, is to manage the chicken tractor rotations in a way best suited to providing the needs of the soil, the chickens, and the farmer. This means that we don't want to leave the chickens in one place too long, lest they deposit more manure than the soil can immediately handle. That could lead to toxicity and perhaps even runoff or nitrate leaching.

If it is necessary to leave the chicken tractor in the same place for a prolonged period, then add carbon material such as straw or dry hay. This carbonaceous material acts as a buffer, a primitive yet very effective biofilter, to dilute the effects of the nitrogen-rich chicken manure.

How Much Organic Matter Do We Need in the Soil?

I've always thought of organic matter as being the heart of the soil. It provides food for the soil dwellers, who in turn make the nutrients available to the plants. Organic matter acts as a buffer against wind and water erosion. A soil that is only one percent organic matter will be continually at risk of blowing or washing away unless it is continually covered with plant life. A soil that has five percent organic matter will have a crumb structure suitable for withstanding wind and water erosion.

A rich soil having a five percent level of organic matter absorbs many times more rainwater before eroding and will retain water much longer. Plants growing in a soil with sufficient organic matter will be far less stressed by lack of water between periods of rainfall. The effects of drought would be lessened. Weather patterns haven't changed all that much over the past couple of centuries. We have probably the same cycles of wet and dry spells for most of the continent; yet today, even a few weeks without rainfall is spoken of in tragic terms as a "killer drought". One reason is because we have burned up and used up all the native organic matter in our soils. The organic matter acts like a living sponge. It is a giant reservoir that holds the water and releases it slowly for plant use.

Organic matter starts the process whereby the soil becomes more fertile, enabling the grower to achieve increased yields from crops. In one test I did several years ago I found that tomato plants in soil containing less than one percent organic matter would yield about two pounds of fruits per plant. In the adjacent plot—where soil organic matter stood at 5 percent—the tomato plants yielded from seven to 20 pounds per plant.

Each type of soil has an optimum and a maximum yield potential. To maximize yields you usually need to add extra fertilizer, particularly nitrogen, to the soil. This added nitrogen often has an unwanted side effect of causing excessively rapid decomposition of the soil organic matter. In the short term, of course, crop yields often increase, sometimes dramatically, but in the long term the soil dies. I think it's better to strive for <u>optimal</u> production yields. Ask the soil to produce yields that are sustainable without costly and degenerative applications of nitrogen.

To achieve optimal production yields—versus maximum--requires us to replenish the soil organic matter on a regular basis, either annually or biannually, depending on the crop we are growing. The fastest and most complete way to add organic matter to the soil is with applications of well-balanced compost. Other ways to achieve increases in soil organic matter are through rotational grazing livestock, cover cropping green manures, and with sheet mulching. All of these are effective, but none are as immediately effective as compost.

Using Compost to Increase Organic Matter in the Soil

Depending on soil type and parent material, there are about 2,000,000 pounds of soil per acre foot. When you have a soil test done, be sure to ask the laboratory to test for the percentage of organic matter in your soil. Anywhere from less than one percent to more than 40 percent of the top layer of the soil is organic matter. The dry, sandy soil of the arid West is often lower than one percent organic matter. The muck soils of southern Canada may have as much as 40 percent organic matter. Most soils in the United States are somewhere between one percent and five percent.

Adding 20 tons per acre of compost to the soil will increase the organic matter by about one percent. Each pound of compost will contain about one-half pound of organic matter, with the rest being made up of water and air. This one percent gain in soil organic matter will require about one pound of compost per square foot of land.

Compost weighs about 1,000 to 1,100 pounds per cubic yard, depending on the moisture content and the origin of the raw materials. Therefore, you will need about 40 cubic yards of good compost per acre. In your garden beds this amounts to about three cubic feet of compost per 100 square feet. That's about a one-inch layer.

In soil reclamation you will want to apply this amount of compost each year until the soil organic matter measures above five percent. Then you can decrease compost applications to every other year or every third year. This will enable you to expect optimal yields on a sustained basis.

Sometimes the question comes up about how much organic matter can you put in the soil before you "overload" it. The answer has more to do with timing than with amounts. Whatever organic matter you use, be it sawdust, leaves, old hay, or grass clippings, you need to leave it alone long enough for the soil microbes to turn it into humus. If you plant too early the organic matter is still breaking down and will tie up all the available nitrogen in that process. Putting the material down the year before and letting it decompose slowly over a few seasons is better than applying the material, then trying to plant right away. The soil life can't react that fast. They need time to carry out their function as decomposers.

In the long term you probably can't put enough organic materials on your land, simply because you won't have access to that much material. As an example, the University of Connecticut has for years been carrying out soil reclamation trials using leaves as organic matter. The soil in some of the garden beds now has over 12 percent organic matter and is producing crops abundantly. In those beds they can stop compost and leaf-mulch applications for many years before the level of organic matter will drop to non-productive levels again.

Making good compost requires that you have the right combination of air, water, carbon materials, and nitrogen materials. Introduce air to the compost pile by turning it or with venting pipes or layering in materials such as cornstalks that will naturally move air through the pile.

Water can come from natural rainfall. During dry periods you may want to add water to the pile. During heavy rainfalls you might want to cover the pile with plastic to retard leaching. The compost pile needs to be damp, like a wrung-out sponge. If it is too dry or too wet, the decomposers—bacteria, fungi, earthworms—can't do their job.

The proper carbon-to-nitrogen ratio in the compost pile is about 30:1. As an example, add one-part leaves (C/N 50:1) to one-part green grass clippings (C/N 10:1). The resulting C/N is 30:1. You arrive at this number by adding the materials together, for example, 50:1 plus 10:1 = 60:1 divided by 2 = 30:1.

Leaves	50
Grass	10
	60 divide by 2 = 30

Well-balanced compost—made from proper combinations of carbon and nitrogen materials—will have an N-P-K ratio of about 1:1:1. This means each of the macronutrients—nitrogen, phosphorus and potassium—is about one percent of the total volume. The following chart shows the carbon to nitrogen ratio of a few common materials.

Ratio of Carbon to Nitrogen in Common Materials

Carbon Materials:	Carbon to Nitrogen Ratio:
Leaves	50:1
Straw	80:1
Dry hay	50:1
Sawdust	300-500:1

Nitrogen Materials:

Green grass clippings	10:1
Food waste	10:1
Livestock manure	10:1
Slaughter waste	10:1

Under most circumstances the decomposition process in the compost pile will reduce the volume of materials by about 50 to 80 percent. In other words, if you put in ten cubic yards of raw materials you'll get back about two to five cubic yards of compost.

If we add 20 tons per acre of compost to the soil, and the compost contains one percent nitrogen (N), we are adding 400 pounds of N per acre. Is that too much? No. The nitrogen binds to the organic matter of the compost, where it remains available for slow release. Only about 50 percent of the nitrogen value of the organic matter will release during the first year. In the following year another 50 percent will release, and so forth, until the nitrogen store is depleted.

The organic matter will hold the organic N until the plants need it. Inorganic N, on the other hand, is immediately available for plant use. The inorganic N that isn't used quickly by the plants will be susceptible to leaching.

Chickens Add Fertilizer and Organic Matter to Soil

If you use the chicken tractor system to raise chickens in your garden you can expect soil fertility and organic matter content to increase in your garden beds practically overnight. This happens because the chicken is not able to convert all of its feed to either meat or eggs. Chickens excrete an average of 75% nitrogen, 80% phosphorus and 85% potassium that is in the animal feed.

A mature hen will eat about 80 to 90 pounds of feed per year, and produce about 50 pounds of nutrient rich manure. A broiler will eat about 15 pounds of feed and will excrete about ten pounds of manure over an eight week period. About 40 percent of this manure is organic matter.

Therefore, if you raise ten hens in a 40-square-foot pen, and move the pen daily, the hens will be depositing about 500 pounds of manure per year on your garden beds. You can rotate these ten hens from bed to bed in a 30-day cycle. That means they will spend one day on each site and not return to that site for 30 days.

This rotational system will cover 1,200 square feet, about the size of a 30 by 40-foot family garden. Thanks to the nutrients and organic matter in the chicken manure you will have fertile beds next year in which to grow your garden.

Use the deep mulch system if you don't have enough garden space to move your chickens each day. The advantage of adding mulch to the chicken tractor daily is that it will interrupt the loss of nutrients to volatilization. If you don't protect the chicken manure on the soil surface, anywhere from 30 to 90 percent of the nitrogen can be lost. Nearly 50 percent of that loss will occur in the first 24 hours. The longer the nitrogen lies exposed the greater the percentage of loss.

Another advantage to the dry hay or straw mulch is to buffer the impact of the nitrogen in the chicken manure. The carbon nature of the mulch will help lock up the nitrogen, releasing it slowly so that the following crop plants don't get an oversupply of nitrogen. Too much nitrogen in the soil can lead to excessive foliage growth in the plants. This may actually retard the yields of the plants. The carbon material helps to buffer any potential nitrogen overload.

Using Rotational Pens to Build Soil Fertility

Using poultry in a rotational grazing sequence is a good way to add fertility to your garden quickly. Each day move the portable shelter-pen to a new spot, leaving behind a residue of manure and organic matter.

As soon as I move my portable pen I broadcast cover crop seed, either buckwheat or winter rye, on the old site. Then I use a garden hoe to loosen the soil, about one inch deep, to cover the seeds I've just sown. Then I apply a light layer of compost, shredded leaves, dry hay or loose straw. This simple, quick technique mixes the newly deposited layer of chicken manure into the soil surface and covers the new seeds to ensure good germination.

By the time the cover crop has germinated and grown to four to six inches height the next batch of chickens is ready to graze this spot. Over the course of the season each spot gets visited by the chickens three times. After the first and second visits I use cover crops. After the third visit I just cover the site with a light coat of mulch to protect it over winter. Next spring this site will be easy to prepare as a garden bed.

This activity incorporates the nutrient-rich chicken manure into the soil quickly so those valuable vitamins and gases don't escape. Covering the newly planted seeds with compost or shredded leaves protects them from birds. The cover holds the moisture in the soil and helps provide the seed-to-soil contact that is so critically important to good seed germination. The root mass left from the previous crop stays in the soil to decay. As the roots decompose they leave channels that feed and house soil life and enhance drainage and moisture capillary action.

Why Not Rotary Till?

I don't rotary till the site before planting. There are only two reasons we ever need to use mechanical tillage in the soil: to break up hardpan or to prepare a seed bed. The very act of tilling itself, if done too often or not done properly, builds hardpan and destroys soil tilth. Pulverized clay and silt particles created during tillage leach in heavy rainfall. Gravity and hydraulic pressure pull the pulverized particles to the underlying firm subsoil where they stratify and compact, forming hardpan.

Hardpan is easy to create, hard to cure, and totally disabling to garden crops. It interferes with earthworm migration from surface to subsoil. It blocks root growth. It holds heavy rainfall near the surface, and blocks the capillary action that brings water from the subsurface water table to the surface when the plants need it during dry spells.

Tillage implements mix good soil (the surface loam), with poor soil (the subsurface sand and gravel). This creates only fair soil, or worse. Too much oxygen pumped into the soil causes oxidation and poor capillary action. It overstimulates soil bacteria and disallows seed-to-soil contact for optimal seed germination.

If the area you are working is too large to work up a seed bed efficiently with a hand hoe, you can still use the rotary tiller. Just run the tiller at a low idle rather than full power. This gives the tines a slow speed. Set the tine depth as shallow as possible while incorporating the top mulch and the cover crop seeds. With a slow rotary speed you will be less apt to pulverize the soil. With the shallow depth you will not be interfering as much with the soil structure or moving the subsoil towards the surface and vice versa.

Another excellent option for soil tillage is to use a spading machine either behind a walk-behind tractor or farm tractor. These spading machines look sort of like a rotary tiller but have longer tines that move in a pattern similar to the way a human pushes a spade into the soil. They don't mix the soil so badly as to pulverize it, yet can prepare a decent seed bed in only one pass, two if you're turning under sod. Spading machines are made overseas, mostly in Italy, but are readily available here in the U.S. (see appendix).

The biomass of roots and top growth of the cover crop that follow the chickens acts as nutrient traps. This holds the nitrogen and other macro and micronutrients in the roots and top growth. The nutrients contained in the biomass return to the chickens in their next grazing rotation. If you till under the cover crop, the nutrients return to the soil. If you mow the top growth to harvest the biomass for green manure you can use it in the compost. I don't have to buy any fertilizer for my garden crops. They get plenty from the residual poultry manure and green matter, and from compost applications.

In recent years quite a bit of research at state universities is pointing out the advantages of mowing versus tilling cover crops. By mowing the top growth and leaving it on the surface as a mulch you are replicating nature. After all, nature doesn't have any mechanical plows or tillers to come in and wreck the soil and turn it upside down. Of course, earthworms are tillers, but they much prefer to come to the surface, find their food, and carry it with them back into their burrow.

Sheet Mulching to Aid Soil Fertility

There are some disadvantages to planting a cover crop after each pen move. Planting the cover crop takes time, labor, equipment, and seeds. In most cases the ground under the chicken tractor is damp enough for seed germination. But you will have to irrigate during the dry seasons, at least until the cover crop germinates and is strong enough to send its roots in search of water below the surface.

The alternative to growing cover crops is to use sheet mulch. After moving the pen, simply scatter straw or dry hay on the site and leave it. The nitrogen and other nutrients in the layer of chicken manure will enable the decomposer bacteria to turn the layer of mulch into compost and eventually into humus.

While this decomposition is going on, the surface mulch gives several other benefits. It protects the soil and soil dwellers from harsh sunlight, and prevents windblown or rainwater erosion. We call this the "sponge effect". The happy reward is richer soil with less work.

When you are rotating your chicken tractor over a 30-day period you just add another layer of mulch to the beds on the second and third rotation through the garden.

You can even use this method in larger farms. There is an attachment for unrolling large round bales that fits on the three-point hitch of the farm tractor. Just drive along the beds unrolling the bales wherever you need them. You can unroll these large bales by hand too, either by rolling them along your garden beds, or unrolling them and tearing off a strip like you do paper towels. These round bales are usually quite cheap or even free if they are a year old. You can often get a local farmer to deliver them, or at least load one of these big biscuits into your pickup truck or trailer. A round bale is equal to about 15 to 20 square bales and weighs 500 to 1,000 pounds.

Through the fall, winter, and early spring the hay will decompose while it is acting as protector of the soil and keeping the nutrients from escaping or leaching. Don't put the mulch on too thick because it is difficult to till under when preparing a seed bed. About one to three inches is enough, I think.

The mulch causes cooler soil that will delay soil preparation in the spring by a few days, but that's not such a problem. It's usually better to wait a few days anyway, until the air and soil temperatures are at the proper levels, before planting spring crops.

The later-planted crops will germinate and grow better, faster, and probably will mature at about the same time, or within a few days, of the early crops. By delaying plantings until the soil warms up you will often avoid cold snaps that might occur late in the spring. Crops planted too early are often lost during a hard frost.

This mulching system can save money on fertilizer, tilling, and compost making. This system works best in permanent beds, and is ideal for the home grower or small-scale market grower.

Wild and Wonderful Earthworms

One component of the successful mulching system is the reliance on earthworms to do a major portion of the decomposition of the sheet mulch. To encourage earthworms to take an active role in your garden program you need to make sure the soil pH is near neutral in range of six to eight.

Earthworms work best in a soil that has a plentiful supply of calcium. You can add calcium to your soil by adding lime. The earthworms use the calcium to make pellets for use in their digestion process. Acid soils interfere with their ability to get calcium. More earthworms will inhabit neutral or nearly neutral soils (pH 7) than they will acid soils.

Earthworm castings are five to eleven times richer in plant nutritional value than the raw materials the earthworms are eating. The increase has to do with the secretions in the worm's digestive tract and calciferous glands.

To encourage earthworm proliferation in your soil, reduce tillage and add organic matter. Tests at the National Soil Tilth Lab in Ames, Ohio, show that a soil with a high population of earthworms can absorb a two-inch rain in 12 minutes. While a soil without earthworms will take 12 hours to absorb a two-inch rain.

Nitrogen Needs of Various Vegetables

A big advantage to using the chicken tractor system is that you don't have to buy fertilizers or compost in subsequent years. This can save you a great deal of money.

Perhaps you will want to buy greensand, rock dust and other amendments, but not fertilizer. You can save up to $300 to $500 per acre in fertilizer and as much as $1,500 per acre in compost.

Trying to determine how much nitrogen to apply per year in your garden beds is difficult, to say the least. The biggest problem you'll have is in trying to figure out how much nitrogen you already have in the soil. Because nitrogen is so mobile, most soil tests don't give an accurate reading. Also, you don't know how much nitrogen it will take to feed the soil life as well as the plants you hope to grow in the soil.

There are some general figures that give you a target to strive for. These figures are for soils that are low in fertility. I use them here primarily as a reference to check the general soil health. This is not a rigid recommendation of exactly what you need in your soil for good crops.

Nitrogen Needs of Common Vegetables

Vegetable	Nitrogen (lb/acre)
Beans	50
Broccoli	100
Cucumbers	100
Lettuce	90
Onions	75
Peas	75
Potatoes	180
Sweet Corn	110
Tomatoes	100
Winter Squash	75

Any nitrogen already in the soil needs to stay in place to feed the soil microbes. Add the amount of nitrogen you need to grow your intended crop without depleting the soil's store of nitrogen.

This table gives the amount of nitrogen fertilizer your crops will need during the growing season. The allowances are for a first year garden that has poor soil. These figures do not account for any nitrogen already in the soil. They also do not reflect the amount of nitrogen in the compost or sheet mulch you are applying to the garden.

In the chicken tractor garden, most, if not all, the nitrogen requirement for these plants is in the chicken manure being made available from your chickens. In the case of low nitrogen feeders such as beans, onions, and peas, you might want to leave the chicken tractor on that bed for less time, perhaps only half a day. In the case of high nitrogen feeders such as sweet corn and potatoes you can leave the chickens on those beds longer to accumulate more manure, perhaps two full days.

As they get older the chickens will deposit more manure. You can move the younger chickens less frequently, and the older chickens more often to adjust the amount of fertilizer per bed.

Seaweed Meal and Seaweed Extract

The key to improved crop yields, both in plants and in livestock, is in building the best soil possible using materials that are at hand. In some cases, especially in new gardens or in reclaiming worn-out land, the soil is just not healthy and fertile enough to provide the macro and micro-nutrients demanded by the plants. Adding fertilizer and lime to poor soil will help a great deal, but in really disabled soil, the plants will still have to struggle to acquire the growth nutrients they need.

In this case, fertility and plant health can be improved, sometimes dramatically, by using foliar sprays containing seaweed extract and fish emulsion. It is available in products such as Foliogro™ and Seamix™.

Seaweed contains growth hormones including auxins, gibberellins, and cytokinins. All of these are chemical messengers produced naturally in minute quantities by the plant. Cytokinins are particularly important, since they increase the speed of cell division and aid the plant in the process of photosynthesis.

Foliar sprays work best when applied early in the morning, especially on a cloudy day. Adding a drop of surfactant to the spray mix can help deionize the leaf surface and aid the stomata in absorbing the nutrients. Stomata are tiny, mouthlike openings on the leaf surface that enable the plant to exchange gaseous aerosols and mists with the surrounding atmosphere. Spraying should always coincide with the stage of plant growth when nutrients are in high demand by the plant but root intake is low. Otherwise you might waste your efforts if the plant isn't in need of the nutrients you are spraying.

Leaves—and their tiny stomata—cannot accept large amounts of macro nutrients such as nitrogen, phosphorus and potash. They can, however, accept valuable, minute quantities of micronutrients and trace elements, particularly the naturally occurring growth stimulators auxins, gibberellins and cytokinins.

There is a complex and not totally understood interrelationship between these stomata and the ambient surroundings of the plant. Authors Christopher Bird and Peter Tompkins, in their book *Secrets of the Soil*, (see appendix) report on the unusual results achieved by Dan Carlson, originator of *Sonic Bloom*. He recorded predawn bird sounds and played them back to crops to stimulate the leaf stomata to open wide for receiving nutrients from foliar spray.

Playing this sound back to the plants *"induced stomata to imbibe more than seven times the amount of foliar-fed nutrients, and even absorb invisible water vapor in the atmosphere that exists, unseen and unfelt, in the driest of climatic conditions."*

Minneapolis music teacher, Michael Holtz, listened to the cricket and bird chirps that Carlson had recorded. After seeing the enhanced plant growth, Holtz said, *"It was thrilling to make that connection. I began to feel that God had created the birds for more than just freely flying about and warbling. Their very singing must somehow be intimately linked to the mysteries of seed germination and plant growth."*

Mohammed Azhar Khan, technical advisor to the Northwest Frontier Provinces' Farmers Association in Pakistan says, *"Using the Sonic Bloom sound frequencies and foliar sprays, I have been able to increase potato yields by 150 percent over the national average and increase corn harvest by 85 percent over the national average."*

Herein lies the message: encouraging the birds and insects to sing in your garden will foster enhanced growth of your plants. I further feel, unscientifically, that chickens and other livestock behave better, are healthier, gain weight faster and produce more nutritious food if they hear the predawn bird sounds that abound in a healthy ecosystem. Who knows, maybe even the raucous, boisterous crowing of the rooster is a signal for plants to wake up and get growing!

It is important to remember that foliar feeding is a supplement, not a substitute for healthy soil and generous applications of organic matter and fertilizers. Seaweed's largest value is in supplying minute quantities of trace elements in a readily usable form to plant and animal digestive systems. In animals, seaweed acts as a catalyst to enable the digestive tract to extract nutrients from the food supply. The same thing happens when we apply seaweed to the soil. It acts as a chelating agent to help plants glean minerals for an adequate diet.

A good rate of application for seaweed meal is one pound per 100 square feet, raked lightly into the soil. You can apply the seaweed directly to the soil in meal form, or you can supply it through the chicken's digestive tract. As we saw earlier, chickens utilize only about 20% of the mineral value of their feed, excreting the remainder. When you are feeding seaweed meal in your chicken feed you will get back a portion of the seaweed meal in the manure. This amounts to about one-third of the total requirement for seaweed in your garden. Add the remainder by lightly broadcasting seaweed meal or by adding several foliar spray feedings scheduled about one week apart early in the season.

It is always difficult to measure the results of this kind of soil amendment. So many other factors play a role in total yields, such as weather, rainfall, organic matter in the soil, origin of fertilizer materials, varieties of plants, and so on. However, as a general rule, I plan on a 10% increase in total yields after applying seaweed meal to my garden.

Permaculture Gardening

One way to measure soil health and productivity is by measuring the vegetable or fruit yields. The upper potential of a <u>healthy</u> soil production is at least seven times greater than the current national average. That means we can grow at least seven times more yields on rich, healthy soil than on poor soil.

If you use chicken tractors to improve your garden beds year after year, you can look forward to developing a fine rich soil that will eventually produce at least seven times what it is producing now. Your first year garden will grow food for one family, but as you make your soil richer and improve your growing techniques you will experience a surplus of food. At that point you can begin decreasing your garden size each year, resulting in less and less work to get more and more food. Or, rather than decrease the garden size as it becomes more fertile, you can start selling the extra food to your friends and neighbors and create a market garden.

If you can grow extra vegetables to sell, it is a simple matter to grow extra chickens to sell, too. However, there is an upper limit to the number of chickens you can grow in your backyard. At some point your little piece of land will become so rich that you just can't add any more chicken manure to it. So, as you add families to your marketing network you will need to add land for growing chickens.

At this point it is time to consider making yours a more holistic project by adding enough land to include grains in the crop rotations. The chickens can fertilize the grain land as well.

Remember, as the land receives more organic matter it will grow richer, will need less irrigation water and be more flood resistant. The soil will be able to hold more of the natural rainfall that occurs. The idea is to make your garden soil structure such that it can soak up the rainfall. Then the soil acts as the reservoir for both nutrients and moisture. Mmmm, your plants will love it!

Chapter 6: Keeping Hens in the Chicken Tractor

Egg layers need certain things that broilers don't, primarily a roost, a nest box, and extra light if you want to maintain egg production in the winter. They also need additional winter protection in most parts of the country.

A. Light, Egg Laying and Chicken Health

I think of light as a nutrient—just as important to the health of the chickens as vitamins. Light has a huge effect on all life, and it's particularly noticeable in chickens. The length of the day's light affects the egg-laying cycle. In nature, when the days begin to shorten, the number of eggs they lay gradually decreases. Sometimes, egg laying will stop entirely in the wintertime. In the natural reproductive cycle, most poultry lay eggs in several batches when the light increases from spring to summer.

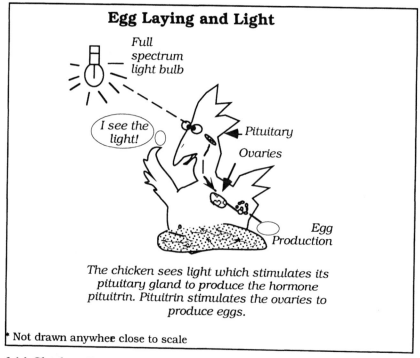

Egg Laying and Light

Full spectrum light bulb

I see the light!

Pituitary

Ovaries

Egg Production

The chicken sees light which stimulates its pituitary gland to produce the hormone pituitrin. Pituitrin stimulates the ovaries to produce eggs.

* Not drawn anywhere close to scale

The domestic hen will produce eggs for a much longer time than do her wild cousins. However, she will need supplemental light if she is to lay eggs during the shorter days of winter.

Measure light in intensity and length. The longest day of the year is the summer solstice in June, with daylight lasting about 17 hours. You might want to provide artificial light from July onwards through the spring (vernal) equinox when the days are of equal length. This occurs around March 21st of every year.

Light intensity is the measure of light's brightness. Use a light meter to measure it in unity of lux. Ten lux is equivalent to natural sunlight.

A dimmer is important to give the birds some warning that it will soon be dark. Chickens are just like us. They need time to find their perches and settle in for the night. If you don't have a dimmer, use a very low watt night-light, so the birds can see to get on the roosts.

B. Roosts and Perches

Broilers don't need perches, but they will sometimes use them if they are part of the pen. Hens love them, and will

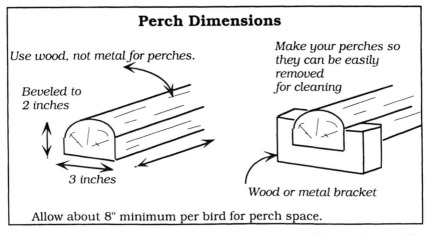

Perch Dimensions

Use wood, not metal for perches.

Make your perches so they can be easily removed for cleaning

Beveled to
2 inches

3 inches

Wood or metal bracket

Allow about 8" minimum per bird for perch space.

appear uncomfortable if roosts are not available. It is essential to give them roosting space so they can live naturally. Their toes have evolved to allow them to lock around a perch so they can sleep without falling off.

A good perch is about three inches wide with a bevel of about two inches at the top. The bevel gives the roost a more natural structure for the chickens to grip. It also eliminates the sharp 90-degree angle that can be uncomfortable for the chickens. Our neighbor Lawrence Gibson makes very nice-looking poultry roosts from young poplar saplings about two-inches in diameter. He installs them at knee height for his chickens and shoulder high for his guineas.

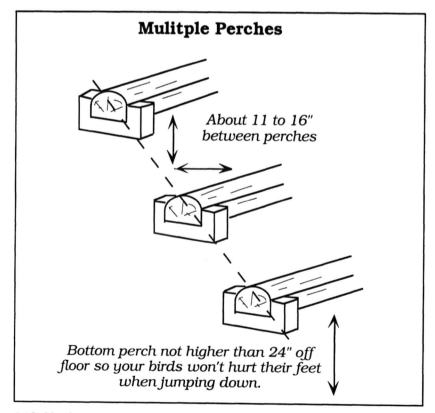

Mulitple Perches

About 11 to 16"
between perches

Bottom perch not higher than 24" off
floor so your birds won't hurt their feet
when jumping down.

You can either use old wooden closet poles for perches or you can make them as shown in the following diagram. Don't use steel or aluminum pipe since the birds will have trouble gripping it and their feet can freeze to metal in the winter.

Perches are best at less than two feet from the ground. This is so the heavy hens won't hurt their feet from continuously jumping down. Small cuts in the feet can result in infections and foot abscesses, commonly called bumblefoot.

Make multiple stepped perches about 16 inches apart. Allow a minimum roosting space of eight inches per bird and preferably even more.

Multiple Perches

If the chickens or pullets you buy are from a commercial grower and have been in cages all their lives you might have to show them how to roost. Put them on the perch. Once one pullet gets the idea the others are soon to follow.

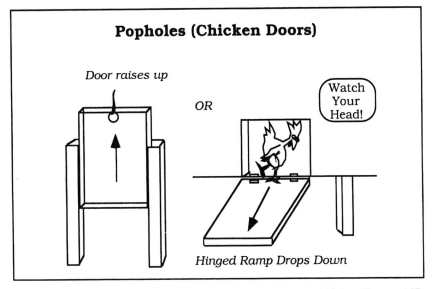

Popholes (Chicken Doors)

Door raises up

OR

Watch Your Head!

Hinged Ramp Drops Down

C. Popholes (Chicken Doors)

Chickens need doors, too. A pophole is a chicken-sized door designed especially for the chickens to enter and exit their house. Build several popholes to open and close in a planned sequence to give access to the appropriate paddock(s).

With the use of a timer and solar panel, you can even have automatic opening and closing popholes such as the one on the Esalen Institute chicken house in Big Sur, California.

In paddocks that are muddy or wet, a ladder-type ramp can also help the chickens to wipe their feet going in— much like a mud mat on your front door. The slots also allow the manure to fall to the ground instead of on the ramp where you would have to clean it. No, I've never seen a chicken intentionally wipe its feet before entering, but I once knew a cranberry farmer in Massachusetts who taught his black lab retriever to wipe her feet before jumping in the truck!

Raised Pophole with Ramp

Raised pop-up door

Slotted ramp helps clean feet before entering the chicken house and manure falls to the ground for fertilizer.

Wider entrance for more chickens

Is it my turn yet?

Wheels or skids for portability

For larger flocks you would want to install a larger pop-hole so that several birds can enter and exit at the same time. Otherwise it could become "ambush pass" for chickens to harass each other.

You can use your chicken tractor in the garden during the day to let the chickens roam around searching for insects. Just install a pop hole in the middle or on the end of the tractor to let them in and out. This works best in a maturing garden, of course. The chickens will eat a few leaves while they are looking for bugs, but probably less than the bugs themselves will eat.

This method works best if you let the chickens out in late afternoon. Most of them will have already laid their daily egg in the nest boxes by noon, so you don't have to hunt

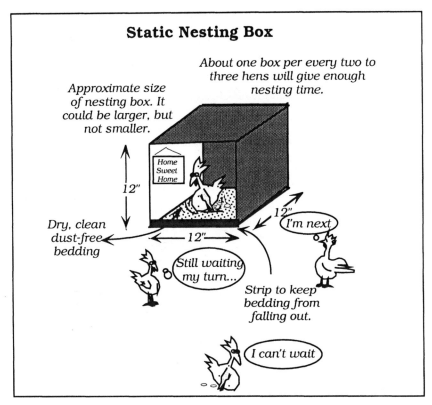

Static Nesting Box

About one box per every two to three hens will give enough nesting time.

Approximate size of nesting box. It could be larger, but not smaller.

Home Sweet Home

12"

Dry, clean dust-free bedding

← 12" →

12"

I'm next

Still waiting my turn...

Strip to keep bedding from falling out.

I can't wait

all over the garden to find any wayward eggs. As dusk begins the chickens will make their way back to the chicken tractor and you can go out in the evening and close their pop hole door.

D. Nesting Boxes

A nesting box provides a quiet, dark, secure place for hens to lay their eggs in privacy. Would you want to lay an egg with everybody looking? No! You would probably use a nesting box, too.

Nesting boxes for bantams (small chickens) generally are about 12 inches high and deep wide. Larger hens, like the Buff Orpingtons, need larger boxes at least 14"-16" high, deep and wide or bigger.

We found our chickens prefer to have the nest boxes at least six" or higher off the ground. However, some of them also use dark corners and lay their eggs directly on the ground in a makeshift nest. You might say different yolks for different folks...is this another chicken yoke?

You want to remove eggs from the nesting area frequently so that they do not get broken. Sometimes hens learn to peck at the eggs—especially broken ones. They like the

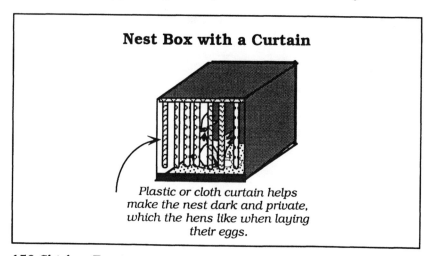

Nest Box with a Curtain

Plastic or cloth curtain helps make the nest dark and private, which the hens like when laying their eggs.

eggshell as a source of calcium. Having the nest dark helps prevent the hens from pecking and eating eggs. One way to make the nest darker is to put a curtain over the front of the box. Other ways to keep hens from pecking eggs is to not overcrowd them, and to collect the eggs frequently, at least once a day, or more often in freezing weather.

Make sure your layers have an adequate source of calcium - oyster shell is a good source. Once a hen starts pecking eggs it is best to cull her from the flock. She probably won't stop and the others can pick up the egg-pecking habit, leaving fewer eggs for you.

The threshold strip will allow the hens to enter and exit easily. This also helps the hens feel more secure and content while they are laying. A three-inch strip along the bottom helps to keep the nesting material from falling out when the chicken leaves the box.

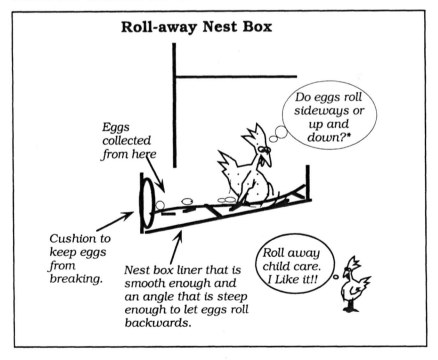

*Poultry Riddle for Zen Study

One box for every three hens is a good ratio. When they are not nesting, they will be very comfortable on the roosts.

There are two types of nesting boxes—static and roll-away. The static box is level so eggs don't roll anywhere. The roll-away box, as its name implies, slants backwards so the eggs roll to the back for easier collection.

I have not found the roll-away box to be practical for small henhouses or chicken tractors. By the time you get the angle steep enough for the eggs to roll backwards, the hens are on unlevel footing. Additionally, the nest box bedding must be smooth enough to allow the eggs to roll. I prefer the natural bedding of straw, hay or wood chips. These materials would not help win an egg race to anywhere.

Other nest boxes I have seen include a trash can on its side with straw inside. Turkeys especially like this size. I have also seen file cabinets, wooden wine crates, and five-gallon buckets used for nest boxes. You can use almost anything that gives the hen a safe, clean, dry, private, semidark place to comfortably lay her eggs.

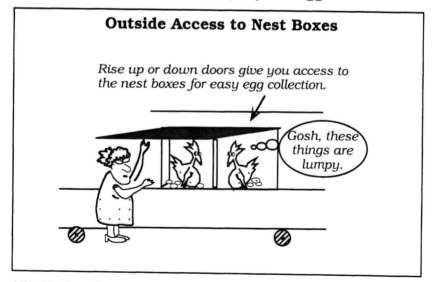

Outside Access to Nest Boxes

Rise up or down doors give you access to the nest boxes for easy egg collection.

Gosh, these things are lumpy.

It is much more convenient to have access to nest boxes from outside the egg mobile or chicken tractor. You can do this by using a hinged waterproof access door that opens directly to the nesting box from the outside.

5. Nesting Materials

You can use anything that is relatively clean, dry, and dust-free as nesting material. Sawdust tends to be too fine and dusty. You can use wood shavings, but never from pressure-treated lumber because of the risk of arsenic poisoning. Chopped straw or hay is very good as long as it is free of mites. Also keep the nest area dry so that mold doesn't form.

There are also synthetic nesting materials, some that resemble grass. The advantage of these is that you can remove them for cleaning. The advantage to the natural materials is you can put them in your compost pile and enrich your soil. We prefer to use all natural materials.

Chapter 7: Marketing

Making an Income by Gardening with Happy Hens and Healthy Soil

It is entirely possible to start a small-scale, part-time poultry business for less than $100. The profits you earn won't be large, but you will make enough money to make it worthwhile.

I first started growing food to sell to my neighbors years and years ago when I got into a yearly cycle of buying and raising three feeder pigs. I planned on one pig for my own freezer and two to sell. The two that I sold each year brought in more than enough money to pay for the piglets and all the feed bills and even some of the butchering costs. By selling the two I usually made enough income to pay for the one I put in my freezer. It takes just a tad longer each day to care for three pigs than for one, so my time wasn't a factor in whether I made a profit on the two pigs that I sold.

Now I do the same thing with chickens. I grow 120 chickens and keep 35 for my freezer. The 85 I sell bring in more than enough money to pay all the costs of my poultry operation. This is probably the "homestead" level of poultry production. This year—our first one in North Carolina—we branched out a little bit and grew 50 turkeys to sell, along with 25 pheasants for our own use. We put some of the pheasants in the freezer and released the remainder to repopulate our land and that of our neighbors' as part of our conservation and wildlife program.

We sold about 30 of the turkeys for $2.25 per pound, and donated the remainder to local churches for Thanksgiving dinner. We also donated some for a banquet at the Southern Sustainable Agriculture Working Group conference in Gainesville, Florida.

We decided to raise turkeys as well as broilers because when we moved to North Carolina we just assumed that we would be able to buy a freerange turkey for our Thanksgiving dinner. North Carolina is number one in U.S. turkey production. There are more turkeys (and pigs) in North Carolina  than there are people. All of these turkeys and pigs are raised in intensive feedlot confinement operations. As it turned out, the only naturally raised turkey we could buy came from the health food store in Asheville, about 50 miles from our farm. And, that turkey was raised in California, some 2,500 miles from our place. You can bet there is nothing sustainable about the practice of raising huge numbers of turkeys in one state and selling them half a continent away.

The people who bought our turkeys this year were used to the supermarket variety. Everyone was amazed at the taste difference in our pasture-raised birds. Comments ranged from "excellent" to "superb" and most of this year's buyers have already signed up for one or more turkeys for next season. Even in the rural county (population 14,000) where we live I'm sure we could sell several hundred pastured turkeys if we were of a mind to raise that many.

Like so many of our backyard livestock adventures we didn't keep exact track of all our time and expenses. But, I'm sure we made more than enough to pay for the chicks and poults, the feed, and all the chicken tractors we built. Next year with most of our up-front start-up expenses paid we'll be in a much better position to earn a tidy profit.

If you are currently at the "homestead" level of poultry (just growing your own stock) and you want to make some spending money from your efforts, just increase the size of your poultry project to the "market garden" level. With an initial investment of about $1,000 you can expect to earn a net income of about $3,000 in a typical six-month season after you pay all expenses. This net income might be large enough to pay your house taxes or mortgage each year, or take you on a long-awaited vacation if you want. The $3,000 income you earn can also be seed capital for expanding your business in the following year.

If you have $10,000 to $20,000 to invest you can build a sizable backyard business where you can earn a respectable five-figure, full-time income. Joel Salatin in Swoope, Virginia, is an example of this size business. With a $20,000 investment and 20 acres of land, he and his wife, Theresa, earn over $25,000 net profit annually from their broiler business. We highly recommend you read their book, *Pastured Poultry Profits,* and watch the companion video (see appendix) for an exciting and encouraging description of how they manage to do that.

Practice Ensures Success

Every backyard chicken grower that I know has more eggs or meat birds than they need for their own family, so they sell the extras. In most cases it's just enough income to help with the feed bills, but sometimes my friends do make quite a bit of money from their poultry project each year.

I'd like to encourage you to spend your first year practicing. Learn how to grow chickens for your own use before you haul off and try to start even a tiny-scale commercial poultry business. I think it's wise to do this for several reasons. First, you won't try to start your new poultry business too big. This is important because there is a learning curve in raising chickens just as there is in any other endeavor. Learn on your own time, make any mistakes quietly without anyone else relying on your performance. There will be plenty of time later to grow poultry for sale, either as a part-time or full-time endeavor.

Secondly, if you don't have any experience growing chickens for eggs or meat, you will need this first practice-year to get comfortable with the techniques. You will learn most of what you need to know about raising chickens from the first batch you grow. It is comforting and safe to start small and let your business grow slowly.

Growing chickens for your own table will give you the chance to find out several things. First, do you really like growing chickens, and do you want to do it as a business? Just as important, you will learn how wonderfully delicious these homegrown chickens are. If you know they are good to eat then you will be able to convince your potential customers. There's nothing like being sold on the product first to enable you to sell it easily to your family, friends, and neighbors.

This is especially important since you will sell your birds for a premium price. We currently sell ours at $2.35 per pound, dressed weight, even though our customers are used to paying much less than that for commercially raised birds. Your task is to convince your customers that your birds are worth much more on many levels than factory farmed birds.

During the first season you will become much more familiar with all the costs and how much labor it takes. You will get a better idea of the land and buildings required for the business and you will gain the actual experience of producing your first batch of birds.

The average family will eat from one to two chickens per week. A four-pound broiler will be enough to feed four hungry adults at dinner. Patricia and I eat 25 broilers per year, about one every other week. With just the two of us we generally get at least two meals out of each four pound bird. We also plan on an extra ten birds per year for dinner parties and special occasions.

If we were to buy these 35 free range broilers from the store we would have to pay about $280 and the flavor and freshness would not be nearly as good. Since we grow them ourselves the real cost is about $175, not counting our labor. Besides, we don't really consider it labor, since it's one of our hobbies and we get a great deal of enjoyment out of it, along with super-rich garden soil.

We always raise extra chickens to sell. This helps to pay all of our expenses and get our own freezer birds for free. If we raise an extra 85 broilers each year, and make six dollars net profit per bird, we earn $255, more than enough to pay for the chickens we want for our own use as well as pay for feed, chickens, equipment, and processing.

You can raise 100 broilers per year using just one four-foot by ten-foot chicken tractor. This requires 20 chickens per batch, and five batches per year. Raising five batches per year is fairly difficult in the colder climates, though. It makes more sense to use two chicken tractors, with 20 birds each, and raise three batches in one tractor and two batches in the other tractor. To make a little extra money, you can raise 120 broilers, with 20 per batch and three batches.

These 120 birds will pay all your overhead and operating expenses and pay for about 35 birds for your own use. You wind up with about $50 to $75 net profit. Please keep in mind that these cost figures are from my experience in my geographic area. I think the two big differences you might find in your area are the cost of feed and the cost of processing.

When Patricia and I lived in Vermont we paid $20.50 per hundredweight for certified organic chicken feed. Here in North Carolina we haven't been able to locate a source of organic feed yet. Therefore we are buying our feed from M & C Feed Mill in Chesnee, South Carolina, just across the state line from us. They don't have access to organic grains, either, but they are mixing conventional grains for us without fillers, antibiotics, or hormones. The price averages about $13 per hundredweight. I understand that other parts of the country have feed for as little as $11 per hundredweight.

For processing, I have paid as high as $2.75 per bird if I want them vacuum-packed in a freezer-duty plastic bag. Growers in other parts of the country are reporting as little as $1.50 per bird for processing.

You can see from the table below that your up-front costs are just over $700 to start this small-scale business. At first glance this might seem like a large investment to make, but the return is very good, indeed. You will earn only $66 in cash, but you will have 40 chickens—worth $320—in your freezer. That's over 50 percent return on your investment, much better than a bank savings account or the stock market. However, if you learn to do

Sample Budget for a 120-Broiler Business.

Item	Cost
4 x 10 tractors (2)	$10 per year *
120 chicks	$60 to $100
Feed	$198 (1,800# x 11¢/#)
Brooder lamp	$2 per year *
Feeders/waterers	$4 per year *
Processing	$300 (120 x $2.50 each)

Total $574

Income $640 (80 x $8 each)

Net Profit $66 plus 40 free broilers for your own use @ $8 each = $386

Total cash required: $718

(Includes up-front costs of tractors, feed, equipment, chicks, and processing.)

* Equipment has a useful life of five years, so I spread the cost over that period of time.

your own processing you can earn an additional $300 from this model. The best part of this deal is the wonderful, full-flavored food you are producing and the manure for your garden soil which gets richer and richer each year.

What if you don't have $718 to get started? Simple. Just presell your birds. Contact all your friends, family, and neighbors and sell them on the idea of hiring you to grow their poultry for them. If you like the flavor and healthfulness of these homegrown chickens, then you can easily persuade your friends to buy from you. Share your budget with them as a way to encourage them to pay you up front.

This method of farm marketing, called Community Supported Agriculture (CSA), is becoming increasingly popular across the country. It's a simple marketing method in which the consumers pay the farmer to grow their food for them. It works equally well with poultry, beef, vegetables and just about anything else you can imagine, even orchard fruits.

Your new customers may not want to pay you all the money up front, but you don't need it all in advance anyway. In the beginning all you need is to buy materials to build the pens, buy the chicks and brooder equipment, and enough feed to last a couple of weeks. This means your customers can pay you in weekly or monthly installments. Spread the payments out any way you like, just so you have the money to spend when you need to buy more feed or pay for the processing.

Keep in mind, too, that you are growing three different batches of birds, 40 to the batch, over a six-month season. Since you have to buy the equipment and build the pens initially your first batch of 40 chickens will cost you $345. Then the second and third rotations will only cost $186 for each batch of 40 birds.

Now, what if you want to make a great deal more income per year by raising broilers for sale? Let's say you want to make $3,600 per year to pay the real estate taxes on your property, or part of your mortgage payment. You can earn this much by growing 1,200 birds to sell, if you can make a net profit of $3 per bird.

With this many birds to raise you might want to consider a different pen size. A 4-foot by 10-foot pen only holds 20 chickens (30 if you phase the harvest at ten birds every other week, for example). You'll be doing three batches of chickens of 400 each batch, so you will need 20 pens of this size.

However, you can build a 10- by 12-foot pen that will hold 80 birds at a time, so you only need five pens. Since 1,200 broilers per year require more land than the typical garden, you will need access to a pasture or field of about two acres.

Keep in mind that you won't need all the $6,720 to start your first batch. Rather you will need enough money to buy the equipment and the first 400 chicks plus feed and processing costs. This totals $2,840. The second and third batches will each require only $1,940 up-front cash.

I've added $100 per batch for hiring someone with a large truck or trailer to haul the birds to the processor. This many birds, 400 per batch, won't fit in a pickup truck. You can hire a local hauler with a livestock trailer, or you can rent a large U-Haul truck and put straw on the floor. If you use a U-Haul truck be sure to prop the door open for air to ventilate the chickens during transit. Use a fence panel across the open door to keep the chickens from hopping out.

You can save a great deal of money if you process the birds at your farm, thereby not having to pay a hauler or butcher. We will discuss this at length in the following chapter. For the moment just keep in mind that you can easily double your net income per year simply by processing the birds yourself, even with the cost of processing equipment and hiring one or two helpers.

It's important to look at these figures carefully before you decide to haul off and start a 1,200-broiler business. The most important figure, of course, is the number of birds.

Sample Budget for a 1,200-Broiler Business

Item	Cost
Chicken tractors (5-10x10) @ $100 each	
$100 (5 x $100 / 5 years) *	
Chicks	$540 (45¢ each)
Brooder lamps	$30 ($150 / 5 years) *
Feeders/Waterers	$50 ($250 / 5 years) *
Feed (18,000 x 11¢/pound)	$1,980
Hauling to processor	$300
Processing	$3,000
	======
Total costs	$5,940
Income	$9,600
Net Income	$3,600

Cash Required up front $6,720

Return on investment = 53.6%, not including your labor.

* Equipment has a useful life of 5 years. Spread the cost over that number of years.

Can you really sell that many in your area easily? If the average family needs only 20 to 40 broilers per year, then you will need to find at least 30 to 60 households willing to pay that price and take that many.

What you will probably experience is some customers want only five or so, while others want fifty to a hundred. In my area there are many one and two person households. They buy smaller quantities than larger families.

Not only do your customers have to be willing, they have to be able. This means they need to have the money available when you ask for it, and they need freezer space to handle the number of chickens they are buying from you.

In the best of cases, your procedure will be to deliver the chickens to the processing house early in the morning. Then you pick up the processed birds in the late afternoon, and your customers come to your house that evening to pick them up from you.

There's quite a bit of phone-calling involved in this, since you want your customers to come on time. Otherwise you will have left over-birds to freeze to keep them from spoiling. Chicken spoils more quickly than most other meats, sometimes within hours of processing, especially in really hot weather.

Nowadays, most families do not have a freezer, other than the small one in their refrigerator. This might mean you will have to provide freezer storage for your customers. You can either do this by buying large freezers, or you can rent freezer space at a nearby cold-storage facility.

Most larger communities do have a cold-storage facility. You can store your chickens there for several months and once each month you can withdraw enough to make deliveries to all your customers. Make sure you will be able to rent space there, and find out how much it will cost. Then add these costs to your total production figures. Also, be sure to calculate your cost of traveling to the facility every month and pulling out chickens for your customers to pick up. The time you spend doing this can add quite a bit to the cost of your broiler operation.

In my area the cost of storing frozen chickens in a cold storage facility is $15 per month per pallet. Each pallet holds about 150 chickens. This adds about two cents per pound to the cost for each month the chickens are in frozen storage. Then I add another five cents per pound to cover my time in going to get them and having them available for my customers to pick up.

You might want to invest in several freezers if you have room in your basement, barn, or garage. A large freezer that will hold 150 four-pound broilers will cost about $600, plus the electricity to run it. You might be able to buy one used for less money. Just be sure it is in good condition and dependable. You certainly don't want to lose a freezer-full of broilers if the freezer stops working.

Here's How to Sell Your Chickens Before They Hatch

There's an old adage that says a "salesman" has a product and tries to get a customer to buy it. A "marketer" has a customer and finds the product that the customer wants to buy. It's a big distinction, and one that will guide you to finding your customers before you grow the chickens. Wouldn't it be terrible to grow 1,200 broilers and not have anybody to buy them?

Before you even order the chicks you need to know how many you can sell. To be on the safe side you might even want to have deposits or even full payment for the number of birds your customers want. Interestingly, if you go out to your friends and neighbors with your business idea, and they don't buy from you, it's a really big reason not to start a poultry business. On the other hand, you might find such a strong demand for homegrown broilers that you can expand your crop and earn a larger income from it.

Two marketing words you might not be able to use in marketing your chicken-tractor chickens are "organic" and "free-range". To use the word "organic" means you raise you birds according to strict regulations—including feeding them certified-organic grain—and are inspected and certified by a recognized agency. Otherwise you can't use the word in your advertising or packaging. Most likely you will not be able to use the term "free-range" for your birds, either. Because you grew them in portable pens rather than on wide-open "free" range. I don't agree with the logic here. In the chicken tractor system the birds get a new patch of fresh grass to graze each day, which in my estimation is better for them than typical "free-range" conditions. In Vermont we solved this marketing challenge successfully by calling our birds "Vermont Range Raised". Joel Salatin calls his birds "pastured poultry". The important point here is to be able to use words that your customers will recognize as meaning high quality and good flavor.

The most powerful word you can use to sell your chickens is "homegrown" and it's the one word the regulators can't take away from you. Use the phrase, "old-fashioned flavor, homegrown goodness" and people will get the message. The only real consumer protection against grower fraud is for the grower to know the consumer and vice versa. Check with your state department of agriculture for up-to-date regulations and interpretations.

How many birds can a grower sell without state or USDA approval? This varies all over the country. Three examples, Vermont, North Carolina, and Pennsylvania, have widely differing views.

Vermont and North Carolina growers can only sell 1,000 chickens locally each year without having them processed in a state-inspected processing facility. If these growers want to sell their chickens across the state line they need to have them processed at a USDA-inspected facility.

On the other hand, the state of Pennsylvania allows a grower to market up to 10,000 birds annually without being state or federally inspected. Pennsylvania is the fourth largest commercial poultry producer in the country. You'd think there wouldn't be much room for a local grower to sell birds, but that's not true. One grower, Mike Yoder, sells hundreds of chickens each year in the shadow of the big producers. He gets $2.25 per pound when big producers with an inferior product are getting something like 65¢ per pound. You can do it too if you take the time to develop your market and find the right people who value nutrition and taste above cost and convenience.

Once you have practiced and learned the art and science of growing chickens for your own use, you are ready to learn how to market chickens to your friends, family, and neighbors. I don't encourage anyone to try to sell home-grown poultry at wholesale. "At wholesale" means you sell poultry to restaurants, brokers, supermarkets who then resell the product to customers at retail. The price you will be able to charge at wholesale is generally too low for you to cover all your expenses and make any profit. State and federal regulators are more stringent for wholesale suppliers.

Still, I don't want to discourage you from at least looking at the available wholesale markets in your area. Some growers have told me they can get wholesale prices as high as $1.75 per pound from their local specialty-foods store or health-food store.

One grower-friend of mine, John Kleptz at LaPlatte River Angus Farm in Shelburne, Vermont, regularly sells 1,000 broilers per year to the local IGA supermarket at $1.75 per pound. At that level he still makes two dollars per bird, which he feels is more than enough to compensate him for his time and effort. The chickens are merely a sideline for his beef farm, and a hobby for John. The store marks up the chickens to $2.19 per pound, and they say the response is great. They always run out of John's chickens before they run out of buyers.

For the beginner though, I recommend you sell your chickens directly (for a retail price) to a select group of purchasers. You can easily find people who are willing to pay a fair price for your chickens. Just talk to all your friends and neighbors, spread the word that you have delicious homegrown poultry or eggs for sale, and you will get plenty of buyers.

How much you charge for your birds is entirely up to you and your customers. If free-range and organic broilers are selling in your area supermarkets for two dollars per pound then that's what you should charge for yours. In some cases you can even charge more, depending on the market area that you are in.

However, I never advise charging more for your birds than the general market is willing to pay. First, if your price is too high you won't sell many birds. Second, when your price is too high your buyers will be continually looking for other suppliers who have homegrown birds and are selling them for more realistic prices.

In my area free-range and organic birds are selling for $2 and $2.25 per pound respectively. At this price I can make about $3 per bird in profit if I pay someone else to process them. That's enough for me, my customers are thrilled to get quality birds and don't mind a paying premium price, and I can sell all the birds I want to raise on a part-time basis.

High prices per pound are what it takes to make the small-scale operation practical and feasible. However, a price that is too high will be counterproductive. High prices per pound are not sustainable in my view because the market is small and fickle. High-priced vegetables and meats become available to only a limited few who have the money to pay the price.

On the other hand, you don't want to sell your birds too cheaply. They cost you money and time to grow and you want to earn a fair return for the effort.

Poor diet is a national problem and we won't solve it by raising prices unnecessarily and beyond the ability of people to pay. However, low prices have no better impact on diet because the farmers don't make enough money and either go out of business, or government subsidies become necessary.

While I doubt if any of us will ever get rich by growing and selling birds in our backyard, I do feel that you can make a very satisfying hourly wage by doing it. For the hundred or so birds I raise and sell each year I make enough to continue the research on chicken tractors, along with getting my food for free.

Buy Local Because

When you go out to find a market for your birds use the "buy local because" marketing plan. This involves persuading your customers to buy from you because:

1. You are a local farmer, helping to keep productive land in use, and keeping their food-buying dollars in the local economy.

2. You are maintaining and preserving open space in your community.

3. You are buying your chicken feed from local farmers, helping them keep their farms open and profitable.

4. You deliver your chickens fresh the day you harvest them instead of days or weeks later like the supermarkets.

5. You raise your chickens humanely, rather than in confined, battery-cage systems.

6. Your birds have that homegrown goodness and old-fashioned flavor that makes them delightful to cook and eat. They are lip smackin', finger lickin' good!

7. You are helping restore the environment by decreasing the pollution caused by factory-raised birds and excessive transportation from out-of-state broiler factories.

Nationally, 250 million people consume 2.5 billion chickens per year. If we developed a cadre of small-scale growers, each producing 10,000 birds per farm per year we would need 250,000 broiler producers here in the United States. Compare that possibility with the five huge producers we currently have in this country.

With excellent-tasting, healthy birds the consumption might increase, even double. This increased demand for poultry would then provide small-farm opportunities for yet another 250,000 producers. People (and poultry) could get out of the factories, find some marginal, inexpensive land, and go in the broiler business for less than $20,000 per farm, and make a good living at it.

Who Is Your Market?

Members of your extended family, your neighbors, associates at work, and general acquaintances are all good potential customers for your homegrown poultry. What I've found happening is that my original customers—primarily my friends—like these homegrown birds so much they brag about them to their friends, who then call me up to buy some. This is word-of-mouth advertising and is quite possibly the most powerful marketing tool available to you.

Get it started by hosting a dinner or cook-out and serve some of your homegrown finest. Then ask your dinner guests to be your marketing crew. Sure enough, they'll buy some and get their friends to buy some, too. Then, you're in business.

Sell Them Other Products, Too

You can use your core group of broiler customers to help you expand your business. Get them to help you sell other products from your backyard market garden or small farm. It may be that you are already selling vegetables or other products to your friends and neighbors. If so, you can expand the number of items you sale and sell many other commodities to your group. Examples are, eggs, laying pullets, turkeys, rabbits, geese, ducks, even pork and beef if you have enough land.

Once you've taken the time and effort of developing a core group or buyer's club, it will be a simple matter for you to expand the quantities and types of food you can grow for them. If you can grow most or all the fresh and stored food for these families, then you can increase your gross income per year to the $50,000 range. You can earn your full-time living from a very small piece of land. Then you will be doing what you really want to do, growing good food for good people.

Raising Pullets for Resale

Some of folks want to grow poultry, but not eat it. If you are in this category, then you can start growing pullets––young hens—for folks who want to have hens for eggs but don't want to bother with the time and effort to raise them from chicks. A pullet is about 20 to 22 weeks old before she starts laying eggs. During this 5 month period you can use these young hens for your soil fertility program, then sell them once they start laying. People who buy them from you will be able to use them to add fertility to their garden soil, and enjoy fresh eggs to boot.

A laying pullet sells for about five dollars. Unlike broilers, you don't have the expensive processing to pay for. If you can sell 100 pullets per year you will make a nice net income for yourself and get plenty of manure for your garden. You will also make it possible for a whole new group of families to become partially food self-sufficient by having hens and getting their own fresh eggs.

Using Brochures to Educate Your Customers and Promote Your Products

We found that a little information for our customers can go a long way to help sell our products. We include a flyer that describes why our birds are superior and what to expect from non-commercially raised meat. The following pages are a modified example of the flyer we produced for our turkeys. The original is an 8.5 by 11" page designed as a tri-fold. Feel free to use any of our wording that fits your farm or situation. And we'd really like to get a copy of any flyers or brochures you produce about your operations. Points to remember when designing advertising include:

1. State clearly what is in it for your customer and why they should buy directly from you.

2. Establish your credibility — say a little about your farm and your self. This will give your customers confidence in you and familiarity often breeds loyal customers. Also get your farm's name to register in your customer's mind as synonymous with quality, nutritious food. Develope brand recognition for your farm.

3. If you can, gather information. That is why we included the survey. This also gives the customer an idea about what we have (or could have) available.

What Makes Our Turkeys So Special?

I'm different and special!

We believe our turkeys, chickens, beef, and pigs are the BEST you can buy. Here are just a few of the reasons why:

How They Are Raised & Handled Regarding:

- Sunshine
- Fresh Air
- Free-Range
- Fresh Organic Pasture
- Natural Pesticide Control
- Humanely Processed

What They Eat & Don't Eat:

- No Antibiotics
- No Hormones
- No Artificial Food Additives
- Natural Vitamins & Minerals
- Lots of Fresh Organic Pasture Without Pesticides or Herbicides

What You Get:

- Wholesome, Nutritional Food
- Certified Antibiotic and Hormone-Free
- Leaner "Heart-Healthy" Meat
- From a Farm That Does Not Pollute Your Environment
- Heritage Breeds of Livestock Helping to Preserve the Gene Pool
- Locally Produced

In summary, our farm's operation is designed to mimic an animal's natural lifestyle as much as possible. This gives them a high quality of life with low stress and optimal nutrition. This translates directly into a healthier food for you and your family.

A few things to note about your free-range turkey: They are a semi-domestic breed called Double Breasted Bronze. We chose this minor breed because of their natural intelligence, heartiness and foraging characteristics.

Our turkeys have a leaner, firmer meat than commercially raised turkeys. We recommend that you leave the skin on when baking. Also, unlike white, factory turkeys, the Bronze turkeys have black pinfeathers. Just ignore the pinfeathers, as you would with the white turkeys.

These turkeys have had the best nutrition we can provide, including nature's best bugs, seeds, and exercise. You should notice quite a difference in the texture and taste of our birds compared to factory-raised turkeys. These birds will taste the way turkeys did when your grandparents had them: wholesome, natural, full-flavored and nutritious.

Be sure to reserve your turkey, chickens, pork, or beef for next year. We always sell out. Also, please share this brochure with your friends or family if they are interested in wholesome, humanely raised, quality food.

With Thanks!
Pat n' Andy

About Green Creek Eco-Farm

This 47 acre farm, owned and operated by Patricia Foreman and Andy Lee, is in its third year of operation. We are located in the isothermal belt of Western North Carolina and have dedicated our farm to conservation land and as a wildlife preserve. Green Creek Eco-Farm is utilizing permaculture principles, ecological design, and humane livestock raising throughout its operations, including:

• Pig Tractors (for pasture) and Bush Hogs (to clear brush). The pigs we have are Tamworths, a heritage breed, great for outdoor pig production.

• Chicken, turkey, pheasant, and guinea tractors. Our poultry not only supply eggs and meat, but also help us with forming garden beds, providing fertilizer and natural pest-control.

• Sheet-mulched Market Garden

• Solar-ventilated beehives for pollination, apitherapy, pollen and honey production.

We plan to expand our operations next year to include grass-fed beef. If you are interested in any of our products or workshops, just give us a call or drop us a note and we'll put you on our mailing list.

Andy Lee is a nationally known speaker on sustainable agriculture, appropriate housing, rural economic development and microenterprise employment strategies. He taught permaculture, market gardening and biointensive gardening at the University of Vermont, and has authored two books, *Backyard Market Gardening* and *Chicken Tractor: the Gardener's Guide to Happy Hens and Healthy Soil.*

Pat Foreman has a bachelor's degree from Purdue University in animal science with concentrations in genetics and nutrition. She also is a pharmacist and Fulbright Fellow. She has for many years worked as a nonprofit primary health care consultant in over 30 countries. She has been the course director for many international/transcultural courses and specializes in adult education.

Yes, I want to know about Green Creek Eco-Farm's activities, workshops and products. Please put me (or my friend) on your mailing list!

Name _____

Address _____

City, State & Zip _____

Phone/fax_____

E-mail _____

I am especially interested in buying (mark all that apply) :

___ Chicken (broilers) ___ Eggs

___ Turkey ___ Guinea ___

___ Pheasant

___ Pork ___ Beef

___ Vegetables (specify)

___ Honey or pollen

Other _____

I would like to learn more about:

___ Permaculture

___ Organic Gardening & Farming

___ Ecology & Environmental

___ Other _____

Green Creek Eco-Farm, LLC
PO Box 160
Columbus, NC 28722
Phone & Fax (704) 863-2288
eMail: goodearth@igc.apc.org

Chapter 8: Here's How to Build Your Custom Chicken Tractor

At the risk of sounding redundant, I must insist that there is no one perfect way, or one way more superior than another, to build a chicken tractor. My advice is simply to design the size pen you need, use the materials, tools, and skills you have at hand, and just do it. Then let me know what you learned so I can know about it too.

However, there are a few things we've tried that worked, and some that didn't. Therefore, I'd like to show you how to build a chicken tractor like the one I use in my own garden. This exercise will help you determine just what your needs are and what you hope to accomplish with your portable shelter-pen.

Before designing the pen, you need to know the needs (what goes in) and products (what comes out) of the chicken tractor system you envision. Some of the many questions you'll want to ask and answer as you design your shelter-pen are:

1. How many chickens do you need to feed your family or to sell each year?

2. Do you want egg layers, fryers, broilers, turkeys, guineas, pheasants, or a combination?

3. Which breeds?

4. Which chicken tractor system and model?

5. What materials are available and what more will you need?

6. Size of garden and how big do you want it to become?

Let's say you want to raise 20 broilers for your own freezer. You might also want to grow enough extra broilers to sell to friends and neighbors. This way you can earn the money to recover your start-up costs. In this example, you'll need to grow 40 extra chickens to sell in order to break-even financially.

Since each batch of broilers will be in the brooder for three weeks and in the tractor for five weeks, it's possible to get four or even five batches in rotation during a long season. In Vermont where I used to live we had a fairly short growing season, so I only planned on growing three batches per season in each chicken tractor. In North Carolina, where I now live, we can raise chickens almost year-round in this relatively mild climate.

Let's assume you have a garden like mine, that has four-foot wide growing beds that are 20 feet long. There are grassy pathways between the beds. A typical four-foot by ten-foot chicken tractor covers 40 square feet. Each batch of chickens is in the portable pen for about 35 days. If you want to move the chicken tractor each day, you will need a total of 1,400 square feet to graze your chickens. If you move the chickens every other day, instead of daily, you will only need 700 square feet of range space. Therefore your total garden space can be about 1,400 square feet, with half each year dedicated to chickens and the other half to vegetables. Then you simply rotate halves in following years.

Learn By Doing

It's easy to get carried away with the building of these chicken tractors. The first one I made is very sturdy, but entirely too heavy. It is so heavy it takes two or even three

Third Generation Chicken Tractor

*Outside dimensions are
4' wide, 23.5" high and 8' long.*

Put 1" chicken wire on all sides, but not the bottom or top.

2 PVC roof panels (use a light color).

Hang water and feeder from the upper braces so you can move the tractor without taking them out.

For small flocks put a pop-door on the end or sides to let the birds out to work in other parts of your yard, garden, or orchard. They will return to roost at night on their own. Only let them out if you are sure they will be safe from predators. This is not practical for larger, commercal operations.

of us to move it, with much huffing and puffing and jostling. I don't recommend you use this model because it is so overbuilt, but let me describe it to you so you know the process. My first generation pen is 3-1/2 feet high, four feet wide and 12-1/2 feet long. The frame is made of 2 x 4 inch boards, with 3/8-inch plywood nailed on the north end and west side, and half of the east side.

On this early prototype the top is framed with 2 x 4 inch boards, with the north half covered with plywood and the south half covered with 1-inch poultry netting. The pen has 1-inch poultry netting on the south end and half of the east side, where the plywood covering ends. The plywood is exterior-grade and stained with a wood-preserving stain. While this pen is far too heavy for use as a portable chicken tractor, it still works as a deep mulch pen and as a semi-portable brooder pen.

The third-generation portable pen we now use is 3'x4'x10' — three feet high, four feet wide and ten feet long. For turkeys it needs to be a little larger, 3'x6'x12'. We wrap the sides of the pen with chicken wire then cover it with a lid made with a sturdy frame covered by plastic roofing panels. In earlier prototypes we used chicken wire on the lid and covered it with blue polypropylene tarpaulin. We found the poly tarp deteriorated rapidly and required quite a bit of maintenance. The plastic panels we now use are much easier to install, don't require chicken-wire reinforcement, and—because of their rigidity—help stabilize the lid frame so the substructure can be lighter weight.

We use the three feet height because that's the standard height of the one inch poultry netting that we use to surround the sides and ends of the pen. Three feet is also a good height for hanging the waterer and feeder from the upper cross brace. We use three-gallon waterers, but if you use two-gallon waterers you can get by with only two feet pen height. The chickens don't seem to care one way or the other how tall their pen is. There is no bottom wire because we want the birds to have access to the ground beneath the pen.

Use one inch galvanized chicken wire for the chicken tractors. You can use the plastic-coated chicken wire that is more expensive, but will last a lot longer. The larger two inch poultry netting is not suitable since smaller varmints such as weasels can easily get into the cage, and racoons can reach in and grab the birds sleeping close to the edge. Little chicks can also get out of two inch netting.

Secure the wire carefully to the pen with galvanized poultry staples. Some of the varmints that will try to get into the pen are quite strong, raccoons especially, and can easily rip the staples out unless you hammer them in securely.

Cover the whole pen, except the bottom and lid, with chicken wire. The plastic roof panels are inexpensive, light-weight, easy to work with, waterproof, and provide shade and wind protection. Some panels are made from fiberglas and are translucent, to let sunlight through. We found the translucent panels let in too much heat in and the tractor literally became an oven, baking the chickens way too soon. Besides, the fiberglas panels are too expensive. Dark panels also absorb too much heat in our southern climate. We like the white or beige panels to use on the chicken tractors. They look clean and don't cook my birds prematurely.

Other coverings you might consider using are tin or fiberglass roofing. Joel Salatin uses tin roofing exclusively but I've never tried it. David Stickney used salvaged tin roofing on his straw bale henhouse with no problem. My only concern is the tin seems to conduct heat more than plastic. This might cause the birds to overheat. I have tried plywood and found it to be too heavy. I've never used fiberglass panels because I think they are too expensive.

We now construct all our pens with panels screwed with galvanized decking screws. This way we can disassemble them in the fall for winter storage out of the weather. This will extend their life a great deal. Even without winter storage out of the elements, these pens will last from five to ten years with only minor maintenance each year.

In the early part of the season you can use the chicken tractor as a sun trap or windbreak for growing plants. You can use the pen for firewood storage, too. A 4- x 10-foot pen that is three feet high will hold one cord of firewood.

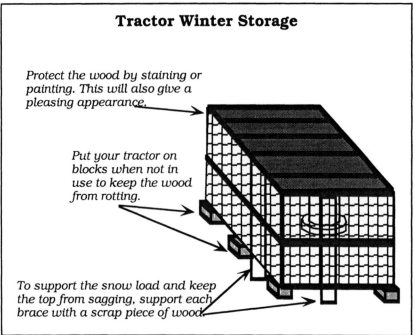

Tractor Winter Storage

Protect the wood by staining or painting. This will also give a pleasing appearance.

Put your tractor on blocks when not in use to keep the wood from rotting.

To support the snow load and keep the top from sagging, support each brace with a scrap piece of wood.

If you remove the plastic roof panels and replace them with plastic greenhouse film you can use this chicken tractor as a portable cold frame or grow tunnel.

I have built all my pens with flat roofs. I find that water runs off the roof easily. Adding a sloped, peaked, or rounded roof to the portable pen is extra work and expense, and not at all necessary.

Over the winter set the chicken tractor up on blocks to keep the wooden frame from contacting the ground and getting wet and rotting. The chicken wire and roofing-panel covers will last for many years exposed to the weather as long as they aren't damp for extended periods of time. In the winter support the flat, hinged lid against heavy snow loads. I just prop a scrap board under each cross brace.

1. Size, Configuration, Space Per Bird

Each broiler requires 1.5 to 2 square feet of space for optimal growth and ease of management. In a 4- by 10-foot tractor you can easily grow 20 birds each batch. Laying hens need twice as much space to be comfortably uncrowded, so plan on having only ten hens in this size pen. You can <u>start</u> two or three times this many chickens in the pen. As they grow larger you will want to separate some of them into other pens, process, or sell them.

Turkeys are much larger and need much more room to maneuver. If you want to grow the large turkey breeds that have a wingspan of six feet, you might consider using a larger pen such as our 6'x3'x12' duel-wheel model. We separated the lid into two sections so it's easier to lift. We raise 15 turkeys per pen but let them out into a fenced yard during the day. We installed turkey-size pop doors in the ends or side of the tractor. The turkeys are easy to herd back into their tractors at dusk. We use long sticks for arm-extenders to help herd them where we want them to go.

Last year we fenced in our new orchard to let the turkeys browse during the day. They enjoyed foraging on the various bugs and slugs that might have otherwise harmed our apple, peach, and pear trees. We also had to wrap a 3-foot high chicken-wire shield around each tree to keep them from killing the young trees.

2. Construction Materials

You can build your 4- by 10-foot chicken tractor on a Saturday and start using it on a Sunday. Materials to build

Materials and Tools You Need
to Build a Chicken Tractor

- **Lumber,** kiln-dried spruce or fir
  Five pieces 2 x 4" x 10'
  Five pieces 2 x 4" x 8'
- **Hinges**, three heavy-duty, piano-type door 3" hinges, galvanized steel (screws usually come in the hinge package)
- **Chicken wire**, one-inch galvanized poultry netting, 28 feet of 36-inch width. Most hardware stores or farm supply stores will have these widths in stock and will cut them to length for you. Galvanized poultry wire will last several years. You can even buy PVC coated wire that will last virtually forever, although it is more expensive.
- **Roofing Panels** two pieces 2 x 10'. Light colored PVC TuffTex™ or similar panel.
- **Screws**, 100, three-inch galvanized
- **Roof Screws**, one pound with neoprene washers
- **Staples**, one pound, one-inch galvanized poultry staples
- **Hasp lock with keeper,** to hold the lid closed.
- **Saw,** hand or power
- **Hammer**
- **Drill,** with screwdriver head
- **Framing square,** or speed square
- **C-clamps,** pipe clamps or furniture clamps
- **Tape measure**
- **Wire-cutting pliers,** or shears
- **A Keen Eye and a Steady Hand**

the pen will cost less than $75 in most parts of the country. Plan to stain or paint your chicken tractor for uniform appearance and weather protection. You will need to let the paint or stain dry for at least 24 hours before using the pen.

The keys to building a successful portable pen are:

- make it light enough to be portable.

- heavy enough to withstand repeated usage, wind and varmints.

- attractive.

The main ingredients in the pen are:

- boards.

- chicken wire.

- plastic roofing panels and

- nails, screws, or bolts to hold it all together.

I use standard, kiln-dried two-inch framing lumber for the frame of the pen. These boards are readily available and, with an annual coating of stain or wood preservative, will last indefinitely.

You might want to use pressure-treated lumber. I don't usually use it because of the negative environmental effects of the arsenic used in the treating process. Chemicals used to pressure-treat the lumber are toxic to humans, animals, and plants, and create huge pollution problems at the pressure-treating facility. Additonally, sawdust and fumes given off when you saw or burn pressure-treated lumber are especially toxic. Do not breathe these fumes.

However, there are times when pressure-treated lumber is merited. In the western North Carolina area the humidity (64 inches of rain per year average) and termites make me consider using pressure treated lumber where the tractor meets the garden. In our climate, bottom boards wear out much faster than the rest of the frame; pressure-treated would last longer.

So far there doesn't appear to be any great advantage to using pressure-treated lumber for the entire frame. The portable pens I built three years ago show absolutely no sign of deterioration.

Here's a list of materials and tools needed to construct the 4-by 10-foot chicken tractor. Note that typical "2 x 4" lumber actually measures only 1.5- by 3.5-inches. At the lumber yard check through the pile and reject any boards with splits, crooks, or large knots. You will rip some of these boards in half lengthwise, so you want the best boards you can get.

Ripping the framing boards is much easier if you have a table saw. But you can almost as easily rip boards with a hand-held power saw equipped with a ripping fence. Rip fences are available for most hand-held power saws. You can buy them at hardware stores or tool stores for less than ten dollars.

Use a saw to crosscut the boards to the proper length. Sawhorses and C-clamps make the task of ripping boards easier. You can also use overturned buckets or milk crates to support the work while you are sawing. A ripping blade or a combination rip and crosscut blade will work fine to do the cutting. Of course, the ripping goes much more easily if you have a table saw.

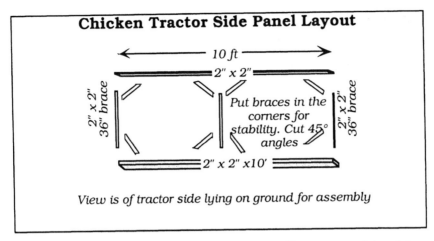

Chicken Tractor Side Panel Layout

10 ft

2" x 2"

2" x 2" 36" brace

Put braces in the corners for stability. Cut 45° angles

2" x 2" 36" brace

2" x 2" x10'

View is of tractor side lying on ground for assembly

A 16-ounce carpenter's hammer is all you need to drive in the staples. You can also use it to start screws in the soft wood, then use the power drill or screwdriver to drive the screws tight.

Use C-clamps or furniture clamps to hold runners and braces in place while you are screwing them tight. The best way to achieve structural rigidity is to have square end cuts and tight screws. Once the frame is erect, the cross braces combined with the poultry wire and roofing panels will serve to further reinforce the structural integrity of the frame.

Use 2 x 2" boards to frame the bottom runners on both sides and the ends. Make the 2 x 2" framing members by ripping 2 x 4" boards in half lengthwise. This makes the unit lighter while still maintaining structural rigidity.

If you lack carpentry skills it may be best to ask a friendly skilled neighbor to give you a hand, at least with the first frame. It's not important to create a masterpiece of architecture and carpentry, but it is necessary to create a frame that will withstand continuous moves, heavy winds and snows, and any varmints that might try to break in.

The job of pen construction is certainly possible by yourself, but it will go much easier and faster if you have a helper to hold pieces in place for sawing and assembling.

Step 1: After all your materials and tools are on site, you can begin the task of building the chicken tractor by ripping the 2x4 boards to make the 2x2 runners, end braces and lid frame and braces. You need to make:

- six pieces of 2x2"x10' feet for the top and bottom long sides of the tractor and the long sides of the lid.

- eight pieces of 2x2"x45" long cross braces for the bottom, middle and upper braces at each end.

- four pieces of 2x2"x36" long for the side braces.

- two pieces of 2x2"x48" long for the sides.

- one piece of 2x2"x36" long for lid prop.

- save extra pieces for corner braces; cut ends to 45°.

After all your boards are ready, you can stain them with a fast-drying, exterior-grade wood preservative. This will add years to the life of your pen and will make it more attractive.

Step 2: After the stain or wood preservative has dried sufficiently, start assembling your pen. On a level surface such as a garage floor or driveway, lay out your first side. Place on the ground a ten foot 2x2", this is the bottom runner of the first side.

Then place a 2x2x36" piece at each end, on the outside of the long pieces, to form a 90° angle. Lay a 2x2x10' piece across the top and a 2x2x10' piece in the middle. The assembled pieces resemble a gate lying on the ground.

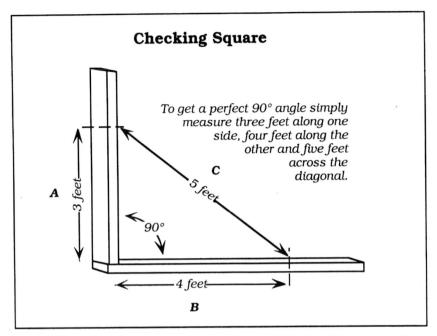

Checking Square

To get a perfect 90° angle simply measure three feet along one side, four feet along the other and five feet across the diagonal.

A — 3 feet

90°

C

5 feet

4 feet

B

Step 3: Use the carpenter's square to make sure that each corner is exactly 90°. This is important throughout the project to ensure the "carpenter's trine" of square, level, and plumb, so the structure is attractive, rigid, and stable.

Another way to check for square is to use the 3-4-5 technique. Measure down one end three feet (a) and along the side four feet (b). The diagonal (c) should be exactly five feet. If it isn't, just scoot the frame one way or the other to make the measurements come out correctly (see diagram).

Step 4: Use the three-inch galvanized screws and the screwdriver to attach the framing members to each other. Use two screws at each end of the 2x4" bottom board, and two screws at each end of the middle brace and top board. You can use a hand screwdriver for this task, but it is much easier and faster with a power drill or power screwdriver. Recheck the frame for square, then tighten all screws securely. It is certainly faster to nail the frame, but the screws will hold tighter and last longer.

Step 5: Set the first side out of your way and build the second side, following steps 1 through 4.

Step 6: Set the two side panels upright. Space the side panels parallel and 45" apart.

Step 7: Have your helper hold the side panels upright while you install the end braces. Install the following:

2x4x45" bottom end brace at each end

2x2x45" middle end brace at each end

2x2x45" upper brace at each end

Continually check for square as you screw the end braces in place with 3" galvanized screws, with at least two screws in each joint.

Step 8: Now install two 2x2x45" cross braces between the upper braces of the side panels, measuring in 42" from each end. These braces will provide lateral stability and a place to hang your waterer and feeder. Install braces on each side to support the load of the cross braces that hold up the waterer and feeder.

Step 9 (optional): If you are building your chicken tractor for laying hens you will want to install two 2x2x45" roosts between the middle braces of the side panels, measuring in 14" from each end of the pen. These roosts provide roosting space for ten or twelve hens. Half of them will be at each end of the pen. This will help distribute the manure evenly and will lessen crowding.

I put roosts in all my tractors. I view it as a quality-of-life asset for the birds to be able to roost. Design specifications of roosts are in the chapter about keeping hens. For laying hens you will also need nest boxes in one end of the pen. Three nests will be plenty for ten or twelve hens. I prefer to make nest boxs about 14" wide by 14"s high by 14" deep. You can install them near the top of the pen so that the eggs are easy to pick by simply raising the lid.

You now have a boxed frame that should be square and level, and ready for installing the chicken wire on all four sides.

Step 10: To install the 36" chicken wire, lay the frame on its side. Have your helper hold the chicken wire in place while you nail it securely with 1" galvanized poultry staples every eight to twelve inches. Be sure to square the chicken wire with the pen so that you can get a continuous wrap around all four sides. This will ensure stability, and it's easier and faster to install if you don't have to cut the wire in sections to get it square on the frame. A tip: use the staple gun to hold the wire in place until you get it nailed securely with the 1" poultry staples.

After installing the wire on the first side, roll the wire around the end and flip the frame to its other side. This is much easier to do if you have a helper. Then, continue stretching the wire around the frame and securing it with poultry staples. An alternative is to apply chicken wire to the panels before assembly. Then you can just screw the four panels together and take them apart easily for winter storage.

Step 11: Now, set your nearly finished chicken tractor upright, check it for square, and get ready to build and install the lid.

Step 12: To build the lid, lay out the 2x2x10 framing members parallel on your work surface 45" apart. At each end install a 2x2x48" end brace. Measure in 42" from each end and install a 2x2x45" cross brace. Check the lid frame for square, screw the pieces together and place it on your chicken tractor.

Step 13: Install the hinges along the back side of the lid and attach them to the upper brace of the rear wall. Place the hinges 12" from each end, with one in the middle of the lid. Then, install the latch in the middle of the front of the lid, with the latch keeper mounted on the upper brace of the front wall.

Use a good quality latch with a positive lock mechanism. This will keep heavy winds from shaking the latch loose. This happened to my second-generation pen. The lock hasp failed and the hinges broke when the lid blew off backwards in a strong wind.

Step 14: You are now ready to install the 24" roof panels on the lid of your chicken tractor. Use galvanized nails with neoprene washers. If the nails are too long, slant (toe-nail) them into the wood

Step 15: Install a 1.5 x 1.5" x 3' stick to prop the lid open while you are taking care of the chickens—similar to the hood prop in your car. Mount this on a center brace, with a keeper on the bottom end to hold it in place while the lid is open, and to store it when you close the lid.

Hold the prop in place with a screw through the cross member, and attached to the lid frame with a hook and eye screw. This will prevent knocking the lid loose while you are inside the pen and having it fall on you. It will also prevent the wind from catching it and blowing it backwards off the pen.

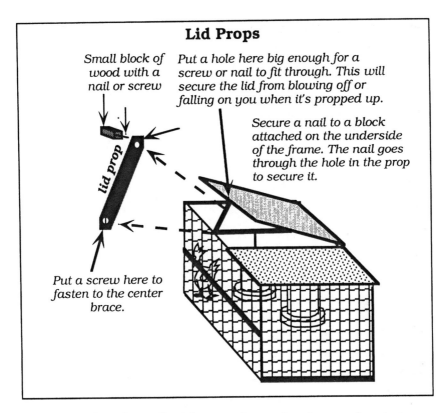

Lid Props

Small block of wood with a nail or screw

Put a hole here big enough for a screw or nail to fit through. This will secure the lid from blowing off or falling on you when it's propped up.

Secure a nail to a block attached on the underside of the frame. The nail goes through the hole in the prop to secure it.

lid prop

Put a screw here to fasten to the center brace.

Step 16 (optional): It's much easier to apply stain or wood preservative to the boards before assembling them, but in some cases I've left the staining until the last step. Having done it both ways, it makes more sense to stain the boards first, then touch up any scratches or bare spots after assembling the pen. I use a cedar-colored stain that is very attractive. Your pen is now complete and ready to use.

To use your chicken tractor frame as a cold frame or growing tunnel, you should screw the roof panels rather than use nails. Then, when you want to take the panels off to install greenhouse film it's a simple matter to unscrew them to make the changeover.

Step 17 (optional doors): We have retrofitted all our tractors with turkey-size popdoors. With small flocks we let the birds out of their tractor to work in a particular section of the garden or orchard. They keep themselves very busy scratching and clearing bugs. This also gives them more exercise and a chance to sunbathe. They naturally go back to their tractors at night, or we can herd them back in if we need to leave during the day. We train them so that when we throw some scratch into the tractor they go in after it.

You can use the same construction sequence and building techniques for creating whatever size pen you choose to make. It costs about $75 to build a 4x10' chicken tractor that will hold 20 broilers or ten laying hens if you use all new materials. It will cost three times that much to build a 10x12' pen, but the larger pen will hold four times as many chickens. The per bird cost is lower in the larger pen. If you plan to grow a large number of birds on open range, this bigger pen can make a difference. You can decide which size pen suits your needs after you've developed your business plan.

Use any materials you have on hand to build these pens. The materials I've listed above are ones that are readily available in my area at fairly low cost. In developing countries the chicken tractor system will work wonderfully, except for one circumstance: oftentimes, there is no access to chicken wire and dimension lumber to build the pens.

In this event, substitute native materials, such as bamboo poles, for framing, bamboo splits or vines for weaving the fence, and fronds from trees such as palms to provide cover from rain and sun.

Step 18 Install the Chicken Furniture: Hang the waterer and feeder from the cross brace under the roof. Arrange it so you can raise the buckets as the chickens get larger, keeping the lip of the feeder tray about chest-high on the birds. This will help keep much of the feces and dust out of the water and feed, and make it harder for them to waste feed by brushing it out as they eat. They have a habit of tilting their heads sideways as they peck, and raking food out onto the floor.

Suspend water and food containers about chicken chest high to keep them cleaner.

3. Moving Your Chicken Tractor

Dragging

By the use of narrow framing members and light sheathing, the pen is light enough for one person to move, yet heavy enough to resist wind, varmints, and repeated usage. To move the pen, just pick up one end and drag it slowly as the chickens walk along inside. For a larger pen you may need a helper to lift the other end and help scoot the pen forward.

Wheels

Without a helper the best way to move the larger 10x12' foot pen is to place a set of wheels, such as a furniture dolly, under one end, then walk to the other end of the pen and pull it where you want it. Poultry grower Mike Yoder, in Pennsylvania, had his welder friend make up a yoke, with lawn mower wheels on it, for $18.

You can install wheels from a junk lawn mower. We got several pairs from the local flea market.

Furniture Dolly

We use a furniture dolly in combinaton with skids to move the tractors. We find the dolly also has numerous farm uses such as hauling firewood, feed bags, bales of hay, blocks, etc.

Scoots

It's even simpler and less expensive to use wooden scoots. Cut these out of two 2x4 boards into a half-moon shape. Cut a notch in the top of the scoot board so the bottom end runner of the pen can fit in it. This also holds the scoot in place while you are moving the pen.

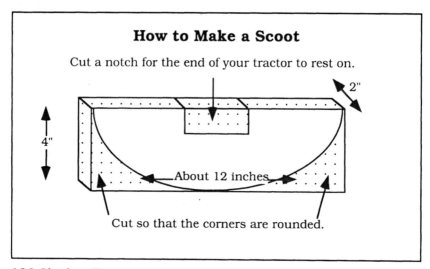

How to Make a Scoot

Cut a notch for the end of your tractor to rest on.

2"

4"

About 12 inches

Cut so that the corners are rounded.

How to Move a Tractor with Scoots

Tie a rope or put handles on the front so you can pull the pen along.

Chickens walk along inside and will be eager for the new graze.

I'm going to enter the tractor pull contest.

Hi ho, Hi ho, it's off to graze we go!

Put scoots under the back corners of the pen. Use two so it doesn't wobble. Remove the scoots when your are done so you can use them to move other pens and so there won't be a gap for critters to get under.

Walk backwards so you can watch to see if any birds get caught under the pen while it's moving.

Chapter 9: Processing Poultry

When it comes time to harvest your broilers you have two choices: you can either butcher them yourself, or take them to a slaughterhouse in your area. Check with your local county extension office for slaughterhouses in your part of the country. Sometimes they advertise in the local paper or you can ask around the feed stores and ask other growers for the names of local processing places.

Having the chickens slaughtered in a USDA-inspected slaughterhouse will set you back anywhere from $2 to $3 per bird. There are two advantages to using an inspected facility. First, the inspector will tell you if your birds have

Madame Chicken LeClaire´

any diseases, and secondly, you can legally sell your dressed poultry to the public through retailers and across state lines.

I talked to Chuck DeCorley recently over at *Small Farm Today* magazine. He says his state, Missouri, has a real lack of processing houses. That surprises me. I grew up in southwestern Missouri at a time when every county had one or more slaughterhouses. Times have really changed, even in the conservative Midwest.

This same thing became apparent when I moved to North Carolina. There just aren't any chicken processors in western North Carolina near where I live. The closest one I've found is in Duncan, South Carolina, about 30 miles away. The end result of this is that I now own processing equipment and butcher my own birds here at the farm and make a larger net profit per bird than I used to.

Before buying the equipment, however, I checked with the North Carolina Department of Agriculture to see what limitations applied to private poultry processing. North Carolina has adopted the federal minimum that allows any grower to produce, process, and sell up to 1,000 birds per year without a license or any inspections. Without inspection, I can only sell these birds off the farm to private buyers. I cannot sell them to stores or restaurants for resale.

As I interpret the law, too, you can have more than 1,000 birds on your farm if they are in different ownership, such as your spouse"s or partner's or children's name. This way several growers (or joint venture partners) can share a more sophisticated processing facility and still be within the limits of the law.

This does not apply to pheasants and quail, however, since they are game birds and are not subject to processing or marketing regulations. In other words, you can grow as many as you want and process and sell them any way you want, at least according to the state department of agriculture. However, you might also run afowl (sic) of state board of health regulations that say you can't sell any food product that is not processed in a state-inspected slaughter facility. This is clearly the case in Tennessee, and they do enforce it. So, be on the safe side and call your state department of agriculture and ask for guidance. At the very least, keep your bird numbers to 1,000 or less per ownership name, or build a facility that can be inspected.

As I said earlier, you can make more money faster with a poultry processing business than you can by growing the birds. It might be that the laws in Missouri or other states make it prohibitively expensive to start an inspected processing facility. In that case look into the possibilities offered by designing and building a community-owned, portable processing facility.

It isn't clear if that 1,000-bird federal limit applies to "per person", "per farm" or some other parameter. Nothing in the law prohibits you from jointly owning a processing facility with other like-minded farmers. The way I interpret it is on a "per farm" basis. As a farmer I can grow a thousand birds, then I can also rent a small piece of farmland to my spouse who has a 1,000 bird commercial flock. That enables us to legally grow 2,000 birds per year. Then, children, brothers, sisters, parents, and so forth can all get in the act by renting a little bit of land and growing a 1,000 birds each. Then we can all share the processing equipment and chore of butchering.

One good example of this method of joint venturing is in McPherson, Kansas. Six farmers, led by Russell Groves, banded together and built a portable processing facility on a trailer. They tow it from farm to farm, or from field to field, to process birds as needed. Each of the farmers produces only 1,000 birds, but they combine their purchasing, processing, and marketing in such a way that the work and the equipment get shared profitably by all.

An interesting side note to this is that they made almost all of their equipment from cast-off junk. They made killing cones from those bright orange traffic cones you see at hgihway construction sites. The scalder is a derelict hot-water heater, and the plucker is a modified, thrown-away commercial washing machine. Finally, the stain-less-steel eviscerating table is a former salad bar. They put the equipment on an 8-foot by 16-foot trailer for pulling from farm to farm. The whole shebang cost less than $3,000. To purchase it all new would cost closer to $8,000.

When the trailer arrives at a farm to process chickens, the first thing they do is plug in the hot-water heater. It takes about an hour to bring the scald water up to an optimal 145° F. The heater requires a 220-volt 50-amp circuit. (Other heaters are available that run on propane). The picker runs on a 110-volt extension cord. Water comes from a garden hose attached to the farm house. Wash water drains out a 4" PVC drainpipe attached to the bottom of the eviscerating table.

A trailer crew of two can butcher 30 birds per hour, faster if more people are available to help out. This is much faster than the 12 birds per hour that David and I have been able to achieve with our wood-fired, galvanized-washtub scalding vat and one-bird-at-a-time plucker. Next year, David and I plan to increase our productivity with a better layout of our tables and vats, and with a propane-fired scalding tank. Using our "homestead-scale" equipment we plan to be able to do 15 to 20 broilers per hour, up to 500 per season. We also raise turkeys, which take about twice as long to butcher as a broiler. We estimate 75 turkeys will take us about 15 hours total processing time, spread out over three or four days just before Thanksgiving.

Another rolling abattoir I've recently become acquainted with is Ray Garciain Littleton, New Hampshire. He started his business several years ago and has become quite well-known in his area for providing prompt, clean, and relatively inexpensive poultry processing. His trailer and equipment set him back about $7,000. He and his helper can do up to 50 turkeys in an afternoon, at $7.50 per bird. He charges $2.00 per broiler, and sells freezer-proof bags to customers who want them. He pays special attention to cleanliness and quality processing so that year after year he keeps his customers and adds new ones. He hasn't given up his day job yet, but the weekend poultry processing business is certainly profitable.

Do-It-Yourself Poultry Processing

If you do your own butchering it will help if you have proper equipment. Doing all the steps by hand can easily take one-half hour per bird, at least in the beginning. Even after you've had some practice you'll still be able to only do about four birds per hour by hand.

With a killing cone, thermostatically controlled scalding vat and a one-bird-at-a-time plucking machine you can undress and butcher a chicken in less than five minutes. This equipment will cost about $600 to $1,000. But it will last you forever if you keep it clean and stored properly, and, paraphrasing Gene Logsdon, "if you don't back your pickup over it".

I think that building your own small-scale processing facility might not make economic sense unless you are processing at least a hundred broilers each year. When I lived in an area where poultry processors were nearby it was easier for me to have them process my birds. After all, they had already made the investment in processing and chilling equipment, they had the time to do it, and they were helping support their families with the income they could make. In those days I found it easier to take the broilers or turkeys to the slaughterhouse the night before processing since it didn't interfere with my work schedule. I think it also helps the flavor of the meat if the chickens get a chance to calm down after their ride in the truck. Excited chickens tend to build up lactic acid in their muscles. It's better to let them sit a few hours in their new surroundings before being processed.

John Adams, a Vermont processor, tells me this delay in butchering makes the birds calmer and helps the feathers come out easier during the plucking process. He also said it's easier to remove the entrails if you withhold feed for 12 hours before processing. Never withhold water, though; the chickens are apt to die on you.

I've done it both ways, and found that it is easier to transport broilers at night rather than in the daytime. At night they are asleep and it's easy to pick them up and put them in the truck. When I harvest the chickens at night I put them in my pickup truck cap and make sure they have bedding and water, and plenty of ventilation. Then, I either drive them to the processing plant that evening or early next day. I can only carry up to 50 chickens at a time in my compact pickup truck. If I have more than that to haul I either rent a big U-Haul truck or hire a local livestock hauler who has a cattle trailer.

Some growers I've talked to use wooden chicken crates to move their broilers. These crates are expensive and hard to build, so I've always relied on either handling the chickens loose, or putting three at a time in used banana boxes. I get the boxes free from the dumpster behind the supermarket.

If I have to catch chickens in the chicken tractor in the daytime I use a large paddle made from a sheet of 1/4" plywood. This paddle traps them against one end of the pen where I can reach in and pull them out two at a time. I use the paddle to get the chickens out of the pickup truck cap, too. Just stick it in through the window and nudge them back towards the tailgate where my helper can catch them and unload them.

Design and Build a Small-Scale Poultry Processing Facility

Last year when Patricia and I moved to North Carolina to build our permaculture farm we were surprised to learn there aren't any poultry processors in the area. As it turns out, however, this is a blessing. It caused us to buy our own equipment and enables us to double the amount of money we used to make on each bird. Not only that, we also took on the dealership for Pickwick processing equipment as a sideline.

We know we can produce better quality meat if it is processed as close to its pen as possible. We avoid the stress and trauma to the bird of being caught and stuffed in the truck for a 20-minute ride over bumpy roads to a strange facility. The birds are calmer and process easier if they are not stressed or alarmed. I think the ideal system might even be to have a little slaughterhouse mounted on wheels so you could pull it alongside the chicken tractor and do the work right there.

Here the question of humane treatment comes up. Should you allow living birds to see the killing and processing of their penmates? Good question, and one that I don't have a clear answer for. My experience has been that it doesn't seem to matter. Last year when we were processing broilers our laying hens came wandering around the corner and came over, as is their curiosity, to see what we were up to. I had to shoo them away so they wouldn't pull entrails out of the bucket.

Then David had to chase them away from the plucker because they were underfoot, pecking at the feathers. We finally put them back in the henhouse to get them out of our way. We were both surprised that the hens didn't display any concerns at all for their fellow fowl. They seemed totally unconscious about what was happening. I guess it's up to individual growers to decide how far from the chicken pen they want to set up their processor.

Another question that always comes up is should you have an enclosed building to set up your processing equipment? My answer is yes, if you can afford it. Last year we processed all our broilers, pheasants, and turkeys using sawhorses and planks set up in the driveway beside the house. To heat the scalding water we put a $17 galvanized washtub on top of the Weber grill and built a good hardwood fire under it. It takes about an hour to get enough hot water this way, and it can be smoky to work around. It was inexpensive and worked just fine, but next year I hope to upgrade our equipment with a propane heater for the water.

Butchering chickens in the backyard was okay, except for hot sun on us and the birds, and no window and door screens to keep out the yellow jackets. The yellow jackets came from all over, attracted by the odor of blood and flesh. They were especially bothersome when we were trying to bag the birds. If we weren't careful they'd fly into the cavity and then we'd have to rinse the bird again to get the wasp out, or use the vacuum cleaner to suck it out. I wasn't concerned about getting stung, especially since Pat keeps bees for pollination and apitherapy. But I for darn sure didn't want to leave one of those yellow jackets in the cavity and have a customer find it on Thanksgiving Day!

This year we definitely plan to have some type of screened and roofed butchering area, even if it's just one of those screened patio houses that you buy at department stores. They cost two or three hundred dollars, but are probably much cheaper than any other structure you could build. I think we'll still do the killing, bleeding and scalding outside, since it's messy. But once we pluck the bird we'll bring it inside for evisceration and chilling and packaging.

Of course, if you build a commercial facility approved by the state department of agriculture you'll want to work with them from the beginning. They will have design guidelines you will need to follow. These government-approved buildings aren't easy or cheap, though. Some requirements are washable walls, ceiling and floor, stainless-steel equipment, separate kill and processing rooms, hallway to bathroom, full septic system, hot and cold water, separate closet for storing cleaning supplies such as bleach, windows and doors with screens, and so forth. If you have more than just a few employees you might also have to install a second bathroom.

At first glance you might feel like they are simply making it so hard and expensive to do that nobody will want to do it. When you explore the reasoning, however, you will probably see the wisdom in such a building. It is about the minimum equipment and size you will need in order to process the 20,000 or so birds per year that a commercial facility needs to break even.

However, for poultry growers in the "homestead" or "market garden" level of production, this big, expensive building isn't necessary. If you plan to do more than 1,000 birds per year then you can look into the rolling abattoir model. You can look around for a cargo trailer or cargo box off a truck. One of my neighbors uses a refrigeration cargo box off a meat delivery truck to chill the deer he and his family harvest each year. It comes complete with a refrigeration unit that plugs into his house so he can chill the carcasses. If you don't plan to travel around with your chicken processor then you could remodel a corner of your barn or garage, or build a small building.

The guidelines that you want to consider when designing and building a place to butcher poultry are:

1. Keeps you out of sun, wind, rain.

2. Easy to clean, especially the evisceration table and floor. Use stainless steel or galvanized equipment.

3. Fly and wasp proof—includes access door and windows for daylight.

4. Cold water supplied by garden hose from your house.

5. Entrails, blood and feathers go into your compost pile or you can bury them where the dogs won't dig them up.

6. Easy for at least two people to work in. Six- by eight-feet is about minimum for two people. Eight by twelve might be more realistic.

7. Killing, bleeding, and scalding can happen outdoors.

8. If the unit is on wheels you can move it close to your chicken pen. You can store it in the barn, and you can even loan it to neighbors or friends.

9. Access to continual cold water for chilling, or plenty of bagged ice.

10. Attractive building that won't cause your customers to cringe. Use the bathroom in your house.

In the beginning "homestead" poultry project you can probably get by with just processing the birds by hand without any expensive equipment. Butchering poultry by hand is slow, for sure. But you will learn a lot about the business, and about yourself, if you process your first hundred or so broilers or turkeys one at a time the old-fashioned way.

Begin by laying out your work area so that everything flows from one step to another. First, you need to catch the chickens and pen them briefly nearby to where you will kill and bleed them. You can catch broilers with a long, wire "chicken catcher" made from number 9 wire, with a long hook in the end that will catch their leg but not slip over their foot. This method usually terrifies the birds and makes them harder to handle.

Another way to catch them is with a large fisherman's pole net. We always keep one of these handy for loose birds. It is much more reliable than the "hook" but nearly as traumatic. The way I prefer to catch chickens for butchering is by herding them into a corner of the chicken tractor with my wooden paddle. I then reach over and pick one up by grasping its legs firmly. They will squawk and struggle a little bit, but when you hang them upside down they generally submit and quiet right down. Turkeys, of course, are much easier to catch since they will walk right up to

Hope St. Peter likes chicken!

Killing Cone

you. They are stronger and will struggle harder than a broiler, so make sure you have a firm grasp on their wings to keep from getting beaten. Also watch their legs to keep from getting scratched by the sharp talons.

Once you have the bird in hand, bring it to your workbench. Either place it in the killing cone, or tie it by its legs to the edge of the table. Put a bucket under the bird's head to catch the blood, then prepare to cut its jugular vein. Use a sharp knife that has a stiletto-type point. We use one manufactured by Pickwick that is double-edged and shaped just right to slip in and slit the vein without cutting the head off. If you cut the head off the bird will die quicker and not bleed out thoroughly. It's best—though difficult—to cut the vein without severing the windpipe, too. Probably you will have a hard time cutting one without the other at first, but with practice you can learn how to do it. I also feel cutting the jugular vein is a more merciful way to kill a bird than chopping off its head.

As you pull the head down through the killing cone you can gently squeeze the throat and feel the vein separate from the windpipe. Insert the knife between the vein and windpipe, then turn it sideways and cut through the vein and the neck skin to release the blood. If you cut the windpipe inadvertently there is some chance the bird will inhale blood into the lungs, making it harder to get a proper bleed-out. Also, if you cut the windpipe the bird will struggle more and will die faster. This inhibits proper blood flow for bleed out. If you sever just the jugular vein and the neck skin the bird will bleed out slowly and die without undue stress or struggle.

Let the bird bleed out for at least a minute, or until blood stops dripping. Turkeys take up to twice as long. Then remove the bird from the killing cone and proceed to scald it in hot water to loosen the feathers for plucking. Proper water temperature is between 142 and 145° F. Place the chicken in the hot water and swish it around for 45 to 60 seconds, then test the feathers. Again, a turkey might take twice as long. If the feathers come out easily, then proceed to remove them in large gobs with your fingers.

After all the main feathers are out, rinse the bird with fresh water; then begin picking out the smaller pinfeathers. These are especially difficult along the legs and wings.

David Stickney Scalding a Turkey

A pin knife will help considerably. This is a dull knife with a wide blade. You use it by catching the feather between the blade and your thumb and pulling it out.

White-feathered birds are easier to pick clean than dark-feathered birds. The white feathers are less noticeable on the finished bird. The black feathers sometimes look like black specks. Unless you plan to eat the skin it isn't necessary to get absolutely all of the pinfeathers out. If you do want to eat the skin then you can scorch the feathers off with a wide flame on a handheld blowtorch or by rotating the carcass over a candle flame. Some old-timers brush or pour melted paraffin or wax over the carcass and let it cool. Then they pull off the hardened wax removing the pinfeathers with it.

After getting all the feathers off you can turn your attention to taking off the head and neck. Use a heavier knife or a set of pruning shears to remove the head. Just cut between the vertebrae of the neck up near the head to

Feather Plucker by Pickwick

remove the head, then cut again where the neck enters the body to remove the neck. Place the neck in chilling water where it can later be packaged with the carcass.

Remove the feet by slicing through the skin at the leg knuckle. Watch how the skin forms around the joint as you move the knuckle back and forth and you will see just where to slice to expose the joint itself. Once you see the joint you'll be able to separate it with your heavy knife so that the feet come off easily. Discard the feet into the entrails bucket for adding to the compost pile. (Keep in mind that some people in some cultures consider the feet a delicacy, or boil them for a soup base.)

Turn the bird on its stomach facing away from you and look for the oil gland just under the skin at the base of the tail. It's important to get this oil gland out intact so it doesn't taint the meat. It is tricky since the gland is right next to the bony part of the back which sometimes interferes with your knife blade being able to get under the gland and lift it intact. Some folks have better luck if they chill the birds first, then remove the gland and rinse just before packing the carcass for the freezer.

Next, turn the bird on its back and make the incision to remove the rectum. Once you cut the rectum loose—don't cut it all the way out or you will severe the intestine—then continue the incision up the belly to the beginning of the breast cavity. Now you can open the cavity and begin moving your hands in to loosen the entrails away from the rib cage. Smaller hands are quicker at this, but just keep practicing and you'll get fairly fast at it after awhile.

Once your hand is all the way into the bird and you can touch the neck opening, then begin pulling your hand back to roll the entrails out in a bunch. Don't pull hard or you will rupture them. Just firmly tug them back out the opening, working them away from ribs and backbone as you go. Once the entrails are all out you can separate the gizzard and liver and heart for cleaning and chilling. Package these in the cavity of the carcass because a lot of folks use them for giblets in gravy.

Rinse the cavity out with fresh water so you can see the lungs which are still attached to the rib cage. Use the lung puller to gently persuade the lungs away from the ribs. Try not to break the lungs open so you can pull them out intact. The lungs will also be attached to the windpipe, so work it loose from the neck so it will come out gently. You can use the lung puller to the outside edge of the lungs and gently roll them towards the backbone then pull them out the vent. Many times the crop and the windpipe will remain lodged in the neck area, so use a small pair of pliers to pull them loose.

You now have an undressed bird that is ready to rinse thoroughly and double-check for clean removal of feathers, entrails, lungs, windpipe and crop. If you're satisfied that the bird is as clean as you can make it then place it in chilling water for two to four hours to drop the body temperature below 40° F.

When the carcass has cooled sufficiently you can remove it from the chill tank and prepare it for freezing. First, put a neck, gizzard, heart and liver in a small zip-lock baggie, remove all the air (see below), close the baggie, and insert it in the cavity. Then put the bird in a freezer bag, remove the air, tie off the bag, and deliver it to your customer or to your freezer.

All that you need to do now is clean up your butchering area. Wash everything thoroughly and resharpen the knives. Put the viscera into your compost pile and cover it well so dogs won't dig it up. Then put all your tools away until next time.

Vacuum bagging

Now that I process my own birds I find that vacuum bagging is fairly simple. I use a small handheld vacuum cleaner with a thin nozzle on it to suck the air out of the bag, then tie off the bag with a strong rubber band. I use the vacuum packing for two reasons. First, it makes a very presentable package for my customers. Second, I think it extends the freezer life and flavor of the bird. Because of these advantages I feel the extra cost of 45¢ or 75¢ per freezer bag is okay.

Last year we didn't have freezer-quality bags so we simply used kitchen-sized plastic garbage bags and double-bagged each bird. That worked okay, but I think the heavy-duty freezer bags are better, simply because they are vaporproof and don't let the meat get frosted inside the bag which can lead to freezer burn.

If you don't have a vacuum cleaner to do your vacuum bagging you can get pretty good results by putting the bird in the bag, then submersing all but the open end in a bucket of water. This squeezes out all the air except what is trapped in the bird's cavity. Other people I've talked to simply insert a plastic straw in the bag and suck out the air. I don't recommend this practice because of sanitary reasons and fear of bacterial contamination.

Processing Equipment

If you continue to grow poultry, you might outgrow your ability and desire to do all the butchering by hand. Then you will want to find a local processor to do it for you, or you will want to buy equipment to make the job faster and less tedious. With entry level equipment costing less than $1,000 you can process up to 100 birds per day. Even with a good helper it's not easy to process this many birds in a typical eight-hour day. You want to be equipped and organized as well as you possibly can to have a smooth-flowing work area.

My friend David Stickney and I have worked out a routine that seems to work for us without overworking us or making the task too tedious. We work together to catch five or six broilers into our wheelbarrow-mounted holding pen. This is a simple two-wheel box-cart with a screened top. We use it to move the birds from their pen to the butchering area.

Then David bleeds one bird at a time, then scalds it and runs it through the feather plucker, then passes it off to me for evisceration. As we work we usually talk about what we're doing and about how things are going in our lives. We sort of entertain each other so the day goes quickly and we enjoy the work rather than considering it a drudge.

I must admit to two things. First, I don't enjoy killing the birds, especially the turkeys. I can do it, but I'd rather not. Secondly, if I can help it I never butcher poultry before lunch. I know it's a silly thing, but I can't enjoy my food after killing and gutting chickens. I need time to shower and shave and separate myself from the smells and sights and sounds of the killing and butchering. I suppose as time goes by and I get more used to slaughtering livestock, this might pass. In the meantime we just allow ourselves the freedom of planning our butchering after lunch and we do other farm chores in the morning.

In the beginning you will be frustrated and annoyed at how slow you are, and how much work is involved. The first broiler I processed took me nearly half an hour. After doing a couple of dozen though, the mystery disappeared and my skills increased. Now David and I working together can process about 15 broilers per hour or five turkeys using our "market garden" level of equipment.

Organization—and practice—is the key to quick and efficient poultry processing. First, you will need a workbench or table that is high enough to be comfortable. I'm 5'10" tall and my workbench is simply made up of two 2x12x14' foot planks laid across sawhorses that are 36" high. This is still a tad low, so next year I'm moving up to 42" high sawhorses.

This year we did our butchering in the driveway next to the house. We used five gallon plastic buckets to catch the blood and viscera and just let the rinse water run out on the lawn. However, if you are in an enclosed area you will want to have a gutter on your workbench so that water flows to a drain that leads to a catch basin or septic tank. I'm currently shopping around for a used, stainless-steel, salad-bar-type workbench that already has a gutter and drain built into it. If necessary, though, I can build my own onto my workbench with a plastic gutter and a backboard. This will be especially important if we do go ahead and build a small butchering shed.

You will need a killing cone or tie strap for bleeding out the birds. The cone is made from galvanized sheet metal and shaped like a cone. It has nail holes at the top rim so you can secure it to your workbench with screws or roofing nails. You place the bird into the cone head first with its head hanging out the bottom and its feet sticking out the top. This way the bird is immobilized so it won't thrash around and bruise the meat or interrupt the bleed-out.

Commercial cones are about $15, but you can make your own from any cone-shaped object, such as traffic cones. There are three commercial sizes: one each for broilers, turkeys, and pheasants. I've not been happy with the turkey size because it's too small in the breast area for today's double breasted turkeys. The pheasant cone is also too small for pen-raised birds, although it's probably suitable for wild birds that are rangier and not as plump as pen-raised birds.

For pheasants I simply use the broiler cone, and for turkeys I just hang them by a strap around their legs and tied to a sturdy nail on my workbench.

Put a nail or cup hook in a convenient place on your work-bench to hold your garden hose nozzle within easy reach for rinsing. You will be constantly reaching for the hose to rinse carcasses or your hands, and for washing off the work surface.

Your workbench will also hold your knives, pruning shears, scissors, sharpening stone, lung puller, pliers and other hand tools you might need. Keep everything within arm's reach distance so you won't waste time going to get what you need. It's especially important to have good knives. You can buy them locally or from companies that sell poultry processing equipmetn by mail. Expect to pay over $50 for a good set of killing, boning and pinning knives, but they will make your task much, much easier. Remember, too, to have a whet stone on hand to touch up the edges as you go through the day.

We use five-gallon plastic buckets that we scrounge from the landfill, for catching blood and viscera. For chill tanks we use 35-gallon plastic trash barrels with tight-fitting lids. Our ice comes from the local convenience store, and our cold water comes from a garden hose hooked to our deep well.

For scalding the birds you will need at least a five-gallon metal container for broilers and pheasants, and a ten-gallon metal container for turkeys. We use a 20-gallon galvanized wash tub. To heat the water we put the tub over our Weber barbecue grill and use small chunks of firewood to get the water hot. Other folks I've talked to use variations on propane camp stoves. Next year I plan to graduate to some sort of stove because the wood fire in my Weber is smoky and requires careful tending to keep the scalding water at just the right temperature of 142 to 145° F.

Up until now we've talked primarily about the sort of equipment you'll need even if you're only processing five or ten birds each day. Once you get above that level, however, you will probably want to add a feather plucker to your equipment lineup. Feather pluckers come in sizes ranging from a tabletop model that sells for $300 up to semi-commercial units that can pluck five birds at a time and cost about $3,000.

The plucker I use here is the Pickwick Hom-Pik D, which can do broilers and turkeys up to 15 pounds. We can even do 20 pound turkeys if we team up, with one of us holding the weight of the bird while the other guides it over the rubber picking fingers. Otherwise we're apt to let the full weight of the bird down on the plucking fingers and get the skin ripped off.

The drum of the plucker has rubber fingers that are moderately stiff. As the drum rotates and you hold the bird lightly against the fingers the feathers will come off so quickly it will surprise you. Within seconds you can pluck even a 20-pound turkey right down to bare skin and a few leftover pinfeathers.

It's important that the birds and feathers be wet as you place them against the drum. They usually go directly to the plucker from the scalder and are dripping wet. But, you can get a cleaner pick if you rig up a small hose and misting nozzle over the plucking drum. When the bird is wet the skin isn't so easily damaged and the feathers will come off more quickly.

We've found that the portable chicken pluckers sometimes don't pick the bird clean on the first pass. So we do a second, lighter pass to clean off any feathers missed in the first go-around. Sometimes I'll also hold a wing or leg separately to get those last few little stubborn feathers. We don't bother with the feathers at the knees or at the head since they come off when we de-head and de-feet the bird.

After the birds are dressed you need to chill them as quickly as possible before freezing them. Poultry spoils very quickly so it's important to lower the body temperature as soon as possible to less than 40 degrees F. It's not a good idea to freeze them before they are chilled because the meat will turn darker, especially around the bones. Incidentally, the same effect happens if you don't bleed the birds thoroughly, especially in the wings where blood will pool and coagulate. This makes the meat less attractive when you cook it.

After all this work to humanely raise and process your birds you can enjoy your reward. You will find poultry raised this way has superior taste, texture, and nutrition. All your friends and family will be impressed.

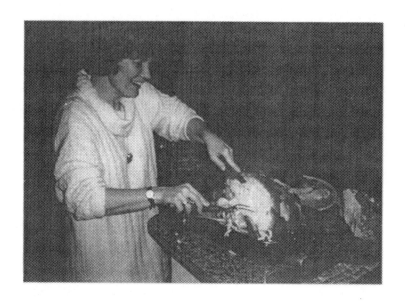

Our former neighbor, Gail Shaw, getting ready for Thanksgiving dinner with a tractor-raised turkey.

Chapter 10: Selecting Chickens for Your Tractor

Breeds to Choose From and Best Choices

There are many more breeds of chickens to choose from than you will ever need. One breeder catalog—Murray McMurray Hatchery—lists ten layer breeds, 30 different bantam breeds, 30 dual-purpose breeds and four meat breeds. They also list over 30 show breeds, as well as partridge, pheasants, turkeys, ducks, and geese. Another breeder, Marti's Poultry Farm, lists 60 different chicken breeds, many of them old-line heritage breeds. (See appendix for addresses).

Your choice depends entirely on which breeds intrigue you, and whether you want meat, eggs or show birds. Buy layers if you simply want eggs. Buy meat birds if you only want meat. If you want both, then consider buying a standard, dual-purpose breed such as Plymouth Barred Rock. You get eggs or fryers from the females and fryers or broilers from the males.

If you want fast-growing meat birds for market, choose one of the hybrid meat varieties such as Cornish Cross, Kosher King, or Silver Barred Cross. These hybrids have a high rate of feed conversion and are fast growers. Any hybrid's offspring will be throwbacks to the original parents and will likely be worthless for either meat or egg production. If you want to keep a rooster for fertile eggs, you will need to keep the standard breeds.

One factor that is most important to the chicken tractor garden is the foraging characteristics of the breed you choose. All the standard breeds will be aggressive foragers, eating bugs, weeds, grasses, and worms. Their ability to forage for food helps save a great deal of grain you would otherwise have to buy.

On the other hand, the hybrids, particularly the high maintenance, hybrid meat birds will be very poor foragers, preferring to get their food from the feed bucket. My experience corresponds to the experience of other growers who say that their hybrid meat birds won't even go outside the coop to walk about or graze. They are just too lazy.

For the chicken-tractor farmer I'd recommend you stick with the standard breeds if you want mostly eggs and only occasionally, meat. Use the hybrids that are chacteristically more aggressive grazers. Especially the old-line breeds that are in danger of becoming extinct, such as those listed in the "Give Me That Old-Time Chicken" chapter.

Many of the old-line standard breeds are only available from small local hatcheries. I think we should all do what we can to keep the independent hatcheries in business. Most of them are family-owned-and-operated and are carrying on a lineage of service to their customers that has been in their families for decades, even generations.

These hatcheries also have a tremendous amount of information at their fingertips and can help you over the rough spots with your poultry problems, especially disease and nutrition questions. If we don't support these hatcheries, then another part of our country's heritage will eventually fade from the scene and we will lose many of the old-line poultry breeds forever.

One of the most satisfying aspects of raising your own poultry for meat, eggs, or show is that you can breed your own hens. Just put a rooster in with the hens gather the eggs, and hatch them either under a broody hen or in an incubator. By doing this year after year you will improve your flock. You can even create a new strain, based on your own criteria and specific needs.

Following is a partial list of the commercial breeds that are readily available through feed stores and mail-order catalogs. This is not a complete list. Instead, these are varieties that are available from commercial breeders and that have proven to be capable of performing well for their purpose.

Words really can't describe the beauty and presence of these distinctly different breeds of chickens. My primary hope in including this list is simply to give you an idea of the enormous range of poultry breeds available for meat or eggs, for dual-purpose, and for show or exhibition. There is a separate listing of turkeys, partridge, pheasants, ducks and geese in Chapter 11, along with a list of rare breeds published by the American Livestock Breeds Conservancy.

Breeds Available from Commercial Hatcheries

Bantams

Light Brahma	Pure white with black-laced tail and hackle feather
Buff Brahma	Golden buff with black tails and laced hackles
Dark Brahma	Silver-penciled, greenish-black base and very white on neck, saddle and tail
Silkes	Available in buff, black, white, and blue
Booted Bantams	Bearded and non-bearded
Mille Fleur	Reddish bay, feathers tipped in white

Porcelain	Pale blue tipped in white
Sultan	Features beard and muffs, feathered legs and five toes
Cochin Bantams	Buff, partridge, red, barred, black with green sheen, golden-laced, red, white, black, mottled and blue
Gold and Silver Sebrights	Golden Bay and Silver White
Japanese	Black, buff, and white with black tail
Old English Games	Very cocky
Quail Antwerp Belgian	Brownish black-tinged with straw color
White-Laced Red Cornish	Clean legged variety
Silver-penciled Rock	Brown eggs, hatch well
Dark Cornish	Excellent to eat
Partridge Rock	Partridge color pattern
Partridge Wyandotte	For show, brown eggs, or hobby
Rhode Island Red	Deep, mahogany color
White Crested Black Polish	Bright white top hat
Araucana Bantam	Lays blue-greenish-colored eggs

Heavy Breeds dual-purpose-meat and brown eggs

Silver Laced Wyandottes	Hardy, vigorous, good winter layers, productive
White Orpingtons	Pure white, gentle, good layers
Buff Orpingtons	Glistening golden plumage, good layers and mothers, and excellent to eat
Turkens	Naked necks, good layers and winter hardy, tasty.
Black Australorps	Australian heritage, good layers and table birds, gentle
Rhode Island Reds	Prolific layers, dual-purpose

Red Star — Sex link, red females, white males, good layers, good to eat

New Hampshire Reds — Handsome and vigorous, good dual purpose birds

White Rocks — Good year-round layers, fryers and roasters

Partridge Rocks — Excellent setters and brooders, eggs, meat or show

Barred Rocks — Dual-purpose, America's favorite layer and roaster, reliable

Buff Rocks — Pure golden buff, fine winter layers and good setters

White Giants — Slow to mature heavy roaster, good egg layers

Black Giants — Exhibition, layer, table use, good cold weather variety, extra heavy at maturity

Speckled Sussex — Beautiful utility bird, for showing, eggs, or table

Dark Cornish — Superb meat qualities and hardy foragers

White Wyandottes — Snow-white plumage, ideal for table, early to finish, good for northern climates, good layers, wonderful dual-purpose bird

Columbian Wyandottes — Medium size-birds, good layers, setters and brooders

Light Brahmas — Old Asian breed, gentle, cold hardy, good layers, slow to maturity roasters, fine quality meat

Columbian Rocks — Black on white, very nice for show

Breeds Available from Commercial Hatcheries (cont.)

White Egg Layers

Blue Andalusians   Spanish origin, blue-laced plumage, not good brooders, excellent for exhibition and fly tying

Silver Spangled Hamburgs   Small size, alert, graceful, elegant and beautiful, great foragers, easy keepers

Red Leghorns   Rare show hen, not good setters, rich red plumage, graceful

Anconas   Excellent layers, lustrous black plumage with white tips, old Mediterranean breed

Single Comb Brown Leghorns   Colorful, chicks are striped like chipmunks, lively, good layers, non-setters

Rose Comb Brown Leghorns   Combs are low, solid, thick, and covered with small rounded points, less likely to suffer frostbite, good range bird

Black Minorcas   Large Mediterranean, large eggs, non-setters

Buff Minorcas   Rich, golden buff color, large eggs, non-setters

Araucanas   "Easter Egg Chicken", Chilean, medium size, extremely hardy, eggs colored turquoise to deep olive

Pear White Leghorn   Prolific, long-lived hybrid, good feed-to-eggs conversion, hardy, outperforms most standard breeds

Highland 55   Hybrid cross between heavy breed males and large White Leghorn females, hardy, prolific egg layer

Crested Breeds White egg layers, ancient breeds from Poland

White Crested Black Polish	Black plumage, white crest
Golden Polish	Ornamental, very showy
Buff Laced Polish	Golden buff laced with creamy white. Showy, gentle, both bearded and non-bearded
White Polish	Snowy white crests and rounded white bodies look like snowballs. Dainty and pretty
Silver Polish	Striking appearance, non-setters
Sultans	Southeastern Europe origin, crest, muff, beard, feathered shanks and five toes
Crevecoeurs	Normandy, France, origin, all black plumage, lay white eggs
Mottled Houdans	France origin, lovely black plumage tipped with white, five toes, delicious eating and good layers

Cochins

Black Cochins	Coal-black, exhibition
White Cochins	Giant snowballs, quiet
Buff Cochins	Poor layers but great setters
Partridge Cochins	Orange-red, show and setting
Blue Cochins	Rare and beautiful
Silver Laced Cochins	Silver laced plumage

Feather footed breeds

White Langshan	Stately, white plumage, brown eggs, showy
Black Langshan	Asiatic, large, glossy black, gentle, showy, brown eggs
Dark Brahmas	Striking, gentle, silver-penciled gray and black with silvery white

Buff Brahmas   Large, gentle, regal, brown eggs, showy, will set

Salmon Faverolles France origin, novelty, showy, large-sized

Rare and Unusual Breeds

Silver Gray Dorkings Ancient Rome, long body on short legs

Sumatras   Island of Sumatra, Asia, long-tailed, beautiful

Golden Penciled Hamburgs   Fine, small, active, white eggs, non-setter

White Laced Red Cornish   Handsome, blocky Cornish, slow to mature

Phoenix   Imperial Gardens of Japan, long tail feathers

Lakenvelders   Germany and Holland, small, quick, active

Buttercups   Sicily, excellent for show

White Faced Black Spanish   Graceful and stylish, slow to develop, oldest of the Mediterranean's

Golden Campines   Belgium, small, distinctive

Red Caps   English, large rose comb

Silver Leghorns   Silvery-white and lustrous black, good layers and very vigorous, outstanding show

Golden laced Wyandottes   Formerly called "Winnebagoes", showy

Dominiques   American, also called "Dominiker", very hardy, good layers

Silver Penciled Rocks Exhibition, ideal fly-tying feathers, single comb

Silver Penciled Wyandottes   Showy, fly-tying, rose comb

Egyptian Fayoumis Small, active, Nile in Egypt, quick to mature as layers and broilers

Breeds Available from Commercial Hatcheries (cont.)

Meat Birds
Cornish Game Hen. Harvest at 2.5 pounds live weight for delicious eating.

Jumbo Cornish X Rocks. Rapid growth, feed-efficient, dress from 3 to 4 pounds in 6 to 8 weeks, pullets take 1 to 1.5 weeks longer to reach maturity for slaughter, not good foragers.

Cornish Roaster. Fryer or roaster, slower maturing, fewer leg problems, more active than Cornish Cross, better forager, dress at three to four pounds in eight to nine weeks.

Chapter 11: Give Me That Old-Time Chicken

...and It's Good Enough for Me

Stepping Backwards Into The Future

Since time began, poultry, and especially chickens, have provided food and valuable products for humanity. However, new technology including refrigeration, transportation, large brooders and incubators, trade associations, and contract growers have changed the way we think about and raise chickens.

Ma, Pa & Little Jo

The industrial meat and egg factories have resulted in a drastic decline in the farm flocks and small hatcheries. Independent hatcheries have closed by the hundreds across America, paralleling the alarming decline in farm flocks and farm families.

Current industry standards favor hybrid crosses over pure breeds. It's true that per bird production in both eggs and meat has increased, while feed consumption per bird has dropped. It's just as true that flavor, nutrition, disease resistance, foraging abilities and weather hardiness have also declined. Consumers have to settle for bland, flavorless—often contaminated—produce from the supermarkets. To get good-tasting poultry we have to grow it ourselves or buy it from a nearby farmer who still practices humane, sustainable livestock husbandry.

According to the American Livestock Breeds Conservancy, there are about nine companies that control the breeding stock for all commercial meat and egg chickens in North America. We currently have endangered breeds of livestock in just the same way we have endangered wild life. As with other animals and plants in the world, some breeds of chickens are at risk of extinction and we are rapidly losing genetic diversity.

Hybrid industrial breeds, designed for commercial production, are very fragile. They require antibiotics in feeds, and extra management to prevent diseases. They require a high protein diet and they suffer in confined housing. This housing requires a tremendous amount of energy for heating and cooling. So what if the new hybrid freaks can out-produce the old heritage breeds? They are doing so at great harm to our environment. Grain farms are in one region and broiler houses are in another. This requires a tremendous amount of long distance trucking. The broiler and layer factories themselves are in states with low wages and lenient pollution laws. Worst of all, the new hybrid breeds just aren't "real" chickens.

Howard W. "Bud" Kerr, Jr., Director of the Office for Small-Scale Agriculture at the USDA, told me a story about trying to use free-range chickens for pest control in his peach orchard. He got some hybrid broilers from a commercial breed, but when he put his portable pen in the orchard, they would not go outside! The only thing these ultra-hybrid birds know how to do is gain weight quickly in protected confinement housing with continuous feeding.

I'm not saying you can't raise the high energy hybrids if you want to, but the chicken tractor system works best with "real" chickens. The standard breeds are aggressive foragers. They withstand changing weather better than the hybrids and they taste better. You just cannot deny the lower fat, better flavor, and healthier texture of the old line breeds. Just like your grandmother used to cook, hmmm gooood!

Also, the old-line breeds of chickens display physical characteristics and personality traits more than the new hybrid breeds.

> *"Most of these older breeds, besides being productively versatile, are also beautiful! They have a satisfying aesthetic value that alone merits their keeping and it gives joy just to have them around."*
>
> Donald Bixby, DVM
> American Livestock Breeds Conservancy

Today, changing global economic conditions and trade agreements are affecting almost every individual somehow. Our climates are shifting. I don't know of a single country that has not had unusual weather in the last several years. We need these harty older breeds and we need to actively preserve them. I support the American Livestock Breeds Conservancy (ALBC) for their efforts in saving the endangered farm breeds and I encourage you to contact them to find out more about their programs and rescue efforts. The best place you can begin to preserve the past, for a brighter future, is in your garden—with old-time breeds.

Preserving Heirloom Poultry Breeds

by Donald Bixby, DVM
Executive Director of the American Livestock Breeds
Conservancy

Chickens and other poultry were some of our first domesticated animals. They have provided a widely adaptable food source used by almost every culture. Poultry have been effective foragers living on the scraps of human activity and providing meat, eggs, feathers, down, and pest control. Explorers and settlers carried them everywhere to provide a portable source of fresh meat and to establish flocks at pioneer farms. There was once a time when chicken flocks were on every farm as well as in most back gardens of town and city dwellers. These poultry flocks were profitable for small farms and regional hatcheries, too.

Along with utility, people have always recognized and appreciated the beauty of poultry. A tremendous variety of type, shape, size, color, and feather pattern and comb are available. The skills of breed selection, whether for production or perfection of form, have been widespread historically.

Some Breeds Face Extinction

Following World War II there was a major restructuring of egg and poultry production. Meat and egg production are completely industrialized, resulting in a drastic decline in the farm flocks and small hatcheries. Today, poultry is big business; produced in factory farms, not on family farms. Industrialization has made poultry meat and eggs an inexpensive source of protein. Unfortunately, while poultry consumption is at an all-time high, consolidation of the poultry industry has led to a loss of breeds, genetic diversity, and the widespread knowledge of selection skills.

Genetic selection limited to a few uniform production characteristics with little regard to innate hardiness has led to the decline of the many formerly important breeds. The industry favors hybrid crosses over pure breeds and vertical integration has resulted in fewer people making decisions about breed selection. The result is a very narrow genetic base controlled internationally by only a few companies. Although existing industrial stocks may be suitable for commercial production, they don't do well in less closely controlled conditions. In return for its high productivity, industry-produced poultry requires a high level of input, including substantial veterinary attention, high protein feed, and confinement housing.

As breeds disappear, valuable traits—developed over many generations—are also being lost. Researchers at Rodale Farms hoped to use chickens as biological control of plum curculio in their apple orchard. Hatchery hybrids would not even go outside their henhouse, let alone forage for the pest larvae in the orchard. The valuable traits of foraging and ranging have been bred out! The American Livestock Breeds Conservancy suggested Dominique chickens, American's oldest recognized poultry breed, long noted for its foraging ability. Sure enough, the Dominiques were in chicken heaven scratching and pecking through the orchard debris and foraging insect larvae as well as other morsels tasty only to chickens.

The American Livestock Breeds Conservancy

The American Livestock Breeds Conservancy (ALBC) has been helping to conserve heritage breeds since 1977. We have an active program to conserve the genetic pool for poultry, asses, cattle, goats, horses, sheep, and swine. Many of the traits necessary for survival are not being passed along in the breeding programs of commercial poultry. Specifically bred out are the abilities to brood chicks, forage, produce both meat and eggs, and adapt to climate changes.

The chicken tractor approach fits the small flock grower and hobbyist very well and provides a "habitat" for endangered poultry breeds. These breeds possess the very traits needed for the chickens to forage and thrive out-of-doors. This means we should consider them superior to the commercial hybrids for your garden. Besides being versatile, the heritage breeds are also beautiful. They have a satisfying aesthetic value that alone merits their keeping and it gives me joy just to have them around.

Today there is a growing emphasis on sustainable agriculture that includes locally grown food and humanely raised livestock. Consumers want to know who produces their food, where, and under what conditions. Additionally, changing global economic conditions and trade agreements are affecting almost every individual in some way. There is widespread concern about climate changes and the continued availability of cheap energy. All of these issues affect our ability to meet the agricultural needs of the future. Adaptation is only possible where alternatives have been conserved. Genetic diversity provides these alternatives to selection of livestock to meet changing needs.

"To safeguard our future, we cannot afford to let go of our valuable poultry heritage and the irreplaceable variety of breeds it represents." 1987 ALBC Poultry Census and Source Book.

To encourage and promote rare production breeds of poultry, ALBC conducts periodic updates about sources and the status of particular breeds and rescue efforts. ALBC can also give you information about breeds for maximum conservation of genetic diversity.

Poultry Census Summary

To assess the status of poultry genetic resources in the United States, the American Livestock Breeds Conservancy conducted a survey of 17 production breeds in 1987. Breeds included in the survey are of cultural, historical, or economic significance in America. The survey distinguished between "production" and "exhibition" strains and limited its search for breeder sources of production birds to those listed in the U.S. Department of Agriculture directory of participants in the 1986 and 1987 National Poultry Improvement Plan.

Categories of "critical", "rare", and "watch" reflect the size of the breeding population (the number of females in breeding flocks) and the number of sources of breeding flocks.

• **Critical**—Breeds with 500 or fewer females and fewer than three sources.

• **Rare**—Breeds with 2,000 or fewer females, and five or fewer sources, or a concentration of the breeding population in fewer than three sources.

• **Watch**—Breeds with 2,000 to 20,000 females, but fewer than ten sources, or a declining number of sources.

Endangered Breeds of Poultry

Critical	Rare	Watch
Ancona Rock	Black Jersey Giant	Barred Plymouth
Black Minorca	Brown Leghorn	Black Australorp
Delaware	Khaki Campbell Duck	New Hampshire
Dominique (old type)		Rhode Island Red
White Jersey Giant		Rouen Duck
White Wyandotte		Toulouse Goose
Pilgrim Goose		
Bronze Turkey (unimproved)		

For more information about livestock conservation send a self-addressed, stamped envelope to:

The American Livestock Breeds Conservancy
Box 477
Pittsboro, NC 27312
Phone (919) 542-5704

A copy of the complete 1987 ALBC *Poultry and Census and Source Book* is only $5.00.

Chapter 12: Raising Chicks From Scratch

Where to Buy Chicks

The day the baby chicks arrive is always an exciting time for the poultry grower. They are so cute—little furry balls running about and chirping as if celebrating having survived the journey to your place.

You can order day-old chicks through your local feed store, or from any of the hatcheries that advertise in magazines such as *BackHome, Organic Gardening, New Farm, Small Farms Today, The Natural Farmer* and so forth. Other useful addresses and contacts are available from your state department of agriculture. They will have a packet of poultry information they will send to you on request, including hatcheries located in your state or region.

Generally, you need to place your order about four weeks ahead of the date you want the chicks to arrive. This gives the hatchery an idea of how many chicks they need to hatch to fill all their orders. You can also buy chicks from local feed or farm supply stores. Usually, feed stores place one order in late April or early May for both broilers and egg layers, and sometimes a second order in June for meat birds only. Feed stores often have several varieties for you to choose from. They will tell you what day to come and pick up your birds, and encourage you to not be late.

Whether you order them directly from the hatchery or from the feed store, the chicks will arrive by arfreight or postal service. It's important that you go right away to pick them up. Just before they hatch, the baby chicks will ingest the remainder of the yolk in the egg. This gives them only enough nourishment to survive for up to 72 hours without food or drink. So you need to get them unpacked and into your brooder quickly.

If you've ordered your chicks directly from a hatchery and they are being delivered by mail, the hatchery will notify you which morning to expect your birds at the post office. I've found it useful to let the post office know a few days in advance, and give them my phone number so they can call me the minute the chicks come in. That way there's very little delay in getting them unpacked and into the brooder where they can get fresh water and food.

The minimum order for mail-delivery chicks is usually 25. Over the years hatcheries have found this is the optimal number to ship without losses to suffocation, freezing or other injury. Shippers use heavy-duty cardboard boxes with air vent holes. The boxes can hold 100 chicks, with dividers to limit each section to 25.

If your chicks come through a feed store be sure to look through the chicks for any that are obviously sick, injured or undersized. Leave these with the store. It's easier for the store to get credit on the sick or dead birds than it is for you.

Feed stores will charge you maybe ten cents per bird more than you will pay by ordering direct from the factory. That's okay, since the feed store takes the worry out of ordering and will be willing to help you pick out the needed accessories and feed, and will answer any questions you have.

Prices vary for chicks, from 40¢ per bird for popular

breeds, up to $5.00 each for rare breeds. The meat birds I've bought recently cost 60¢ each if I specify all cockerels. The cockerels will usually grow out to about one pound more per bird than the hens on the same amount of feed and in the same amount of time. If you want all meat birds, the cockerels are definitely worth the extra ten cent premium.

The hatchery staff will do the best they can to separate the hens from the cockerels, but you still may get one or two hens in with your batch of broilers. You probably won't notice this until about the sixth week when the hens aren't getting as large as the other birds, and their combs are much smaller and not as brilliantly colored.

It's okay to get hens mixed in with the cockerels. They dress out to a smaller weight and you can use them as fryers or for grilling. If you are selling meat birds some of your customers will ask for the smaller birds specifically.

One thing I have noticed is that during the seventh and eighth weeks the males will try to mount any females that are in the pen. This may cause a problem in confined areas. The mounting act is fairly rough and the hens may get injured. If they do, just separate the injured hen back to the nursery and let her recover. If it's close to harvest time anyway I just keep the hen in the nursery until it's time for the batch to go to the processor.

Roosters, Hatching Eggs and Broody Hens

If you want to hatch your own chicks you need a rooster to get fertilized eggs to hatch. If you let the rooster run with the hens you can assume he will keep all the hens bred, so any eggs you pick will most likely be fertile.

Eggs for hatching need to be less than ten days old when you place them in the incubator or under a broody hen. They take 21 days to hatch.

Most of the newer breeds of laying hens have had most of the broodiness bred out of them. You will have better luck relying on one of the older standard breeds to do your setting and brooding for you.

If you have fertile eggs but no broody hens, just use an incubator. These are available for $100 or less from the larger mail-order hatcheries. An incubator will last forever if you keep it clean and well maintained.

Incubating eggs is not difficult, and it can be a lot of fun, especially for children, to see the miracle of birth take place. The incubator does need careful attention twice each day, though, since the eggs need turning at twelve hour intervals so the embryo forms properly. The more sophisticated incubators have automatic egg turning which handles this chore for you. The moisture and temperature levels are important, too, to ensure optimal hatching results.

Generally, 50 to 8 percent of your fertile eggs will hatch. It's almost impossible to get 100 percent hatchability due to variations in temperature, humidity, and fertility of eggs. Still, if you have your own breeding flock and pay $100 for an incubator you will be ahead of the game financially after hatching about 150 chickens.

Another advantage of the incubator is that it enables you to maintain your purebred flock, or even create your own strain by matching your best roosters to your best hens.

At our place the first shipment of birds arrives in early May and goes straight to the brooder. They are only one-day old and very susceptible to a whole bunch of different diseases. Some birds become infected at the hatchery. Some of the diseases remain in the pens from one batch of birds to the next. It's important to clean cages and equipment carefully. Many of the poultry diseases transmit through fecal matter and dust. Put down fresh bedding for each new batch of chickens.

After the first batch has moved to the chicken tractor it's time to think about ordering the next batch. Thanks to the warmer weather, the second batch will be in the brooder only two weeks, versus three weeks for the first batch. So, order your second batch to arrive two weeks before you harvest the first batch.

Then, as soon as you remove the first batch to the processing facility you can clean the chicken tractor and move the second batch from the brooder to the field. Following this schedule with your third and fourth

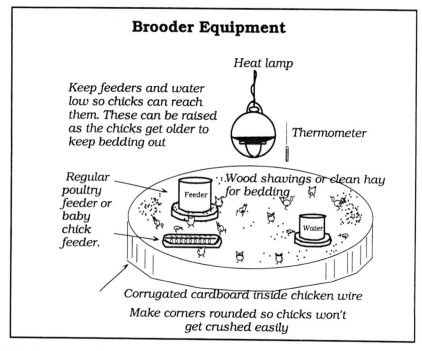

Brooder Equipment

Heat lamp

Keep feeders and water low so chicks can reach them. These can be raised as the chicks get older to keep bedding out

Thermometer

Regular poultry feeder or baby chick feeder.

Feeder

Wood shavings or clean hay for bedding

Water

Corrugated cardboard inside chicken wire

Make corners rounded so chicks won't get crushed easily

batches will have your last batch of broilers finishing up by November 15. Then you can turn your attention to dressing your turkeys for Thanksgiving Day.

Schedule for Multiple Batches of Chickens

May 1 to July 1 — first batch
June 15 to August 15 — second batch
August 1 to October 1 — third batch
Sept. 15 to November 15 — fourth batch.

In warmer parts of the country you will be able to start your first batch on April 1 and finish out on December 1, for five full flights. This will extend your season, your work and your net profits, since you use the same facility for all five batches. In hotter climates it may not be practical to raise chickens during the heat of the summer.

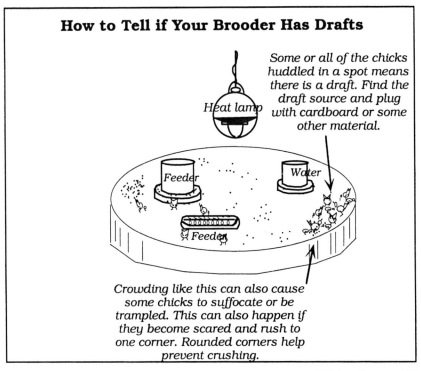

How to Tell if Your Brooder Has Drafts

Heat lamp

Some or all of the chicks huddled in a spot means there is a draft. Find the draft source and plug with cardboard or some other material.

Feeder

Water

Feeder

Crowding like this can also cause some chicks to suffocate or be trampled. This can also happen if they become scared and rush to one corner. Rounded corners help prevent crushing.

If the weather is warm and sunny the chicks can go out to pasture as early as seven days old. However, the first spring batch will probably need to be in the brooder for up to three weeks to get the chicks up to a size and strength where they can withstand the cooler outside temperatures and the damp days of spring.

Moving the two- or three-week-old birds from the brooder to the chicken tractor is an easy matter for me. I spread hay in my pickup truck camper cap. Then I load the chickens, close the cap lid and drive over to the chicken tractor for unloading.

If you don't have a barn, garage, or basement for setting up your brooder, you can use the chicken tractor itself. Just add extra tarps or covers and install a heat lamp. We use old cardboard boxes cut to strips and stapled or taped to the inside of the frame to round off the corners. This

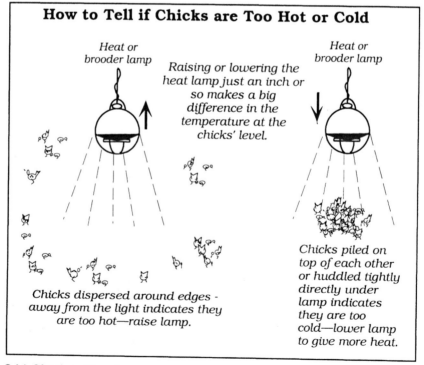

How to Tell if Chicks are Too Hot or Cold

Heat or brooder lamp

Raising or lowering the heat lamp just an inch or so makes a big difference in the temperature at the chicks' level.

Heat or brooder lamp

Chicks dispersed around edges - away from the light indicates they are too hot—raise lamp.

Chicks piled on top of each other or huddled tightly directly under lamp indicates they are too cold—lower lamp to give more heat.

keeps the chicks from piling up in the corners. The cardboard is also a good shield against winds that might chill the young birds.

Equipment and Supplies You'll Need for Chicks

The equipment you'll need to raise baby chicks is neither expensive nor complicated. It consists simply of a circular enclosure about three feet in diameter to use as a brooder, a waterer, a feeder, heat lamp, wood shavings for bedding and a thermometer.

Brooder Space

The "brooder" is the place you keep the chicks from birth until they are old enough to go out to the shelter-pen. Generally, about one-half square foot per chick is enough space in the brooder. An enclosure about three feet in diameter gives plenty of room to brood 30 baby chicks. You will need a brooder are five to six feet in diameter for 50 chicks, and 100 chicks need about seven to eight feet diameter.

I make my brooder in a circular or oval shape using chicken wire with cardboard on the inside. The cardboard is at least 24 inches high and serves as a draft shield. Drafts can chill your chicks in no time, leading to sickness. You can tell when there is a draft in the brooder if the chicks huddle together against one side. The solution is to find where the draft is coming in and plug it with cardboard or some other draft-stopping material.

Light and Heat

Chicks need a temperature of about 90 to 95 degrees for the first week. Install a heat lamp over the center of the brooder cage. Red light bulbs are better than white ones because the chicks tend to peck at each other less under the red light. Fasten the lamp so you can raise or lower it as needed. If the chicks pile under the light they are too cold. Move the light closer to them or add a second lamp. They are too hot if they scatter to the edges of the pen or hide behind the waterer and feeder.

The area directly under the light should be 90 degrees F or a little higher for the first few days. The chicks will adjust their distance to the light to get a comfortable temperature. Make sure your brooder area is large enough for the chicks to move away from the heat lamp if they get too hot.

You can reduce the temperature about 5 to 10 degrees per week until they are comfortable at about 70 degrees. This gives them time to gradually acclimate to colder temperatures.

Water for Chicks

The chicks are only one or two days old when you pick them up at the farm store or when they arrive at the post office. Have at least one gallon of water for 50 birds. As you gently unpack them, dip the beak of each chick in the water before you turn it loose. They will be thirsty and dipping their beaks helps them find the water sooner.

Most baby chick loss occurs because they don't start to eat or drink soon enough. Remember, if your birds arrive by mail every hour counts so get your babies as soon as you can from the post office. We let our post office know when we are expecting birds and have them call us as soon as they arrive. We make a special trip to pick them up before our normal mail would be delivered.

For the first day or two you can add about three table-spoons of sugar or honey to each quart of water to give them extra energy to recover from their trip. **Never let your chicks run out of water**—even after they are full grown. Chickens get dehydrated very quickly and can die before you know it. Always have fresh water available.

Chick Feed

Use a commercial chick starter mash for at least the first two weeks. If the chicks are having trouble recognizing the starter mash just cover the bedding near the feeders with newspaper and spread some feed on it. This will help them find the food. The newspaper will be needed for only about a day or so as they quickly learn to get food from the feeders.

Have at least two feet of feeder space for 25 chicks. Some of the more timid chicks won't get enough to eat other-wise. Check them twice daily to keep the waterer and feeders clean and full. When the chicks move outside in the third week you can start feeding them grower pellets.

> **Never feed lay ration to baby chickens. The extra calcium it contains for the egg layers can seriously injure the young chicks' kidneys.**

Grit for Chicks

All free ranging chickens will eat small pebbles or other grit to help digest their food in their gizzards. Grit that is available from the feed store is tiny insoluble granules of sand, stone or even shell. You can buy grit as limestone, oyster shells or granite. Most feed stores stock grit.

Even chicks need grit. Sprinkle it on their food. Do not sprinkle too much or they will fill up on the grit instead of food. When you are putting it on, think of it like salt; a little bit for seasoning. Do not feed baby chicks limestone grit. It contains calcium that will injure their kidneys.

Baby Bedding

Bedding can be any material that is dry, absorbent and dust free. I prefer wood shavings for bedding because it smells nice and absorbs urine, feces and spilled water quickly. However, you can also use straw, rice hulls, ground corn cobs or dry hay.

Sick or Injured Chicks

Listen to the chirp. Is it loud and shrill or perky and pleasant? Gail Damerow, in her delightful book, *YOUR CHICKENS*, says chickens make at least 30 different sounds. A sick chick will often tell you it doesn't feel well, both by the way it sounds and by its body language. Sometimes you might have some especially fragile chicks that need extra care. Bring these into the house and keep them in a cardboard box with a light bulb to keep them warm and unstressed until they recover. We have saved many temporarily frail babies by simply providing them with a quiet, warm and safe place with a lot of tender loving care.

Sometimes chicks get a touch of diarrhea and manure sticks to their rear ends. This is not unusual nor alarming. Too much protein in the feed can cause this. It is essential to remove this daily. Just gently pull it off. If it has hardened, I get a paper towel or cloth and warm water or olive oil to loosen it and gently wash it off. Pasted rears will disappear after a few days as the chicks grow and stabilize in their new home.

Commercial growers will probably wince when they hear this rather cavalier attitude towards chicken diseases. They regularly plan for at least a five percent loss, and sometimes suffer losses of 25 percent or more. The experience I've had, corroborated by many, many small-scale poultry growers across the country, is that very few birds die in these small home flocks. Nonetheless, you want to take every precaution you can to make sure that diseases don't spread from one batch to another.

Chapter 13: Predators

I've grown chickens in several areas of the country, such as the river bottoms of south-western Missouri and north-eastern Oklahoma, the sand dunes of Cape Cod, the broad lake valleys of Vermont, and the Piedmont foothills of North Carolina. There are several varmints common to all these areas: rats, raccoons, coyotes, feral cats, bobcats, red and gray foxes, minks, weasels, big snakes (not in Vermont) and worst of all, the neighbors' dogs.

Next time I'll bring you a CHICKEN!

In a typical hen yard or on free range, without the protection of the chicken tractor, losses to predators can be high. Just the other day I heard from a poultry grower in Missouri who has lost 200 free-range hens to foxes in the past year.

In my experience, moving the chicken tractors daily seems to make predators suspicious, so they don't bother the chickens. Having said that, however, I need to point out that varmints of all kinds will be eager to take a crack at your homegrown poultry.

Rats and Mice

Rats and mice are common inhabitants of farms and fields. They love poultry feed and will chew holes in feed bags if they have access to them. Rats will also kill baby chicks and drag them into their burrows.

These rodents love hiding places they find in conventional chicken houses. Spaces between walls, under floors and around junk make great rodent hotels. Luckily, with your portable chicken tractors, there are few places for a mouse or rat to set up housekeeping. The chicken tractor doesn't have walls or floors where the critters can hide and build nests.

I keep grain stored in galvanized garbage or plastic trash cans with the lid secured with a bungee cord. This makes the feed for my small flock rodent proof—even raccoon proof, and I have yet to see any rat using the bungee cords to jump off the trash can for a cheap thrill.

Domestic Cats and Dogs

Since I've been using chicken tractors my only problem with predators has been a neighborhood dog trying to dig under the pen when I use it in a deep mulch system. I stopped that by laying chicken wire alongside the pen on all four sides and pegging it to the ground with pins made from bent coat hangers.

My neighbor's Lhasa apso sometimes runs and jumps and barks in front of the chicken tractor, scaring the dickens out of the birds. One way to prevent this, short of tying up your neighbor's dog, is to run a hog wire fence or electric fence around the perimeter of the pens, at least ten feet out. The biggest danger from dogs is their barking and chasing, causing the chickens to crowd in a corner where they pile up and suffocate, or die of fright. Eventually we got the Lhasa apsos to understand poultry etiquette. The dogs actually bonded with the chickens and would keep them herded away from the driveway when the chickens were out foraging.

With the help of the Twelve Step program I've given up chasing chickens!

Even my cats have learned to leave our baby chickens alone—although they will sit and observe the chicks for hours —a kind of kitty TV. All my pets know what NO means and know what is acceptable behavior.

Who Me?

Foxes, Coyotes, Raccoons, Weasels and Other Critters.

Several years ago—before I started using chicken tractors—raccoons pulled the chicken wire off my hen house window to get at the birds. That window was 6-feet off the ground. I think the raccoons climbed a nearby tree, dropped down on the roof, and reached over the roof edge to pry the window open.

If you live in an area where chicken loving critters present a greater than normal problem, you can provide extra

Ways to Predator Proof Your Chicken Tractor

Cover ends, back side and top with plywood or a tarp over the chicken wire so raccoons can't reach through. Chickens are safe from hawks and owls swooping down to grab them. This also gives protection from the weather.

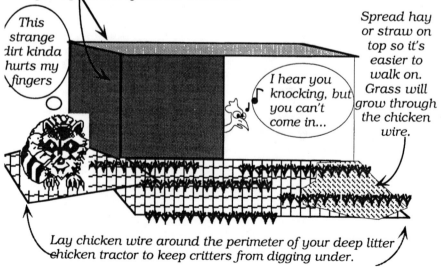

This strange dirt kinda hurts my fingers

I hear you knocking, but you can't come in...

Spread hay or straw on top so it's easier to walk on. Grass will grow through the chicken wire.

Lay chicken wire around the perimeter of your deep litter chicken tractor to keep critters from digging under.

protection for the chicken tractor. Install a portable electric fence around the garden area. The new net-style electric sheep fence is especially effective. Bait the fence with peanut butter so the wildlife will try to lick it off. This guarantees they will get a healthy shock to their tongue that will convince them that these electric fences mean business.

Don't tempt fate and a hungry canine. If you know coyotes or foxes are living in your wood lot, don't put your chicken pens out there without some kind of extra protection. Another way to protect the chickens, if you do need to put them near the woods, is to install a dog run parallel to the field edge and leash your dog to it each evening.

Ohhhooooohhhh I need a place to live too!

A fox will often kill several birds and sometimes leaves them partially buried. Raccoons, for all their fastidiousness, can be gruesome diners. If chickens are sleeping too close to the pen sides, the raccoon can reach its paw and powerful claws through the wire to grab a chicken and will literally pull it apart alive. If a raccoon gets in with the chickens it will usually eat the crops (throats) of chickens and will decapitate some of the birds. Raccoons will return every few days for another dinner if they get the chance.

Minks and weasels tend to kill several birds at irregular intervals. Their trademarks are small bites around the head and neck.

Predatory Birds.

Owls and hawks love chicken dinners. They tend to kill one or two birds, usually at night. However, we recently had a hawk kill a pullet that was free ranging with the TurGuChi Gang. Hawks leave behind the carcass except for the head and neck. Keep in mind that owls and hawks mainly eat mice, moles and other potential pests. They help keep nature in balance.

The ultimate solution to the varmint problem, of course, is to shoot or trap them all. To me this isn't an acceptable option. I enjoy the occasional sighting of the wildlife far too much to ever want to eradicate them from my land. Many of the varmints, too, are predators of mice, moles and other grain eating herbivores that can cause problems in the grain fields if their populations get out of hand. It is far better we coexist with the predators and let them help us keep a healthy balance of natural life in our meadows, fields and forests.

Chapter 14: Chicken Diet

(Theirs, Not Ours)

In a natural setting—full of weeds and grasses, seeds, bugs, worms and so forth—chickens will be able to get an adequate diet. They will thrive on this diverse food intake, at least during the warmer months. Unfortunately, natural settings for chickens to forage are not always available.

Even if it's just on grass, intensive grazing in shelter-pens does give the chickens some access to a natural diet. However, the intensive grazing cannot meet all their dietary requirements. You need to supplement their diet with grain based chicken feed.

How much feed you will need depends entirely on the breed of chickens you're growing, the time of year, and whether you are growing layers, fryers or broilers. To grow the average meat bird to four pounds dressed weight will require from 12 to 15 pounds of grain feed.

A laying hen will require 18 to 20 pounds of feed from birth to egg laying age. Then she will require 80 to 90 pounds of grain feed per year. That seems like a lot of feed, I know, but not so much so when you compare it to one turkey that will eat nearly 80 pounds of feed to reach a market dressed weight of about 25 pounds.

Earlier I pointed out that it is possible to save as much as 30 percent on your feed bill by having the birds on pasture after they leave the brooder. According to Joel Salatin (see *Pastured Poultry Profit$*) you can ensure the 30 percent savings by moving the flock to fresh graze daily.

Make the move early in the morning and withhold grain for 1/2 to 1 hour. The grasses and weeds are most tender and most succulent early in the morning, and the birds are eager to begin morning feeding.

In an ordinary free range system in which the chickens just roam around the field the chickens have continual access to either grain feed or graze. They will fill up on grain, and use the grazing activity to stretch their legs and to satisfy their normal pecking and foraging instincts. In this case, the amount of grain feed saved can be as little as 10 percent. This foraging pattern was noted in several university tests, particularly at the Ohio and Vermont agricultural experiment stations.

Even if your flock is only getting 10 percent of their nutritional requirements from graze and forage, this is probably the most important portion of their diet. The activity surrounding grazing and foraging is important for muscle tone and exercise. Sunlight is important for Vitamin D fixation.

The contact with the earth is important for access to small grit and the vitamins and enzymes in the soil. It also satisfies the bird's normal yearning for earth contact. The green plants themselves contain chlorophyll, a prime detoxifier that enables the birds to cleanse their digestive systems regularly. All of these combine to make a better tasting, healthier poultry.

Some grasses and weeds are better than others for grazing poultry. In a more natural setting, it is best to allow chickens to have access to as many varieties of plants as possible. Some plants are higher in protein, while others are higher in carbohydrates.

Given its choice, the chicken will eat the plants that provide the best diet for its needs. With a diverse variety of grasses, legumes, weeds and herbaceous forbs, the chickens will have access to what they need when they need it. This forage diversity leads to a more sustainable diet for the chickens.

Organic Feeds

My experience convinces me that chickens will excel when grown on organic feeds. Given free choice of organic versus conventionally grown grains, the chickens will become very adept at selecting the organic grains first. They will gain weight faster, have a better quality of meat, and will taste superior to the chickens raised on conventional grain. This is only my opinion, of course. To my knowledge professional research has neither proven nor disproven my position.

Taste is a very subjective thing, with each of us having a particular sense of what tastes good and what doesn't. Chickens have this innate sense of healthy food compared to not-so-healthy food. It is not uncommon to have organically fed chickens gain weight faster by about 10 percent, on about 10 percent less organic feed than conventionally grown chickens.

> **We don't try to find the cheapest feed,**
>
> **we try to find the most nutritious feed.**

Poor feed will stress an animal and it will produce inferior meat or eggs. Inferior feed will also cause a greater mortality loss and health problems.

The problem, of course, is finding affordable organic feed for your chickens. It simply may not be available in your area. If it is available it may be inordinately expensive. In any case, you can use conventional feed grains and still expect reasonable gains and the flavor will still be superior to the poultry you would otherwise buy in the supermarket.

If you have land and time available, it might be worth your while to grow grain and hay for your chickens. If you don't have land and time, consider starting or joining an organic grain cooperative. These cooperatives are buying in grain from nearby farmers in bulk and repacking it for distribution to the cooperative members.

If you are growing a large number of poultry, you might be able to get your local feed mill to grind your feed for you. Usually this service is only available for quantities of two tons or more at a time. If you are part of a grain cooperative, you can split the order among the members to accommodate the needs of the feed mill.

The grain mill where I buy my feed is a small family run business that caters to small scale farmers such as myself. They are happy to mix quantities as little as 1,000 pounds if I ask them to, though I usually get a ton at a time of both pig feed and poultry feed. They can add any additives such as kelp meal that I ask for, and gladly leave out the antibiotics and growth hormones that I don't want.

When mixing your own feed ration—even if you're feeding organic grains—you will want to add a mineral package to the feed. A typical mineral package will contain Vitamins A, D, E, B-1, electrolytes and biotin. These mineral packages are available from mail order companies that sell poultry equipment and supplies.

Researcher H. R. Bird at the Ohio Agricultural Experiment Station found laying hens having access to good pasture can get 12 percent of the protein, 5 percent of the calcium, 100 percent of vitamins A and D, and 100 percent of the riboflavin necessary to sustain good egg production. Sunshine, of course, helps Vitamin D become available. This is a major contributor to the health and vigor of the pastured poultry flock.

It is possible—especially with the older breeds that are aggressive foragers—for the chickens to get many of their dietary needs from gleaning. Gleaning simply means to let your poultry or livestock pick up any grain or vegetables you missed during the harvest. They are particularly adept at snapping up weed seeds and grasses that are encroaching on your garden beds. In some scenarios, you can let the birds loose in the gardens for short periods of time to glean and control insect pests. I've found them especially helpful in controlling slugs in my mulched gardens.

Naturally, you want to let the hens have access to your garden for only a short time, and while you are there to keep an eye on them. It's also a good idea to turn them out in mature veggies instead of in the young succulent seedlings. Otherwise they'll ignore the slugs and wipe out your crops. In my experience, hens are particularly fond of ripe strawberries and ripe tomatoes.

Let the chickens into your garden in late afternoon and they will automatically go back to the pen at dusk. You won't have to chase them around to get them back in their pen. You can also train the chickens to follow you with a grain bucket. Thus, you can move them from pen to field and back a lot easier.

Patricia has trained our tur-gu-chi gang to come when she whistles. It's simple to do this, just give them a morsel of feed as you whistle and pretty soon they'll come to you just like pets. The friendlier chickens will come-a-running while the more aloof turkeys and guineas sort of hang back. This really comes in handy if we are going out for the evening and need to get them back into their chicken tractor or straw bale house before we leave.

Another way to provide a diversified diet for your flock is to hand pick garden pests such as potato beetles and cabbage worms and feed them to the chickens. In areas where Japanese beetles are a problem in your garden your chickens will be a big asset in bug control. Expedite the collection process by hanging the beetle traps in the pen to attract bugs to the chickens. As soon as our chickens hear the beetle fall into the trap they rush over and catch it as it falls through to the ground.

If you don't have pasture available for your flock, you can feed good quality clover or alfalfa hay. What they don't eat will become bedding. The bedding will feed the soil microbes that help turn your chicken litter into rich compost.

Chickens really like a variety of different feeds in their diet. You can feed your chickens many of the items you normally throw in your compost pile. They love leftover baked goods and vegetables, especially tomatoes and lettuce. Chickens can also eat food preparation waste and table scraps. They will even eat meat scraps and peck at bones. Don't feed too many of the strong-tasting foods such as garlic, chives, onions or fish, however, because these can make the eggs and meat taste odd.

Beware of spoiled food too, since it might cause injury or death for your chickens or other livestock. A while back we lost two of our Buff Orpington hens when we inadvertently gave them some spoiled nuts. Within minutes they became paralyzed, vomited then died.

They Will Work for Chicken Feed

Your biggest expense in growing poultry will be feed, so let's look closely at the economics of chicken feed. You can buy chicken feed either as pellets or crumbled mash. There tends to be less waste with the pellets because the chickens have an eating habit of putting their beaks in the feed and tossing their heads spreading food all over. It is easier for them to peck wayward pellets off the ground than it is the crumbled feed.

I usually buy about two to four weeks worth of feed at a time rather than stock it too far ahead. It will get stale, especially in warmer weather. Feed also loses nutritional value as it gets older. Use up all the feed from one bag before you open another. Exposed to air, feed gets stale and can spoil.

I store the feed in a 30 gallon tin trash can and hold the lid on with a bungee cord. This is to prevent attracting rodents and wild birds to the feed. I prefer metal over plastic trash cans because the plastic tends to crack with extensive outdoor use—especially in cold weather.

You Can Grow Your Own Organic Feed

The amount of land you will need to grow grain for your flock depends on the climate, soil characteristics, cultural methods and your skill as a grower. Grain yields can range from as little as 2,000 pounds per acre up to 6,000 pounds per acre. At the lower yields you will need one acre of grain to feed 20 hens for a year. With increased soil fertility you can grow grain for 20 hens on just one-third acre.

One way we've been able to grow grain for our chickens is to use millet, barley, oats or wheat as a cover crop and let it go to seed. Then we turn the chickens in on it to let them peck out the seeds; then we turn the hogs into the plot and let them plow it up and turn the straw under.

Gene Logsdon, author of *The Contrary Farmer* taught us how to grow grain and harvest it whole as loose hay with the seed heads still intact. Store the hay in a barn or shed and give it to the poultry in loose sheaves. They will pick out the grain and leave the straw as bedding in their pen or straw bale house. Small grain alone isn't a complete diet for the poultry, but it supplements their prepared feed, and gives them something interesting to do with their time, and saves you a bit on your feed bill.

You can use any part of your garden or field that doesn't have other food crops on it to grow corn for scratch feed. Corn is easier to handle than the other grains, and you will find it enjoyable exercise to pick and shell the ears and grind them in a hand grinder to make scratch feed. Then turn your pigs or steers loose in the corn patch and let them eat the stalks and any grain you missed.

In most commercial feed rations, corn makes up about 60 percent of the mix. Even on a small piece of land you can easily grow enough corn to lower your purchased grain costs. Harvesting corn is simple, just pull the ears off the stalks, peel back the husk and break it off the ear. Pitch the ear into a wheelbarrow, cart or pickup truck and deliver it to your storage bin.

To get the corn kernels off the cob requires either a hand sheller—which is fairly slow and laborious—or a mechanical sheller. You can buy hand crank shellers for less than $100, or motorized shellers new or used for just a few hundred dollars. Grind the cobs in a hammermill type leaf and yard waste grinder and use them for bedding. You can grind the corn kernels in the hammermill, too. Use a fine screen in the grinder to break the kernels into small enough pieces for the chickens to eat. Mature layers can even eat whole corn.

For those who have larger land holdings and access to equipment, I encourage you to grow some or all of your own grain. You can rotate the chickens through the grain land for extra fertility in alternating years. For an excellent guide to raising, harvesting and feeding small grains, see Gene Logsdon's book *SMALL GRAINS*, published by Rodale Press, Emmaus, Pennsylvania. This book is now out of print but you can get a look at it through your inter-library loan network.

Water In and Water Out of Your Chicken Tractor System

Chickens lose water through sweat, urine and respiration. In close confinement, the water vapor given off by the chickens can build to unhealthy levels. That's why it's necessary to have a well-ventilated shelter.

Chickens need continual access to fresh, uncontaminated water. Unfortunately, growers who use city tap water for their chickens might be doing the birds a disservice.

There are two chemicals added to many municipal water systems that are unhealthy, both for chickens and for humans. These are chlorine and fluoride.

Chlorine kills bacteria, both good and bad. The chlorine in the tap water kills the beneficial bacteria in the bird's intestinal tract. These bacteria are cells. The lymphocytes (white blood cells) have the task of cleaning the system by consuming the dead cells. This overworks the lymphocytes, taking them away from their primary duty of searching for and consuming cancerous cells in the blood, vascular system, muscle and skin tissue and intestinal tract. As a result, many chickens have greater than normal populations of cancerous cells in their body tissues and fluids.

In humans, byproducts of the use of chlorine can cause cancer, liver and kidney damage, heart and neurological effects and can affect unborn children. Lest you think I'm making all this up, the Environmental Protection Agency has just called for a $50 million, five-year research program to find out what to do about at least 13,000 public water supplies that are affected. This clean-up will eventually cost America's taxpayers over $1 billion per year, according to the EPA. Not to mention, of course, the billions of dollars in medical bills and the untold suffering of millions of residents who have become ill after long exposure to supposedly safe municipal water.

Fluoride is just as degenerative as chloride, in the same way. It is an insidious, corrosive poison that is a by-product of the aluminum can making industry. According to medical researchers, fluoride is more harmful to the body than the recently banned Alar. Fifty percent of our municipal water systems treat their water with fluoride, even against overwhelmingly strong evidence that it does very little, if anything, to control tooth decay. In many areas tooth cavities have actually doubled in the last two decades.

In Canada, those communities without fluoride in the drinking water have experienced lower incidence of tooth decay than those which have treated water. At the same time, those communities with fluoride have a 20 percent higher rate of cancer. The myth that fluoride fights tooth decay is just that, a myth. That fluoride helps cause cancers in humans, and chickens, is more accurate by far.

Yes, it is true that the average rate of tooth decay has decreased in some areas since the use of fluoride began. I think we can trace this to better programs of teaching dental hygiene in schools. We also now have better toothbrushes and toothpastes, more dental visits, better diet and more flossing. In my opinion, dental hygiene not flouride is primarily responsible for the decreased incidence of tooth decay.

There are four ways to overcome the hazards of drinking supposedly safe municipal water.

1. Filter the water first through a sophisticated filtering system.

2. Buy bottled water.

3. Dig a well.

4. Harvest rain water.

Filtering is fairly effective, depending on the capacity and cleansing abilities of the filtering apparatus. It's also fairly expensive, considering the cost of the filtering equipment and installation.

Buying bottled water is also expensive. In some areas it costs more than gasoline. Also, there is a chemical reaction taking place between the water and the plastic container, especially when exposed to sunlight. This chemical reaction may result in carcinogens from the plastic being released into the water.

Digging a well is not always practical, possible or cost effective. Drilling the well and installing a pump and water lines can easily cost thousands of dollars. You still need to test the water to make sure there aren't any contaminants.

So, the best choice, in my opinion, is to harvest rain water from the structure closest to your garden.

Harvesting water is fairly simple and straightforward. The easiest place to look for water to harvest is on your house roof. Just put a gutter on the roof and direct it to a holding tank of some sort. If you have gutters already, just direct the downspout to an area where you can build a holding tank or pond.

The holding tank can be something as simple as a 55-gallon drum, or as elaborate as an above-ground or in-ground swimming pool. If you have room you may want to put in an in-ground pond that can hold all the roof water your house receives. For each 1,000 square feet of roof surface (measured horizontally), you will get 627 gallons of water in each one-inch rain.

In New England where we used to live, the typical house can harvest from 24,000 to 30,000 gallons of rain water per year. Here in western North Carolina we can harvest nearly twice that much because of our 65-inch average annual rainfall. A storage facility large enough to handle this volume of water would be huge, compared to what your needs are for chicken watering.

The best scenario, of course, is if you have enough roof surface area to harvest all the water you need into a small pond or holding tank. Some of the best and least expensive temporary water repositories we've found are the 55-gallon plastic barrels that come with food concentrate in them. They are available and cheap, about $5 usually. You can buy hose bibbs at your hardware store and install them at the bottom of the barrel and attach a garden hose for watering and washing equipment.

For more storage capacity simply add more barrels and connect them with threaded 3/4-inch pvc pipe about 12-inches long. Near the top of the barrel bore a 3/4-inch hole, insert the threaded pipe, dope it well with silicon caulk and screw on the nut, then insert the other end of the pipe into the next barrel, and so on. As the first barrel fills with water it will spill over to the second barrel. You can attach a hose bibb to the bottom of each barrel or just to the last barrel in the series.

Concerns about harvesting and storing water are: acidity, oxygenation, freezing, utrophication, algae growth, airborne and water-borne pollutants, child and pet safety, and aesthetics.

Add lime to adjust pH from acid rain. Use a fountain or wind spinner in your pond or holding tank to keep the water agitated. This slows down the algae buildup. Use floating briquettes to keep mosquitoes from breeding, too. A tight fitting lid or a nice fence around your storage tank or pond will keep your kids and pets out of harm's way. Air- and water-borne pollutants can be filtered out with a simple sand filter or carbon filter.

To transport the water to the chicken tractors use a garden hose. If you need to transport water a longer distance than a hose can reach, use a simple wheeled frame similar to a little red wagon, or a garden cart to haul buckets. We are working on a prototype "water tanker" now that will look like a garden cart with a lid on it. A hose bibb in the bottom will let us connect a short length of garden hose for dispensing water.

In a larger poultry business you can move a 55-gallon barrel of water with a pallet fork mounted on the three-point hitch of your tractor. The barrel rides on the pallet. Lift the barrel high enough so you can use gravity pressure to clean and fill the waterers at each chicken tractor. Carry the feed in a barrel in the bucket of the tractor so it's a simple one stop operation to feed and water the chickens.

If you want to grow fish for the table or for sale you can make your pond or holding tank large enough to do double duty. In a typical eight month season here in North Carolina we can start with fingerling Tilapia and have harvestable fish to put in the freezer by fall. Weighing one to two pounds each, they are easy to clean and fillet and make a few good meals each winter. The tilapia will also help keep the water clean and will fertilize it to make it richer for garden irrigation.

We have a water harvesting pond next to our house. The downspouts carry our roof water to the pond. With 65 inches of rain annually our house can collect about 50,000 gallons of water per year. We had the pond dug when our excavating contractor was digging our house foundation, so it cost us less than $1,000 for a 50 x 60 pond that is six feet deep.

My friend John Tieman came up with another simple way to build a water reservoir. He suggests pouring a cement slab the size you want, then building a four-foot high wall around the edge of the pad using four-inch concrete blocks. The first course of blocks is mortared to the cement pad, then following courses are dry-stacked. When the wall is four feet high use cap blocks to form the top. Then connect all the blocks together with a 1/8-inch layer of surface bonding cement.

Surface bonding cement looks like stucco, and has millions of little Fiberglas filaments in it. They turn every which way and create a mat that is unbelievably strong, as much as five times stronger than a mortared block wall. It's also waterproof, so you can just pour the water right in.

A tank that measures four-feet high and four-feet square will hold about 400 gallons of water. Putting three of these tanks in series will give you 1,200 gallons of water holding capacity. In a recirculating system that is closely managed that's enough water to grow about 120 pounds of tilapia per year, and still be able to water your poultry.

You can fill the tanks from roof-water harvesting or from your well or town water. If you use town water be sure to let the chlorine evaporate before you give the water to your fish or poultry.

Comfrey

Comfrey is a feed supplement you can grow yourself, either in the garden bed or as a hedge planted around the garden. Comfrey is a member of the Borage family, and is rich in vitamins and minerals. Its most important constituent is the chemical *allantoin*. *Allantoin* is a primary ingredient in products such as canker medicines, where its ability to aid cell regeneration is important to heal the wound. It is a nitrogenous crystalline substance that appears as white crystals on the dried roots. This substance gives comfrey its remarkable curative, therapeutic and preventive abilities. *Allantoin* aids cell proliferation and helps immunize against infective diseases, both in humans and livestock.

Protein content of comfrey is highest in the spring, when it can be as much as seven times higher than the protein in soybeans. The following chart lists the major vitamins, nutrients and amino acids contained in comfrey. Naturally, different varieties of comfrey and the differing seasons will affect the available nutrients in the plant, with the spring being highest by some 40 percent.

Comfrey is a "cut-and-come-again" herb that is an overlooked and sometimes maligned source of fodder and nutrients for livestock on America's small farms. Herbal teas and tonics and pharmaceutical preparations use most of the comfrey grown commercially in the United States. Over the centuries, comfrey has shown its ability to heal wounds, stop bleeding, treat respiratory ailments, and as a general tonic. Make tea from dried comfrey leaves. Eat young leaves like spinach greens, and use peeled roots in soups.

The plants have a sturdy, upright growth pattern, with leaves shaped like donkey ears. Flowers are creamy-yellow or purple-blue at the top of the 2-foot to 4-foot stalks. Comfrey blooms from April to frost and continues to produce foliage well into the fall season after most other plants die from frost.

In Europe and England, farmers grow comfrey for human consumption and as a forage crop for livestock. It is a favored herb for poultry, goats, sheep and pigs, with cows being only moderately interested, and horses being only slightly interested in it. Yields can be tremendous, often exceeding 50 tons per acre green weight, with three to four cuttings annually.

One report from Kenya (Dr. Lawrence Hill, *Fertility Without Fertilizers*, 1975), claims 135 tons yield per acre in 12 cuttings. Ecology Action in California grows comfrey as a goat fodder crop and for compost materials. Their yields range from 220 pounds up to 339 pounds per 100 square feet. That is 47 to 72 tons per acre per year.

Comfrey is a very hardy perennial that can withstand temperatures of 40 degrees below zero in a mulched bed. It regenerates itself through root development and seeds. It can become a pernicious weed if allowed to grow uncontrolled in the garden. The best way to eradicate a sprawling comfrey patch is to let pigs root it out, or let the chickens continue to eat the new growth until the plant dies from root exhaustion. Individual plants have a life expectancy of four years, and a well cared for planting can last for 40 years or more.

The plants are heavy feeders, requiring annual replenishment of nitrogen, phosphorus and potassium. They respond very well to liberal applications of fresh chicken or horse manure, and demand plenty of moisture. Straw or leaf mulch is an excellent way to keep the soil around the plants moist while providing slow release nutrients for them. Comfrey responds well to seaweed extract as a foliar spray as well.

Comfrey is difficult to start from seed. Most gardeners start it from root cuttings or plants given to them by gardening friends. Starter plantings are also available from several of the mail order gardening catalogs, (see appendix for listings).

Comfrey prefers a rich soil with a pH range of six to seven and can tolerate full sun or partial shade. It is a good crop for stacking under semi-dense shrubbery and deciduous fruit trees. "Stacking" is the practice of growing several different varieties together that have different levels of top growth and different depths of root growth.

Plant root cuttings or young plants three to six inches deep, two to three feet apart in all directions. If you are using enriched, double dug beds, you can space root cuttings 12 inches apart in a hexagonal pattern. This enables you to plant 159 plants per 100 square feet.

In coming seasons you can increase your comfrey patch by simply digging up the roots, dividing them and replanting. If you allow your comfrey plants to set seed, the seeds will fall near the plant and germinate. Extend your comfrey bed by transplanting these young seedlings.

Within a few weeks after planting, the plants will be large enough for selective harvesting of three to five inch leaves which you can eat or feed directly to your chickens. If you plan to harvest and dry the comfrey for later use, the first harvest will be ready about 120 days after planting. Cut the entire plant about two inches above the crown, hang it in a clean, dry, dark place and leave it to dry slowly. Turn the comfrey frequently and try not to bruise the plants since this will allow molds to enter and spoil your crop. Allowing the comfrey to dry in the sun will be faster, but you will lose much of the nutritional value. Comfrey has an aggressive rooting pattern, often drilling down ten

Composition of Comfrey

Nutrient	Percentage
Protein	21.8 to 33.4
Fat 2.22	
Carbohydrates	37.62
Crude fiber	9.38
Ash 15.06	
Total digestible nutrients	86.5

Mineral analysis	Percentage
Iron .016	
Manganese	.0072
Calcium	1.700
Phosphorus	.820

Vitamins present grams	Milligrams per 100
Thiamine	.5
Riboflavin	1.0
Nicotinic acid	5.0
Pantothenic acid	4.2
Vitamin B12	.07
Vitamin C	100
Vitamin E	30.

Other	
Carotene	.170 parts per million
Allantoin	.18 milligrams per 100 grams
Chlorophyll	

Amino acids:
tryptophan
lysine
isoleucine
methionine

feet or more. The horseradish-like root delivers nutrient rich moisture from deep in the sub-soil to the soil surface. Use comfrey sparingly as a forage or hay due to its high mineral content, high moisture and low fiber content. Your chicken's diet can be 10 to 20 percent comfrey.

In reviewing the above composite chart of comfrey, we can easily see why humans and animals can benefit greatly by its consumption. Comfrey is the fastest known builder of vegetable protein and provides up to seven times the protein found in soybeans. Calcium helps to build strong bones and prevent muscle cramps. Chlorophyll, the life force of all green plants, helps heal diseased tissues and detoxify the blood. Comfrey offers four times as much Vitamin B12 as yeast and is the only plant known to take B12 directly from the soil. Vitamin B12 is important for building healthy blood and will help heal ulcers and arthritis.

Does Comfrey Cause Liver Damage and Central Nervous System Paralysis?

Comfrey has received much attention in recent years because of its constituents *consolidine* and *symphtocynoglossine*. These are two poisonous alkaloids found in the larger leaves (above five inches). These have similarities to curare, an arrow poison used by South American Indians. This substance paralyzes the central nervous system.

According to Keats Publishing, New Canaan, Connecticut:

> *The debate and investigation has continued, prompting studies on the alkaloid content and toxicity in three research centers in England. These are reported in an appendix to Lawrence D. Hill's book,* <u>Comfrey: Fodder, Food & Remedy</u> *(Universe Books,*

1976) by Dr. D.B. Long, who concludes: "The use of comfrey as a food for mankind or animals does not present a toxic hazard from alkaloids, there being no evidence of acute or chronic hepatic reactions either to the direct injection of purified alkaloid or to prolonged consumption of comfrey root flour, which has the highest alkaloid content, by rats."

I'm sure that any astute researcher can find other studies that may point a more accusatory finger at comfrey. I'm mindful, however, that very few things in nature, or from the nation's chemical laboratories, are safe for consumption <u>if taken in extreme doses</u>. Given a choice between using comfrey, or using chemically derived feed supplements in my chicken feed, I choose comfrey.

Countless herbalists and stock breeders around the world are using comfrey daily in their ministrations. It is safe, beneficial, easy to grow, and easy to harvest and store. Your chickens will love it and thrive on it. It aids digestion, which will enhance feed-to-gain ratios and creates less offensive odors in manure. It helps prevent pecking and cannibalism and controls some parasite infestation in the bird's digestion tract. It saves you money on your feed bill and gives you and your customers better tasting meat and eggs.

If possible toxicity of the larger, mature comfrey leaves concerns you, just use them in your compost pile. They are an excellent activator and will return their nutrients to the soil on which you spread your compost.

Kelp

One way to overcome micro-nutrient deficiency in our soil is to use kelp meal. You can use it in meal form as a feed supplement for livestock, or apply it directly to the land. In its liquid form you can spray it on plant foliage.

I feel that kelp meal is so valuable that I start feeding it as soon as the baby chicks arrive and keep up the ration right through to slaughtering time. Kelp is a complex natural product high in vitamins and minerals. Its most valuable attribute is its richness in trace elements—organic minerals that are both safe and potent.

Lush and otherwise nutritious grass or grains containing adequate amounts of nitrogen, phosphorus and potassium might still fail to supply the nutritional needs of livestock. On poor soil certain trace elements may be missing or not available for plant uptake. Both pasture plants and grazing animals have delicately balanced needs for these trace elements. Too little may produce deficiency symptoms, too much may be poisonous.

One characteristic of kelp as an animal feed, is that the benefits of feeding it to animals seem far out of proportion to the apparent food value of the kelp itself. This is a matter of experience—it results from the observations of farmers and breeders rather than research workers, although more and more research is substantiating users' claims. The fact that kelp modifies the intestinal flora or bacteria of livestock may be the chief cause for the results obtained.

Kelp has been used worldwide for centuries as a rich source of natural organic minerals and vitamins. The ancient Greeks and Chinese used it for medicines, human food and animal feed. Thorvin kelp (*Ascophyllum Nodosum*) contains over 60 elements, 21 amino acids and 13 vitamins, including Vitamin E and Vitamin B12.

When used as a livestock feed additive, kelp increases production and improves performance. It strengthens appetite and enhances digestion. It promotes healthy fur, coats and plumage, and helps to regulate animal heat cycles, increases the number and durability of sperm, improves conception rates, and increases the percentage of normal healthy births. In general, kelp improves the overall health of the animals.

After adding kelp to poultry feed you can expect brighter plumage, increased weight gain and enhanced general alertness. There will be a marked increase in iodine content in eggs. The yolks will be a deeper color, with better pigmentation, improved hatchability, reduction of blood spots, reduced incidence of coccidiosis, less egg breakage and stronger shells. Your poultry will display better feed conversion and improved overall health, with fewer diseases.

Japanese researchers are currently exploring the reduced levels of cholesterol in eggs from chickens who have received kelp supplements in their diet. I can't prove it, but I think the chickens are happier, fight less and have better dispositions, too.

Unfortunately, you can't grow kelp, but you can buy it from your feed supply store or by mail. You can see in the charts that kelp contains only tiny amounts of any of the various elements. At first it is hard to understand why such minute amounts of any of these mineral elements can be of any significant benefit to crops or livestock. However, the soil only requires these minerals in tiny— sometimes infinitesimal—amounts.

Mineral Analysis of Seaweed
(Norwegian *Ascophyllum Nodosum*)

Minerals	Percentages	Minerals	Percentages
Silver	.00004	Sodium	4.180000
Aluminum	.193000	Nickel	.003500
Gold	.000006	Osmium	.000001
Boron	.019400	Phosphorus	.211000
Barium	.001276	Lead	.000014
Calcium	1.904000	Rubidium	.000005
Chlorine	3.680000	Sulfur	1.564200
Cobalt	.001227	Antimony	.000142
Copper	.00635	Silicon	.164200
Fluorine	.032650	Tin	.000006
Iron	.089560	Strontium	.074876
Germanium	.000005	Tellurium	.000001
Mercury	.000190	Titanium	.000012
Iodine	.062400	Thallium	.000293
Potassium	1.280000	Vanadium	.000531
Lantanum	.000019	Tungsten	.000033
Lithium	.000007	Zinc	.0003516
Magnesium	.213000	Zirconium	.000001
Manganese	.123500	Selenium	.000043
Molybdenum	.001592	Uranium	.000004

Other Elements

Bismuth	Beryllium	Niobium	Cadmium
Chromium	Cesium	Gallium	Indium
Iridium	Palladium	Platinum	Thorium
Radium	Bromine	Cerium	Rhodium

Other Features

Moisture Content	10.7%
Protein	5.7%
Fat	2.6%
Fiber	7.0%
Ash	15.4%

From Norwegian Institute of Seaweed Research

Average Analysis of Kelp Iceland Ascophyllum Nodosum			
Macro nutrients	**Percent**	**Minor Nutrients**	**ppm**
Crude Protein	8.6	Cobalt	5
Nitrogen	1.0	Copper	5
Phosphorus	0.1	Iodine	1534
Potassium	8.7	Iron	622
Magnesium	0.7	Manganese	100
Sulfur	2.8	Molybdenum	2
Salt	9.8	Selenium	4
		Zinc	30

Also identified:
Carbohydrates   alginic acid   mannitol (sugars)
Methylpentosans
laminarin
(starch)   fucoidin
Vitamins: A B1, B2, B6 (niacin), B12,   C, D, E, K

Plant Growth Hormones:
auxins
cytokinins
gibberelins

Copyright 1988 Necessary Trading Company.

For example, only 2 ounces of Vanadium, a minor nutrient, will be enough to provide for about 2,000 acres of crops. Lee Fryer, in his book *The New Organic Manifesto*, says, *"That's something like a 'whiff' per acre."*

Seaweed has a chelating ability that makes nutrients more readily available for plant uptake. This enhanced chelation improves cation exchange in garden soil and helps release locked-up minerals.

Kelp also contains growth-producing hormones and can be applied to plant leaves as a foliar spray. The stomata of leaves absorb the growth stimulants gibberellin and auxin, giving better plant growth and development. Seaweed also helps protect plants against light frost, and against certain insect and disease infestations, particularly fusarium in tomatoes and red spider mite in fruit crops.

Kelp Feeding Rate

As a chicken feed supplement, add kelp meal at a rate of one to two percent of total grain rations. Feed at the higher rate when your stock is under stress, due to travel, disease, weather, reproduction or weaning.

Specific Kelp Feeding Rates – Quantity per day	
Dairy and Beef Cattle	2 to 4 ounces per day
Heifers and Calves	1 to 2 ounces per day
Horses, Sheep & Goats	1/2 ounce per day
Poultry ration	1 to 2 percent of feed
Large Dogs	1 teaspoon per day
Small Dogs	1/2 teaspoon per day
Cats	1/4 teaspoon per day
Not recommended for rabbits	

The best way to mix Thorvin into the ration is when the feed is being ground and blended, otherwise you can "top dress" it onto already prepared feed. A third method is to mix kelp with salt to feed free choice, cafeteria style. In winter, mix two parts kelp to one part salt since the animals eat less salt during the colder months. In summer, reduce the ratio to one part kelp to one part salt. For all range animals, this free choice method may be the most practical. Some farmers choose to mix one part kelp, one part Diatomaceous Earth (see below), and one part salt in their free choice mixture.

Cost of Feeding Kelp as a Feed Supplement

Chickens are, in one measure, poor converters of nutrients. They excrete nearly 80 percent of the nutritional value of the feed, including the kelp feed supplement. I can't prove it, and the multi-million dollar companies haven't researched it yet, but I feel that one of the major side benefits of feeding kelp meal is the improved nutrient conversion of the chickens.

We already know that feeding kelp meal causes total feed consumption to go down while health and weight gain improve. It stands to reason that the kelp is enabling the chickens to become better nutrient converters. They are thriving on less feed because they are more effectively utilizing the nutrients contained in the food they do eat.

Each 55 pound bag of Thorvin Kelp costs $49.50, delivered to my farm. That is 90 cents per pound. Each pound of kelp meal will treat 100 pounds of feed, at a cost per pound of nine cents.

Without the kelp, each chicken will eat 15 pounds of feed to grow to six pounds live weight, or four and a quarter pounds dressed weight. If I am buying chicken feed at 14 cents per pound, the total cost of feed per chicken will be $2.10.

After adding the kelp to the feed, there is a ten percent reduction in feed consumption to achieve the same weight. Total feed consumed then becomes 13.5 pounds per bird. This lowers feed cost to $1.89 per bird, plus nine cents worth of kelp, for a total feed cost of $1.98.

You save money on the feed bill while getting a healthier, tastier bird, better grazing characteristics and richer, less offensive smelling manure to enrich your soil. Quite a bargain, if you ask me.

Diatomaceous Earth

Diatomaceous Earth (DE) consists of the sedimentary deposits formed from the skeletal remains of a class of algae (*Bacillariophyceae*) that occur in both salt and fresh water and in soil. These remains form diatomite, an almost pure silica, that is ground into an abrasive dust. When the tiny, razor-sharp particles touch an insect, they cause many tiny abrasions, resulting in loss of body water and death by dehydration.

DE is 98 percent repellent to insects, yet free of dangerous residues. It is digestible by earthworms and harmless to mammals and birds. The dust contains 14 beneficial trace minerals in chelated (readily available) form. Manure and urine carry these minerals into the soil.

Use DE to keep stored feed free of insects. Feed it to poultry and other livestock to control internal parasites. Laying hens will dust themselves in a box of DE to control fleas and lice. It is a digestive activator that helps to control fecal odors, resulting in less offensive smelling manure.

We use DE in our house to help with flea control. The DE silica spears pierce the eggs of the fleas. We spread DE liberally around where our animals sleep and in our oriental carpets.

Duckweed

Our friend Harvey Harmon is a permaculturist and biodynamic farmer in Bear Creek, North Carolina. He recently turned us on to the idea of experimenting with Duckweed as a possible feed crop. Duckweed grows on water much as algae does, and is a big problem weed in some farm ponds. However, it produces up to 20 tons of yield per acre per year, with a protein content of about 18 percent. Compare that to alfalfa which yields about five tons per acre.

Duckweed is easy to grow on any pond surface and won't interfere with your irrigation or livestock watering needs or your fish farming project. Just skim off enough duckweed each day to supplement your chicken feed. The duckweed will happily reproduce and keep giving you a steady supply all summer until it goes dormant with the late fall cold weather. It springs to life in the spring and goes on giving. We raised a small tank of it this year and our chickens and pigs love it, so we plan to expand our duckweed production next year. Our hope is to eventually replace as much as 20 percent of our feed bill with home grown duckweed.

Chapter 15: Diseases and Afflictions

Good Management Will Prevent Most of Them

Chicken Pox is a virus spread by direct contact with people who have the disease. It is not transmitted to humans by chickens. It is so named because someone with chicken pox has little red marks all over their body and they resemble a freshly plucked chicken.

Over the course of many years of growing chickens, I have experienced only occasional diseases in my home flock. I've talked with other small-scale growers who say this is true for them, as well. The two problems I <u>have</u> had in my broiler flock are curly toe paralysis and breast blister.

Leg Problems and Curly Toe Paralysis

The curly toe paralysis has only been a problem with the fast-weight-gaining Cornish Cross meat chickens. These hybrid birds gain weight so fast their legs can't keep up. Their toes start to curl under and they have trouble walking. Eventually they will lay down and be killed by the other chickens or starve to death. They just can't get to the feed. In the early stages of curly toe move the chicken to the nurse pen and give it extra yeast for riboflavin. Since riboflavin deficiency can be one cause of the affliction it's a good reason to provide plenty of fresh pasture and kelp meal in their diet.

Both of these contain riboflavin.

I think the easiest way to avoid curly toe paralysis is to not buy the breeds that are susceptible to it. A hardier hybrid is the Kosher King, sometimes called the Silver Barred

Cross. It is less susceptible to curly toe paralysis than the Cornish Cross. The Kosher King gains weight nearly as well as the Cornish Cross and is a more aggressive forager. This makes the Kosher King more useful in the chicken tractor system. As far as I know, curly toe paralysis is unheard of in the heritage and standard breeds.

Breast Blisters

The other problem I've had with chickens is breast blister. This is a swelling of the skin in the breast area. One grower I talked with feels it happens to his broilers when they crowd under the waterer where it is cooler in the summer. Other growers tell me it happens when the heavy breeds rock on their roosts. Breast blister is not prevalent in the heritage and standard breeds. Even though I've raised chickens for years I had never heard of breast blister until I tried growing the Cornish Cross hybrids. Since I've switched to Kosher King meat birds I no longer have the problem.

Breast blister, as far as I can tell, is primarily a cosmetic problem on the skin of the breast. It can be trimmed off during processing. It doesn't affect the meat at all and apparently has little effect on weight gain or vigor of the birds.

Coccidiosis is probably the only other chicken ailment that concerns me. A parasite causes this disease. The characteristics of the disease are loose, watery droppings that are sometimes bloody. It usually occurs in young chicks. If I suspect an infection in young chickens I buy commercial, medicated starter mash for the first two to three weeks, then switch to non-medicated grower pellets. The medicated starter feeds have a coccidiostat that helps prevent the disease.

Antibiotics In Feeds

Medicated feed combats diseases with antibiotics. Most commercial growers routinely feed a low level maintenance dose of antibiotics. My concern—one that is being confirmedt in recent research—is that these low level doses will eventually lead to resistance strains of virus that we won't have the medication to control. Also, the drug passes up the food chain, and can end up in the human body, especially the liver, where the toxins can interfere with our natural immune system.

However, I agree that it is okay to use drugs to keep animals from suffering needlessly or dying. This is particularly true in the case of young chicks. The antibiotics—coccidiostats, for example—will have a chance to move out of the poultry before we eat any of the meat or eggs.

The best preventive, of course, is to raise the chickens as naturally as possible. Give them plenty of good food and clean water, access to sunshine and a place to forage and scratch. Fecal dust is a carrier of disease, too, so clean the waterer and feeder each day when you tend the chickens.

For a really good in-depth guide to chicken health you can read Gail Damerow's book *The CHICKEN HEALTH Handbook*, (see appendix).

Pecking and Cannibalism

One horrible vice that chickens sometimes develop is pecking each other and in extreme cases, eating each other. The cause of this behavior can be poor nutrition––including lack of enough water or food. Pecking can also be due to overcrowding, especially with hens. They need more floor space and nesting privacy.

In my experience with chicken tractors, I have had little trouble with chickens pecking or cannibalizing. The time I had 300 chicks brooding in my garage there was a little pecking on two of the smaller chicks that caused superficial wounds. I separated these two from the larger flock and made sure they got plenty of food, water and quiet. They grew quickly and in a week had recovered and gained enough weight to go back to the brooder without further problems.

Debeaking.

This is industrial agriculture's solution to pecking and cannibalism. Debeaking is a typically inhumane modern factory-farming practice, and a clear example of fixing the symptom rather than the root problem. Debeaking is the practice of cutting off slightly more than one-half of the upper beak and blunting the lower beak. This makes it difficult for a bird to grasp feathers or skin.

Nippers (like large toenail clippers) are used to manually debeak a bird. Commercial producers use a debeaking machine that has an electrically heated blade that cuts and cauterizes at the same time to stop bleeding. Debeaking can cause damage to the nerves and blood vessels in the circulatory system of the beak. You can imagine how painful this could be, as well as frustrating to the chicken. Birds use their beaks like we use our hands. They use beaks to explore their environment, clean themselves, play, smell, communicate, defend themselves and eat. Mortality from debeaking can be high because the damaged chicks sometimes will not or cannot eat and simply starve to death. Most producers debeak at about one week old; some do it as early as one day old. In my opinion, debeaking is among the cruelest things you can do to a bird both physically and psychologically.

I don't recommend you debeak chickens in your chicken tractors. They need their beaks to forage for seeds, bugs and weeds. Poultry foraging in your garden is part of the key to the chicken tractor system. The chances of you having pecking problems will be minimal if you provide good nutrition and do not crowd your flock into too small an area.

Debeaking

Slightly more than half the upper beak is cut off.

Those are my lips!!!

The lower beak is blunted making it hard for the bird to pick up or peck at anything.

Chapter 16: Raising Poultry Humanely

Chicken Tractor is one of the most humane, clean, sensible and safe ways to raise chickens and other poultry. The portable shelter-pens allow the birds plenty of exercise, sunshine and fresh air, while protecting them from the weather, predators and inhumane conditions. Using chicken tractor systems you can supply yourself and neighbors with wholesome, humanely raised food while enhancing your garden.

We have included this article entitled "The Truth Behind A Hen's Life" because I have seen first hand how terrible the conditions are for chickens in the egg layer and broiler factories. I know there is a more humane and profitable way to raise wholesome, healthy meat birds and eggs. The way to do this is by raising them locally, using more sustainable agricultural practices such as chicken tractors and pastured poultry. As Dr. Adcock states, "Raising consumer awareness is one of the keys to a more humane world".

Commercial broilers raised "free range".

The Truth Behind "A Hen's Life"

by Melanie Adcock, DVM

Adapted and reprinted with permission from *Humane Society of the United States News*, Spring 1993

The hen is not unlovable or emotionless, but a thinking, sensitive and complex creature. A chicken can recognize and remember about 100 other chickens. Chickens enjoy playing with toys. Chickens like listening to classical music (Vivaldi in particular) while others cuddle up to red mittens for comfort. Knocking on the door before entering a small henhouse will keep hens from being startled by a visitor.

When allowed to roam freely, hens are extremely active during the day—walking, running, flying, exploring and searching for food. At night they roost together, preferring to perch high off the ground.

Chickens are inquisitive animals and will closely investigate anything new in their environment. Hens like to work for their food. Even if food is readily available, hens choose to spend a large part of their day exploring for food and scratching and pecking at the ground.

Chickens are very social animals and form tight social groups. Groups of birds tend to dust-bathe (a grooming behavior) and eat together. They communicate with each other through visual displays and calls. The baby chick begins communicating while still inside the egg, responding to the mother's purring as she incubates the egg.

Nesting is extremely important to laying hens. They prefer to lay their eggs in a private nest, and they perform an elaborate sequence of behaviors while searching for a nest site, building the nest and laying eggs.

Hens raised in a "Battery Cage".
This practice is now illegal in many European countries.

It is hard to imagine a less appropriate housing for the highly social complex and active laying hen than "battery cages" typically found on industrial egg factory farms. These cages are made entirely of wire and are so small and cramped that hens cannot spread their wings. About 98 percent of all eggs sold in supermarkets come from hens who spend their entire productive lives—up to two years—crowded into tiny cages with other hens.

To limit the damage from the aberrant excessive pecking of cage mates in this restrictive, barren environment, part of the hen's beak is removed, a practice termed "debeaking". A hen's beak is critical for preening, exploring, and feeding. Debeaked chickens show behavior changes suggesting short-term and long-term pain. The severed nerve endings in the beak develop into abnormal nervous tissue, and the beak never heals properly.

A hen's nesting desire is so strong that she will go without food and water to be allowed to use a nest when she's

*The crowded, stressful life of a
factory farm-raised laying chicken*

ready to lay. Deprived of nests, hens in battery cages pace anxiously and repeatedly attempt to escape for hours prior to laying an egg. Without privacy or nests, they lay their eggs on the sloping wire floor where they are forced to stand. The birds are bred to be egg-laying machines, continuing to lay even when severely injured.

Hens suffer foot and feather damage from poorly designed wire cages unsuited to their needs. The wire floor doesn't allow dust-bathing, or scratching or pecking at the ground for food. The cramped quarters do not even permit normal preening or grooming. The complete lack of exercise coupled with the demands of high egg production causes bone weakness, predisposing the hens to broken bones. The first time they experience the outdoors is when they are sent to slaughter, often piled five cages high in open trucks.

You are the key and when you spend money at the grocery store you directly influence how food is made and how animals are raised. Every time you reach for a carton of eggs from battery-caged hens, you are telling the grocer and egg industry that you accept that product and the current treatment of industry laying hens. Instead, for just pennies more, you can improve the lives of millions of laying hens by choosing cartons of eggs from humanely raised, uncaged hens.

Today, more humanely produced foods are not readily available in convenient locations such as local grocery stores. To confront this problem the Humane Society of the United States is mounting an "egg effort" in several major cities. They are joining forces with consumer, environmental, farmer and animal protection groups to bring eggs from uncaged hens into grocery stores and to urge consumers to support the more humane egg farmers.

The Humane Society's efforts to empower consumers to improve the lives of laying hens are part of a nationwide campaign asking consumers to "shop with compassion". Because the battery cage is one of the most inhumane systems for raising animals, it is the first target of their campaign. No other farm animal endures such extreme physical confinement and crowding for as long as the hen does. The Humane Society needs your help to spread the word about battery-caged hens and to urge all egg users to buy eggs from free-roaming hens.

To learn more about the Humane Society's "egg effort", contact:

The Humane Society of the United States
2100 L Street NW
Washington, DC. 20037
Phone (202) 425-1100; FAX (202) 778-6132

Chapter 17: Other Animal Tractors

With only slight design modifications you can adapt the chicken tractor idea to other types of livestock, including quail, pheasants, turkeys, ducks, geese, guineas, rabbits, pigs, and even milk cows and beef steers.

Some of the changes you might want to make are to build larger pens for larger fowl such as turkeys, or add netting to keep wild flying birds such as pheasants from escaping when you open the lid to feed and water them.

Turkey Tractors

Almost 100 percent of today's turkeys are produced in confinement without access to fresh air, sunshine, earth contact or fresh grass. While factory confinement production is efficient from an economic and unit production standpoint, this system is often unable to address the questions of flavor, texture, feed and hormone additives and the manure disposal.

We are concerned about the food we eat and wanted to have especially great Thanksgiving and Christmas dinners. So we have begun experimenting with raising turkeys using the tractor model. Raising turkeys is a lot like raising chickens, beginning from the day-old chicks through processing. You can follow the instructions for raising chicks earlier in this book and do fine with turkeys.

Turkeys are a little slower than chickens in almost everything. But they are also friendly and inquisitive. They would follow you or let you herd them just about anywhere. We also grew fond of their soft chortling and cooing sounds they made when foraging and chatting with each other. They are generally quiet. As they matured, a few of the hens and toms tended to peck too hard and turned somewhat aggressive. We have not noticed this aggressiveness with the five keel breasted Bronze turkeys we are keeping for pets and breeding.

Our Bronze turkeys did well in our three-foot high chicken tractors. We put in turkey size pop-doors in all the tractors and let them out in our small fenced-in orchard to graze during the days. At night we simply drove them into the chicken tractors and closed the pophole. They like to be off the ground and used their roosts every night. Ours grew so fast and large that only about 10 would fit in a tractor for the night. Because of daily exercise, we can crowd them in a little more at night. Otherwise these pens would only hold about five to six turkeys full time.

Because of their size our next experiment with turkeys will not be in the box-type chicken tractor but rather we will put a turkey yard where we want next year's garden beds to be. We plan to use a variation of the straw bale chicken house by using four eight feet posts set about one and a half feet in the ground which will support a roof. Turkeys like to roost high so we want this building to be taller than the chicken bale house.

We will run hog fencing around the turkey yard and the space will include part of our woods so the birds can get away from the summer heat more easily. We also plan to put two strands of electric fencing outside the hog fencing to keep predators out.

Turkey Breeds From Commercial Breeders

Broad Breasted Bronze. Stately, large up to 38 pounds, hens to 22 pounds, feathers sheen copper to bronze to burnished gold, six foot wing span.

Giant White. Popular broad breasted turkey, hens to 25 pounds and toms to 45 pounds. Especially dumb.

Bourbon Red.   Beautiful, medium size, slower to mature, good to eat.

Wild Turkeys. Hardy and colorful, good flyers, very tasty, for table or game birds. Check wildlife reguation in your area, you may need a permit to raise these wild turkeys, even for table use, and you may not be able to raise them for market sales.

Excerpted with permission from Murray McMurray Hatchery catalog

Turkey Varieties

The turkey industry relies on only a few breeds of turkeys and virtually all the turkeys in the U.S. are from a single breed, the Large White, also called the Broad-Breasted White. This breed has been specifically bred for rapid growth, large size and is adapted only to the high-input, confinement environments. They also rely on substantial veterinary support. These turkeys have been bred for so much breast meat that they can no longer mate naturally. Every single turkey you buy from commercial growers is a product of artificial insemination. Additionally, the breeding stock for the Large White is controlled by about a half-dozen companies.

According to the American Livestock Breeds Conservancy, Bronze Unimproved and many other strains of turkeys are available without the broad-breasted gene. Because they are standard breeds you can breed and raise them on the homestead.

Until the last 30 years turkeys were raised outside and had to forage for much of their food. They were very useful in pest control in corn, row crops and orchards. The names of these heritage breeds reflect their beauty: Bronze, Holland, Slate, Narragansett, Bourbon Red, Spanish Black, and Royal Palm. All of these except the commercial Large White are in danger of extinction. Yet the heritage breeds have the characteristics you need for turkey tractors. They are disease resistance, broodiness, foraging ability, natural mating and soundness.

Sources for heritage turkey breeds are listed after the breed description.

Bronze, Wishard Line — Wish Hatchery, Box 326, Prairie City, OR; 503-820-3509. This line is naturally mating and selected for range production for over 40 years.

Broad-Breasted Bronze — Cackle Hatchery and Clearview Hatchery (addresses below). These are not naturally mating but are more vigorous and better suited for turkey tractors than the Broad-Breasted White. This is a popular breed for small scale production. Has black pin feathers.

Bourbon Red — Cackle Hatchery and Clearview Hatchery (addresses below). This is a popular ornamental breed with good meat conformation and a light-colored undercoat to dress cleanly.

Black Spanish — Cackle Hatchery and Clearview Hatchery (addresses below). This is a historic breed and was competitive in meat production as recently as the 1930s. Has black pin feathers.

Narragansett — Sand Hills Preservation Center. This is a historic breed and needs conservation efforts.

White Holland — Sand Hills Preservation Center. Medium size white breed with toms from 18 to 20 pounds.

Hatcheries:

Cackle Hatchery (Smith Family) PO Box 529, Lebanon, MO 65536, Phone 417-532-4581.

Clearview Hatchery (David Hartman) PO Box 399, Gratz, PA, Phone 717-365-3234. This is where we ordered our Broad-breasted Bronzes from.

Sand Hill Preservation Center (Glenn Downs), 1878-230th Street, Calamus, IA 52729, phone 319-246-2299.

Turkey tractors system not only eliminates the problems of confinement production but also serves as a habitat for the rare breeds of turkeys and can lead more people to become involved in generic conservation efforts.

The Gabby Guineas

Raising guinea fowl is not hard or expensive. To us they are incredibly funny, almost prehistoric looking with their cone heads. They act like something a cartoonist would create, especially when running. The guineas in our flock remind us of motorcycle helmets with stick legs darting in and out of traffic.

The females can be incredibly noisy with their two-syllable "buck-wheat" call that is sometimes incessant and annoy-

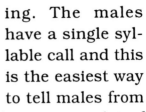

Get out, you trespasser!
BACK OFF! That's my bug!
HAWK ALERT! HAWK ALERT!!
Move over — move it!!

*How a guinea
(Military Poultry)
thinks*

ing. The males have a single syllable call and this is the easiest way to tell males from females. No one has spent a lot of money or time developing guinea breeds for commercial use. If someone did we hope they would select for quiet birds.

The wonderful guinea characteristics that make them worth keeping is that they are voracious, dedicated carnivores who seek out insects, particularly ticks and fleas. We live in a tick belt and since getting guineas we haven't had as many ticks on us or our animals! Given the problems of Lyme disease in our area, that is a huge asset. The flea population on our cats has also dramatically dropped. Guineas are also famous for keeping snakes away.

Guineas are omnivores, but their primary diet is meat, mainly insects and grubs. They also forage the seeds of grass and weeds. In the garden they do not scratch and dig like chickens. They aim their quick pecks more at grubs and bugs than at tender young seedlings.

If guineas are unsung heroes they are quick to announce their own existence. As the military poultry (MPs) of the barnyard they are ever on guard duty. They will give you a loud warning if *anything* is unusual. These gutsy little guineas treed our cats and sometimes even go after the turkeys who are at least five times their size. They are famous for protecting other poultry by driving away hawks, crows and other birds. These feathered watchdogs will scold stray dogs and cats until they leave. In the next few years we plan to do Joel Salatin's Egg mobile and Salad Bar Beef model. We will experiment with including guinea hens in the egg mobile to serve as predator alarm.

With new guineas you will need to acclimate them to their surroundings before letting them all loose. They are notorious for taking off for parts unknown as soon as you let them out. Plan on keeping new guineas in their home for at least a week to get them familiar and bonded with their surroundings. After a week or so of keeping them in, let one out. Guineas don't like to be alone and that one will stay around the pen getting used to the surroundings. After a few days let another one out. If they stay around you can probably let the rest of the flock out safely.

Male guineas tend to be aggressive with other male poultry. We don't keep roosters but the guineas will sometimes chase our turkeys all around the yard and through the woods.

Guineas are good to fry, roast, bake or barbeque, and have their own distinctive, gamey taste. They are best for the table at four to six months and will weigh from 1.75 to 2.5 pounds. You can season them to simulate the relatively rare pheasant, grouse and partridge meat. We have several recipes but haven't tried them yet. Guinea eggs are delicious, having a little richer flavor than chicken eggs and with a thicker shell.

Raise baby guineas (keets) similar to chicks. We raised our guineas with the chickens and turkeys. They bonded. When we let them loose they didn't disappear as guineas are rather famous for doing and roost cozily between the other birds. As far as we know, guineas do not carry diseases that are dangerous to chickens or turkeys.

Guineas. All-dark, gamey tasting meat, easy to raise, live on bugs, insects and weed seeds, very active foragers will eat deer ticks, act as watchdogs.

Purple Guineas   Dark black with purple sheen

Coral Blue Guineas   Polka dots, very appealing

Lavender Guineas   Very striking color pattern

Slate Guineas   Very rare in U.S.

Buff Dundotte and Buff Guineas
Soft buff color with polka dots on Dundotte and no dots on Buff
White and Pearl Guineas
Whites have albino plumage and skin, Pearls are most common guineas with purplish-gray plumage "pearled"

Other poultry you might want to consider are:

Goslings

Toulouse. France, all-dark meat, males 18 to 20 pounds and females 12 to 13 pounds.

White Embden. Germany, pure white, easy to dress, great taste, males 20 pounds, females to 13 pounds, showy as purebreds
White Chinese. Very hardy, good layers, good hatch, showy and make good watch dogs.

Weeder Geese. China, they love weeds but not fruits of garden plants, great foragers and garden companions

Ducks, Geese, Partridge
White Pekin. China, fine meat quality and egg laying, creamy white, large breasted, easy to pick and prepare, males 10-11 pounds, females 8-9 pounds

Rouen. France, similar to wild Mallard, males to 8-9 pounds, females to 6-7 pounds.

Cayuga. New York, Lake Cayuga, brilliant "beetle" green plumage. hens to 5-6 pounds, lay blue-gray eggs, males to 6-7 pounds
Flying Mallard. Smaller, with gamey flavor

Khaki Campbell. General purpose, good layers, mature at 4.5 pounds, easy to pick for table use, excellent foragers and hardy. Fawn and White Runners
Scotland, small, good foragers,

Buff Ducks. England, good layers, not broody, hens up to 7 pounds and drakes up to 8 pounds

Blue Swedish. Very hardy, good foragers, up to 8 pounds, mostly white eggs some blue or gray tinted.

Chukar Partridge. You may need a permit, can be domesticated or wild, a real treat for the table.

Pheasants

Red Golden. Beautiful, China, hardy, easy to raise, valued feathers, slow to mature.

Buff Pheasant. Used for stocking hunting clubs

Lady Amherst's Pheasant. China, very pretty, easy to raise and prized for feathers, slow to mature.

Black-Necked Pheasant. Western Europe, coppery red with dark head and neck and brown shoulders

Afghan Pheasant. Small, alert, quick and good flyers, likes arid climate
Silver Pheasant. Southern China, easy to raise and breed

Reeves Pheasant. China, long-tailed, fast grower in first year

Chinese Ringneck Pheasant. China, beautiful, delicious, will grow wild
White Pheasants. Jumbo size, easy to raise and clean, delicacy

Jumbo Ringneck Pheasants. Larger than Chinese Ringnecks, raised for meat production, taxidermy and ornamental

Excerpted with permission from
Murray McMurray Hatchery catalog

Epilogue:

Empowering the Chicken: When the Old Cocks Crow, the Young Ones Learn

by Howard W. "Bud" Kerr, Jr.

WASHINGTON DC—In 1944, I was in 4-H and I raised chickens for my table. Fifty years ago it really was popular to have "chicken every Sunday". I grew the chickens out in our backyard. With maturity they learned to greet the morning light uttering the characteristic cry of the rooster. These raucous cries usually came from the very ones destined to become the centerpiece on our family dining room table. The pullets enjoyed a more favorable life as they were destined for the henhouse to begin egg production.

My mother's father was a farmer and it must have agreed with him. He lived to 93 years of age. My mother and father's hobby farm was about two acres located in the suburbs of Baltimore, Maryland. My mother lived 89 years and imparted her farming wisdom to me at a very young age. She gave me a favorite saying, learned from her mother, and since passed on to my children.... "As the old cocks crow the young ones learn."

In recent years, families—both in rural and urban environs—have begun to create special opportunities for family enjoyment by seeking enriching activities together. Yesterday's "Yuppie Puppies" are now middle-aged. For som, the rungs on the ladder of success have bent or broken from the weight of stress-filled responsibility. They are now content to live a more peaceful lifestyle at home with the family. Backyards are again becoming a place for pleasure, work and enjoyment. "As the old cocks crow, the young ones learned".

Activities that can be shared by parents and youngsters are not easy. However, small scale gardening and raising poultry fits the bill. Andy Lee, in his book, *Chicken Tractor*, has managed to humorously and creatively combine past methods of poultry raising with today's intensive gardening techniques.

The chicken really is the tractor in today's garden. It enriches and builds the soil so that gardens flourish. At the same time, there are eggs and meat for the family to consume or sell, and even feathers for crafts. All of this leads to a fulfillment of the entrepreneurial spirit that drives the success of small-scale farmers all across this land. "As the old cocks crow, the young ones listened!"

Howard W. "Bud" Kerr, Jr., Director

Office for Small-Scale Agriculture

United States Department of Agriculture

Recommended Books for Small-Scale Agriculturists

The following books are available from your local bookstore or from the individual publishers. If you are unable to locate them in your area contact Good Earth Publications, P. O. Box 160, Columbus, NC, 28722, phone and fax 704-863-2288.

Prices below do not include shipping and handling.

Backyard Market Gardening, The Entrepreneur's Guide To Selling What You Grow, Andy Lee, 1993, Good Earth Publications, PO Box 160, Columbus, North Carolina, 351 pp., $19.95

The Contrary Farmer, Gene Logsdon, Chelsea Green Publishing, Post Mills, Vt., 1993, 237 p. hard cover, $22

Raising Poultry Successfully, Will Graves, Williamson Publishing, Charlotte, Vermont, 192 pp., $10

Raising Poultry The Modern Way, Leonard Mercia, 1990, Garden Way Publishing, Pownal Vermont, 234 pp., $10

Your Chickens, A Kid's Guide To Raising and Showing, Gail Damerow, Storey Comm. Inc., Pownal, VT, 156 pp., $13

Backyard Livestock, George P. Looby, The Countryman Press, Woodstock, VT., 225 pp., $15

The CHICKEN HEALTH Handbook, Gail Damerow, 1994, Storey Communications, Pownal, Vermont

Garden of Microbial Delights, Dorian Sagan and Lynn

Margulis, 1988, 231 page hardcover, HBJ,Boston, MA., $25

Start With The Soil, Grace Gershuney, 1993, Rodale Press, Emmaus, PA., 275 page hardcover, $25

The Rodale Book of Composting, new revised addition, Rodale Press, Emmaus, PA., 278 pp., $15

Introduction To Permaculture, Bill Mollison, 1991, Tagari Publications, Australia, 198 pp., $25

Permaculture; A Designer's Manual, Bill Mollison, 1990, Tagari Publications, Australia, 576 pages, hard cover, $45

Salad Bar Beef, Joel Salatin, 1995, Polyface, Inc, Swoope, VA, 368ppb, $30.

Secrets of the Soil, Christopher Bird and Peter Thompkins

Pastured Poultry Profit$, Net $25,000 in 6 months on 20 acres, Joel Salatin, Polyface Inc., Swoope, Va., 330 pp., $30, companion video, one-hour, $50

Your Money or Your Life, Transforming Your Relationship With Money and Achieving Financial Independence, Joe Dominguez and Vicki Robin, Penguin, NY, 350 pp., $12

Holistic Resource Management, Allan Savory, Island Press, Covelo, California, 564 pp., $27

Farming In Nature's Image, an Ecological Approach to Agriculture, Judith Soule and Jon Piper, Island Press, Covelo, California, 286 pp., $20m

How To Grow More Vegetables Than You Ever Thought Possible on Less Land Than You Can Imagine, John Jeavons, Ten Speed Press, Berkeley, California, 175 pp., $15

The New Organic Grower, A Master's Manual of Tools and Techniques for the Home and Market Gardener, Eliot Coleman, Chelsea Green Publishing, Post Mills, Vermont, 268 pp., $20

The New Organic Grower's Four Season Harvest, How to harvest fresh, organic vegetables from your home garden all year long, Eliot Coleman, Chelsea Green Publishing, Post Mills, Vermont, 206 pp., $18

Taking Stock: The North American Livestock Survey, and *The American Minor Breeds Handbook,* both from the American Livestock Breeds Conservancy, $15 and $8 respectively.

Tree Crops: A Permanent Agriculture, J. Russell Smith, Island Press, Covelo, California, 408ppb, $22. Must reading for everyone in agriculture.

World Wide Web and Internet Resources

There are so many web pages and sites to visit on the web for information about poultry that it is impossible to list them all here. Several of the best sites we have found to date are listed below. These sites have LOTS of links to other poultry resources so have fun exploring!

American Poultry Association. http/ www.poultry.mph.msu.edu. Information about the APA, newletters.

Feather Site by Betty Koffler. This web site has photos and it is virtually an on-line poultry encyclopedia. It also has lots of links to other poultry resources and specialty pages. http:// www.cyborganic,com/people/feathersite

The Sam & Ella Culture Club. Home of the Domesticated Bird mailing list. This "a group of wacky folks who love their poultry...they have banded together from all corners of the globe to talk with each other about their birds. If you love your chickens, train your guineas to attack snakes and skunks or raise giant geese to keep your neighbor's Chihuahua from relieving itself on your petunias then DOM_BIRD list might be for you!" You can find the Sam & Ella (Salmonella - get it!) Culture Club via the Feather Site address above.

Poultry Page. http://www.exoticpets.com. Has information about poultry and rare breeds. Lots of photos.

USDA extension. http://www.esusda.edu

VetNet. Archive and information of interest to veterinarians and others. Has newsletters, publications, conference proceedings. Has specific information about species.

Glossary (Chicken Talk)

Bantams: miniature chickens usually one-fourth to one fifth the size of standards breeds. They weigh only one to two pounds. They have many different types and color patterns. Popular for hobby and urban flocks as they require less space and respond well to human relationships. Eggs are smaller than the heavy breeds but just as tasty.

Broiler-fryer: a chicken less than three months old, male or female destined for a dinner table.

Capon: a castrated male chicken used for roasting. Capons are usually butchered when about 3 months old and weigh five pounds or more.

Chicken: any bird of the species *Gallus Domesticus*.

Cockerel: a young male chicken up to one year old.

Gizzard: the second stomach of birds that helps in the grinding down of food, especially grains.

Grit: tiny particles of sand or stone. Poultry need grit to help grind food in their gizzards.

Hackles: neck feathers often used in making fishing lures. Chickens will "put their hackles up" when feeling threatened or angry.

Hen: a female chicken.

Molt: the natural process of shedding old feathers and growing new ones. The birds sometimes get bald spots on their backs and look rather sickly until their new feathers grow out.

Pullet: an immature female hen less than one year old.

Roaster: a chicken of either sex, about five months old or younger that weighs five pounds or more. These birds have tender meat and a fairly flexible breastbone cartilage. Once a chicken matures to one year old the tip of the breastbone is hard and inflexible.

Rooster: a mature male chicken at least one year old. Also called a cock.

Scratch: a mixture containing at least two grains, one of them usually cracked corn. Once a day, in the late afternoon when the birds are thinking about bedding down, throw scratch on top of the litter. They will stir up the litter to keep it loose, dry and odors down. You can also use scratch to train birds to come when you call them with whistling or your own code.

Chick Producers and Equipment Dealers

There are many more chicken producers than are listed here. If you are a producer and would like to be listed in the next edition of *Chicken Tractor* please contact Good Earth Publications with information about your company.

Abendroth Hatchery, Rick Abendroth
W8697 Island Road, Waterloo, WI 53594
Phone 414-478-2053, Fax 414-478-2004

Clearview Hatchery
Box 399, Gratz, PA., 17030,
Ph.717-365-3234, fax 365-3594

Brower Equipment for Poultry, Livestock and Pets
PO Box 2000
Houghton, Iowa, 52631
Phone 319-469-4141

Picwick Poultry Processing Equipment
1870 McCloud Place NE
Cedar Rapids, IA, 52402
Phone: 319-393-7443 -
Please tell them Good Earth Publications refered you.

FarmTek
RR2 Box 17
Hopkinton IA 52237, 1-800-895-1598
Holderreads' Waterfowl Farm and Preservation Center
P. O. Box 492, Corvallis, Oregon 97339,
Phone 503-929-5338

Johnny's Selected Seeds
Foss Hill Road
Albion, Maine 04910-9731, 207-437-4301
Cover crop seeds, vegetable seeds, books, tools, good advice

Kuhl Plastic Poultry Equipment
P. O. Box 26 Kuhl Road
Flemington, N.J. 08822, phone 908-782-5696

Marti Poultry Farm
P. O. Box 27, Windsor, MO 65360-0027, Ph. 816-647-3156

Mellinger's Inc.
2310 West South Range Road,
North Lima, OH 44452-9731, 800-321-7444, rooted comfrey cuttings, major greenhouse and garden supplier

Moyer's Chicks
266 East Paletown Road
Quakertown, PA 18951, Ph. 215-536-3155

Murray McMurray Hatchery
Webster City, Iowa 50595-0458
Order: 1-800-456-3280, FAX: 515-832-2213

G.Q.F. MFG. Co.
P. O. Box 1552
Savannah, GA 31498-2701

Well-Sweep Herb Farm
317 Mt. Bethel Road
Port Murray, NJ 07865, rooted comfrey cuttings, free catalog

Wild Acres,
HC83, Box 108
Pequot Lakes, MN 56472, Phone 218-568-5748 or 568-5024

Magazines and Publications

Appropriate Technology Transfer For Rural Areas (ATTRA)
P. O. Box 3657
Fayetteville, Arkansas 72702, 1-800-346-9140, free publications on small-scale farming topics

BackHome Magazine
PO Box 70
Hendersonville, NC 28793
703-696-3838

Countryside and Small Stock Journal
N2601 Winter Sports Rd.
Withee, WI 54498 715-785-7979

Bibliography

Fryer, Lee, *The Bio-Gardener's Bible,* Chilton Book Company, Radnor, Pennsylvania, 1982.

Damerow, Gail, *Your Chickens: A Kid's Guide to Raising and Showing,* Storey Communications, Inc. Pownal, Vermont, 1993

Fryer, Lee, *The New Organic Manifesto,* Earth Foods Associates, Inc., Wheaton, Maryland, 1986

Gershuney, Grace and Smillie, Joseph, *The Soul of Soil,* Gaia Services, St. Johnsbury, Vermont, 1986

Harris, Ben Charles, *Comfrey, What You Need To Know,* Keats Publishing, New Canaan, Connecticut, 1982

Holderread, Dave, *Raising the Home Duck Flock,* Storey Communications, Inc. Pownal, Vermont, 1978

Jeavons, John, *How To Grow More Vegetables*,* Ten Speed Press, Berkley, California, revised 1991

Mercia, Leonard S. *Raising Poultry the Modern Way,* Storey Communications, Inc. Pownal, Vermont, 1990

Mollison, Bill, *Permaculture; A Practical Guide for a Sustainable Future,* Island Press, Washington, D.C., 1990

Mollison, Bill, and Slay, Reny Mia, *Introduction To Permaculture,* Tagari Publications, Tyalgum, NSW, Australia, 1991

Organic Gardening Staff, *The Encyclopedia of Organic Gardening,* Rodale Press, Emmaus, Pennsylvania, 1978

Salatin, Joel, *Pastured Poultry Profit$* Polyface Inc., Swoope, Va. 1994

Stockman Grass Farmer, *Alternative Marketing,* audio tape, Grass Farmer Library, Jackson, MS., 1990

Thear, Katie, *Free-range Poultry,* Farming Press Books, 4 Friars Courtyard, Ipswich, UK, 1990

Maine Organic Farmer and Gardener
RR 2, Box 594, Lincolnville, ME 04849

National Poultry News
P. O. Box 1647
Easley, SC 29641, 803-855-0140
A nation wide publication of poultry, exotic fowl and animals

Natural Farmer
Northeast Organic Farmers Association
411 Sheldon Rd., Barre, MA 01005, phone 508-355-2853

NOFA NOTES
Vermont Northeast Organic Farmers Association
P. O. Box 697, Richmond, VT 05477

Organic Gardening
Rodale Press
33 E. Minor Street
Emmaus, PA 18098 215-967-5171

Rural Heritage
281 Dean Ridge Lane
Gainesboro, TN 38562-5039,
Phone and Fax 615-268-0655

Small Farm Today
3903 W. Ridge Trail Rd.,
Clark, MO 65243, Ph. 800-633-2533

Associations to Join

The American Livestock Breeds Conservancy
Box 477, Pittsboro, North Carolina 27312,
Phone: 919-542-5704

American Pasture Poultry Producers Association
5207 70th Street
Chippewa Falls, WI, 54729
Phone: 715-723-2299

American Poultry Association Inc.
26363 S. Tucker Rd., Estacada, OR 97023

Index

57, 69, 116, 124, 270

O

oats, 71
odor, 43, 58
Office for Small-Scale Agriculture, 231
organic feeds, 257
organic fertilizer, 50
organic matter,
    49, 69, 70, 118, 123, 124, 130
Osentowski, Jerome, 20
owls, 77, 85, 254
oxygen, 67, 87, 132

P

Paddocks, 52
partridge, 221, 223
pastured poultry, 83, 166, 255
pecking, 38, 286
perches, 145
Permaculture, 141
permaculture,
    31, 34, 40, 52, 76
permanent pathways, 74
pest control, 47, 231
pH, 268, 272
pheasants, 221, 223
phosphorous, 129, 272
phosphorus, 276
Pickwick processing equipment, 204
Pittman, Scott, 8
plastic film, 67
plucking machine, 202
plum curcullio, 234
Plymouth Barred Rock, 221
poly tarp, 180
Polyface Farm, 83
Polyface System, 52
pop-hole, 148
portable pen, 180
potassium, 129, 272, 276
practicing, 157
predators, 57, 250
pressure treated lumber, 186

processing facility, 200, 203
protein,
    231, 234, 248, 256, 270
Pullets, 172

R

raccoons, 181, 252
Raising Poultry Successfully, 86
Rats, 250
Relative Location, 37
repugnance zone, 83
respiration, 264
Rhode Island Reds, 85
Riboflavin, 284
Robinson, Ed, 86
Rodale Farms, 234
rodents, 250, 261
roost, 146
rooster, 140, 223, 240
Roosters, 33
roosters, 43
rotary till, 132
Rotary tilling, 69
Rotational, 52
rotational grazing, 122, 131

S

salad garden, 55
Salatin, Joel, 83, 156, 166, 181
Sample Budget, 160
Sand Hill Preservation Center, 298
Savory, Allan, 27, 120
scalding vat, 202
scratch, 80, 194
scratching, 38
Seamix™, 139
seaweed extract, 139, 272, 278
Secrets of the Soil, 139
seed bed, 132
seedlings, 67, 89
selection skills, 234
shading, 43

The Coveted

Pullet Surprise
for Poultry Pioneers

Hall of Fame

Joel Salatin
for his book Pastured Poultry Profit$
that is revolutionizing commercial poultry raising.

Sam & Ella Culture Club
and Barry Koffler
for enhancing world-wide-web
communications among poultry lovers

Bruce Johnson
for creativity in chicken tractor design

Andy Lee and Patricia Foreman
for their book Chicken Tractor
that is helping to integrate chickens into gardens

Good Earth Publications, LLC
Established 1989

Featuring books, information, resources and links on sustainable agriculture, alternative building, conservation, preservation of land, and Earth-friendly life-styles.

Visit our book store and see the entire table of contents for each book at:

www.GoodEarthPublications.com

If you enjoyed *Chicken Tractor* you might like other books by the authors:

Backyard Market Gardening:
The Entrepreneur's Guide to Selling What YOU Grow

Day Range Poultry:
Every Chicken Owner's Guide to
Grazing Gardens and Improving Pastures,
including the Management of Breeder Flocks, Egg Handling, Incubating
Secrets, Hatchery Efficiency, Building Shelters, Marketing, Advertising,
Soils Regeneration, Processing Poultry Humanely and Efficiently, and
Much, Much More!

20% of all profits from our book sales
are donated to projects promoting
Earth repair and sustainable life-styles for all beings.
We appreciate your business!

LaVergne, TN USA
20 June 2010
186705LV00003B/7/A

9 780962 464867